THE ATONEMENT

THE ATONEMENT
Its meaning and significance

Leon Morris

INTER-VARSITY PRESS
LEICESTER, ENGLAND
DOWNERS GROVE, ILLINOIS, USA

Inter-Varsity Press
38 De Montfort Street, Leicester LE1 7GP, England
P.O. Box 1400, Downers Grove, Illinois 60515, U.S.A.

© Leon Morris 1983

Unless otherwise stated, quotations from the Bible are taken from the HOLY BIBLE: NEW INTERNATIONAL VERSION. Copyright © 1978 by the International Bible Society, New York. Published in Great Britain by Hodder and Stoughton Ltd, and used by permission of Zondervan Bible Publishers, Grand Rapids, Michigan.

First published 1983

Inter-Varsity Press, England, is the publishing division of the Universities and Colleges Christian Fellowship (formerly the Inter-Varsity Fellowship), a student movement linking Christian Unions in universities and colleges throughout the United Kingdom and the Republic of Ireland, and a member movement of the International Fellowship of Evangelical Students. For information about local and national activities write to UCCF, 38 De Montfort Street, Leicester LE1 7GP.

InterVarsity Press, U.S.A., is the book-publishing division of InterVarsity Christian Fellowship, a student movement active on campus at hundreds of universities, colleges and schools of nursing. For information about local and regional activities, write Public Relations Dept., InterVarsity Christian Fellowship, 6400 Schroeder Rd., P.O. Box 7895, Madison, WI 53707-7895.

Distributed in Canada through InterVarsity Press, 860 Denison St., Unit 3, Markham, Ontario L3R 4H1, Canada.

Set in 10/12 Palatino
Typeset by Nuprint Services Ltd, Harpenden, Herts.
Printed in the United States of America

UK ISBN 0-85110-711-7
USA ISBN 0-87784-826-2

British Library Cataloguing in Publication Data
Morris, Leon
   The atonement. Its meaning and significance
   1. Jesus Christ—Crucifixion—Meditations
   I. Title
   232.9'63   BT450

ISBN 0-85110-711-7

Library of Congress Cataloging in Publication Data

Morris, Leon, 1914-
   The Atonement, its meaning and significance.
   Includes indexes.
   1. Salvation.   2. Jesus Christ—Crucifixion.
3. Covenants (Theology).   4. Atonement.   5. Passover.
I. Title.
BT751.2.M63 1983   234   83-20649
ISBN 0-87784-826-2

19	17	16	15	14	13	12	11	10	9	8	7	6	5
99	98	97	96	95	94	93	92	91	90				

Preface

This book is written out of the conviction that the cross is at the heart of the Christian way. This is the way of salvation and it is the way of Christian living. I have tried to bring out for people who are not experts in theology or in the study of the biblical languages something of the meaning of the great terms used in the New Testament to convey the significance of the atoning work of Christ. The cross is central to Christianity. It is the new and living way into the very presence of God.

The subject-matter is of course that of my previous book, *The Apostolic Preaching of the Cross*. I have often been asked to lecture on the subject-matter of that book, not infrequently to groups of lay people who could make nothing of its technicalities. The experience has led me to believe that there would be some advantage in putting on paper in simpler form some of the things I then said.

But this book is not simply a re-hash of the older work. I have made new points in every chapter and I have included some studies not in the previous book, such as the chapters on the Passover and on the Day of Atonement. I have also introduced a chapter on sacrifice which includes matter in the earlier work, such as the section on blood, but which is written from a different perspective and includes much that the older work did not.

I am indebted to many who have commented on my lectures and asked questions. The discussions have been stimulating and I trust have resulted in some clarifications. I am grateful to all who have helped me. I am grateful also to my former secretary, Mrs D. Wellington, for her careful work in typing out the manuscript.

5

Normally I have used the New International Version for quotations from Scripture, though occasionally I have cited other versions or made my own translation.

LEON MORRIS

Contents

Abbreviations

ASV	American Standard Version, 1901
AV	Authorized (King James') Version, 1611
GNB	Good News Bible, 1976
NEB	New English Bible, 1961–70
NIV	New International Version, 1974–78
RSV	Revised Standard Version, 1946–52
RV	Revised Version, 1881–85

Introduction

Jesus was a Jew. Peter, James and John were Jews. Paul was a Jew. All the first Christians were Jews. Throughout the Gospels it is plain that the whole manner of life of both Jesus and his immediate followers was that of normal first-century Jews. It is true that they did not please the strictest sect of Judaism in some things, for instance in such matters as their attitude to ceremonial cleanness. To give an example, the Pharisees were very pernickety about the way they washed their hands when they came from the market-place and before they ate; they were also particular about washing cups, kettles and the like (Mk. 7:3–4). There was friction between the Pharisees and the little group about Jesus because these latter did not concern themselves about such trifles. Again, the strict Pharisaic rules for keeping the Sabbath were out of this world. Jesus ignored the rules and maintained that the Pharisees did not understand what the Sabbath was all about. If they had understood the significance of some of the directions Moses gave, they would have acted very differently from the way they did (Jn. 7:22–23).

But the fact that the Pharisees did not like this independent attitude did not mean that Jesus was not a faithful and loyal Jew. There were many Jews who did not go along with the strict party in the way they understood the practice of their religion. There was no question of Jesus' essential Jewishness. He had been circumcised in his infancy (Lk. 2:21) and his parents had gone through the standard Jewish purification ceremonies (Lk. 2:22–23). He had been brought up to observe the Jewish feasts (or at least the Passover, Lk. 2:41–42; but if he kept this feast, the presumption is that he kept the others also). It was his custom to worship in the synagogue on the Sabbath (Lk. 4:16). Throughout his whole life he followed the Jewish pattern and his death came about when he was in Jerusalem for the feast of the Passover. It is true that there were some aspects of Jesus' teaching that many Jews found strange, but he said explicitly, 'Do not think that I have come to abolish the Law or the Prophets; I have not come to abolish them but to fulfil them' (Mt. 5:17). It was never his intention to do away with the religion in which he had been brought up.

If we go on to the church that he founded, the story begins with his followers gathered together in Jerusalem to observe another Jewish feast, that of Pentecost (Acts 2:1). They apparently observed the hours of prayer in the temple (Acts 3:1) and such things as purification rites for people who had made vows (Acts 21:23–24, 26). They frequented the synagogue (Acts 9:20; 13:5, 14; *etc.*). Paul never renounced the religion in which he had been brought up and, for example, he pointed out to the Romans that he was an Israelite, a descendant of Abraham and a member of the tribe of Benjamin (Rom. 11:1). He informed the Philippians that he was 'circumcised on the eighth day, of the people of Israel, of the tribe of Benjamin, a Hebrew of Hebrews' (Phil. 3:5).

None of the early Christians seems to have regarded himself as anything other than a faithful Jew. True, they all felt that the Judaism of the day was wrong at certain points, notably in not seeing how the writings of Moses and the prophets, indeed all their sacred Scripture, found fulfilment in Jesus. But they lived as Jews did with no more laxity than many of their contemporaries, people whom the Pharisees criticized but did not excommunicate. But in quite a short time after Jesus' death the Christians were everywhere excluded from the synagogues.

Why?

Why did a movement, cradled in Judaism and consistently claiming to be faithful to authentic Judaism, end by being firmly excluded from the bosom of that religion and even becoming an object of persecution from its adherents (Acts 17:5, 13; 18:12; 1 Thes. 2:14)?

Much could be said in answer to the question. Basically, of course, it concerns the attitude of the first Christians to Jesus. Paul could say that he counted all his proud heritage in Judaism as nothing for the sake of Christ: 'What is more, I consider everything a loss compared to the surpassing greatness of knowing Christ Jesus my Lord, for whose sake I have lost all things. I consider them rubbish, that I may gain Christ' (Phil. 3:8). Such an attitude was plainly the usual one among the Christians, even if they did not express themselves quite as forcefully as Paul did. They put Jesus Christ in the highest place at the same time as they asserted their essential Jewishness.

I have raised the question of the exclusion of the Christians, but I do not intend to pursue it seriously. I simply want to indicate that the emergence of the Christian church as an entity separate from Judaism was not a foregone conclusion. It was neither looked for nor relished by the first Christians. They saw themselves as the authentic Israel, as members of the true people of God. The final split was not their idea. When it came it surprised and grieved many of them.

It was the place of Jesus that made the difference. To see him as the Messiah was to put everything in a new perspective. Not only did the Christians see him as the Messiah, but as the crucified Messiah. For them the central thing was the cross, so that Paul could sum up the message he proclaimed in the words, 'we preach Christ crucified' (1 Cor. 1:23). Whatever subordinate and incidental issues were involved, the essential difference between Judaism and Christianity was the cross (for that matter it is the cross that is the difference between every other religion and Christianity). For the Jews, the Messiah is still to come and when he comes he will be supreme. For the Christians he has come already and when he came they put him on a cross.

It is not at all unlikely that at first the Christians did not realize the full significance of the cross. But in time they came to see that the crucifixion is rightly understood only when it is seen as God's great saving act. It is the means God used to deal with the problem of human sin. The Christians came to emphasize that the way of salvation is not the way of law, as devout Jews held. It is the way of grace. People do not merit salvation but receive it as a free gift from God on the basis of what Christ's death accomplished. That death means something old, for God has always acted by the way of grace, as Paul makes so clear in his discussion of Abraham (Rom. 4); the cross is the continuation of the outworking of his grace. But it also means something radically new, for God had never before done anything like sending his Son to die for people's salvation. That was a new demonstration of God's forgiving love; it meant that sin was really overcome and put out of

11

the way. It meant a new way to God – a new and living way.

We can understand some things about this new way by a close study of some of the words the New Testament writers used to bring out the meaning of the cross. They made use of some vivid picture-words, words that meant much to the people of the day, but which we do not always use in the same way. Thus we sometimes talk of 'sacrifice', or again of 'redemption', but we do not mean by these terms what the New Testament writers meant. It is worth studying the terms in an attempt to rediscover what the first Christians had in mind when they used them.

This book, then, is a study of some of the great words used to bring out the meaning of the cross and is thus a serious attempt to see some of the significance of Christ's atoning work. It is undertaken partly because there is a tendency, in some quarters at least, to minimize the place of the cross. There are not many leading theologians these days who discuss theories of the atonement. We tend to emphasize the incarnation or liberation theology or the reality behind the charismatic movement. With few exceptions people are not writing about the atonement.

But this is to ignore the fundamental New Testament position. Paul could say that Christian preachers 'preach Christ crucified' (1 Cor. 1:23). Again, when he outlines the essential Christian message he begins with 'what I received I passed on to you as of first importance: that Christ died for our sins according to the Scriptures...' (1 Cor. 15:3), and concludes his summary with 'Whether, then, it was I or they, this is what we preach, and this is what you believed' (1 Cor. 15:11). There are differences in the ways the New Testament writers present the facts, but there can be no doubt that for the New Testament writers as a whole it was the cross that was at the heart of the faith. In the literal sense of the term it was 'crucial'. We are saved, not by some fine theory and not by some blinding revelation and certainly not by our own best effort, but by Christ's atoning death.

Therefore any really serious attempt to understand the Christian way must begin with the cross. Unless we come to see what the cross means we do not understand Christianity, real Christianity in the sense the New Testament writers gave to it. The cross is absolutely central. We must give time and attention to our understanding of what it means.

While the New Testament writers are agreed on its centrality, they do not all bring this out in the same way. Some prefer one kind of imagery, others another. I have picked out what seem to me to be some of the more important of the picture-words these writers used and I have subjected them to close scrutiny. As we see what these words meant to those who used them originally, we shall be led into a fuller understanding of the depths of meaning they found in Christ's cross. We will see something of what it cost Jesus to bring about our salvation and something of the meaning of atonement. I do not claim that at the end we will know exactly how the atonement works. Through more than nineteen centuries the church has been working at that problem and it still has not come up with an agreed solution. But at least we shall know a little more of what the New Testament writers are saying to us.

Basically this will concern the meaning of Christ's atoning work. How does the death of Jesus, so many years ago, bring salvation to all his people, those alive then and those alive now? The question is not easy to answer, but the language of the early Christians helps us come closer to an understanding. We see that there are many facets to the cross. It may be seen as a paying of the price, as a bringing of enemies into a state of friendship, as an opening up of a way of access to God, and much more. These great words tell us much about the way of the cross in the sense that the cross is the means of dealing with all our sins.

They also speak to us about the way of the cross in the sense that Christians are people who live in a certain way. We shall be challenged as we come to see more fully what the cross meant to the New Testament writers. Not only is the cross of Jesus the means of bringing us into salvation, but it is a reminder that we are to take up our cross day by day (Lk. 9:23). To understand that Jesus died for us is to understand that we must live for him. Not for those who follow the crucified Christ are the paths of selfish ease.

The new and living way is, first and foremost, the way that Christ made open by dying on the cross for the salvation of his people. But it is also the way in which his people walk. They are different because they have been brought out of their sins into the way of God. This study is concerned most of all with the former aspect, but no-one can study the meaning of the cross without coming to see that it has its implications also for the daily life of every follower of the crucified one.

1
Covenant

It was the last night of Jesus' life. He was at table in the upper room with his disciples. During the course of the meal he took some of the bread that was on the table, gave God thanks, broke the bread and gave it to the disciples with the words, 'This is my body.' A little while later he took a cup of wine, gave thanks over it and gave it to them saying, 'This cup is the new covenant in my blood' (1 Cor. 11:23–25), or perhaps, 'This is my blood of the new covenant' (Mk. 14:24).

As Jesus in this way began the service of Holy Communion, a service which has continued throughout the centuries and has spread throughout the world, he connected the shedding of his blood with the making of a new covenant. There is a slight problem posed by the fact that some ancient manuscripts do not have the word 'new' in the accounts in Matthew and Mark and the whole verse which contains it might possibly be omitted in Luke. The scholars enjoy themselves working out which is likely to be the correct reading in each of our accounts. But for our present purpose we can ignore these delights. There are no such textual doubts about our earliest account, that in 1 Corinthians, and in any case, describe it how you will, any covenant Jesus made had to be a new one, for the old one had been in existence for hundreds of years.

What did Jesus mean by 'the new covenant in my blood'? The answer is not obvious. We use the word 'covenant' today but not in such a way as to make sense of 'the new covenant in my blood' or 'my blood of the new covenant'. The *Shorter Oxford English Dictionary* defines a covenant as 'A mutual agreement between two or more persons to do or refrain from doing certain acts;

sometimes, the undertaking of one of the parties.' It goes on to inform us that nowadays the term is mainly used in a legal or theological sense, and in this latter sense it is 'Applied to engagements entered into by and with the Divine Being, as revealed in the Scriptures, etc.'. But, even armed with all this information, we are not really in a position to make much sense of the words of Jesus about blood in connection with the covenant, nor with the idea that the covenant is a new one.

For that we must go back to the Old Testament, where the concept of covenant is frequent and very important. Covenants go back as far as one God made with Noah (Gn. 6:18; 9:9; *etc.*). Some scholars speak of a covenant with Adam, holding that what the Old Testament tells us about our first father justifies us in thinking that there was a covenant between him and God. Be that as it may, the word 'covenant' is not used in Scripture of this relationship and it is better to confine ourselves to the passages which definitely speak of a covenant.

The covenant with Noah was a covenant between God and a man; but there are also covenants in which God does not feature, covenants between people. It seems reasonable to think that the term was originally applied to such human covenants and that people then reflected that the word could fittingly be applied to God's dealings with them. So it will be profitable to begin with purely human covenants. These covenants are always regarded as very serious affairs. They were a bit like a very solemn business agreement among us, a binding contract, or in many cases like a treaty. But whereas with us such transactions are essentially secular, belonging to the areas of business and diplomacy, with the Hebrews covenants were fundamentally religious. A covenant was an undertaking entered into before God and solemnly ratified with appropriate religious ritual.

In the Old Testament covenant was only occasionally between private individuals. The one purely individual covenant in the whole Old Testament appears to be that between David and Jonathan, and even that may have had wider implications because Jonathan was the king's son and it was presumed that he would be king himself one day. Any solemn agreement into which he entered might then become an affair of state. Whatever be the case with this covenant, all the other covenants were between representative men and they implied that those they represented were equally bound by the covenant. For example, Jacob and

Laban made a covenant (Gn. 31:44–54) and clearly this was binding on the clans of which they were the respective heads and not only on these two men as private individuals.

A covenant was always made with good intentions between the parties. There is never a covenant binding the two to harm one another in any way. A covenant is always a pledge by one, and usually by both, that the interests of the other party will be forwarded. A covenant always means being loyal to the other party; it is never simply an agreement to perform some external duty.

There seems to be no passage in which the method of making a covenant is outlined. The ancients knew quite well how it was done and apparently had no urge to set out the various steps for the benefit of posterity. But if we put together what we learn from the making of a number of covenants a procedure something like the following emerges.

1. Agreement on the terms
Obviously there was going to be no covenant unless the two parties were in agreement on some course of action that bound at least one of them (and more commonly both) for the future. And as we have seen, it bound them to benefit and help each other, never to hurt one another.

2. The swearing of an oath
A covenant was not to be entered into lightly. Each party must know that the other had every intention of carrying out to the full the obligations he was taking upon himself. So both swore a solemn oath that they would carry out the covenant obligations. So important was this that on occasion the whole process could be spoken of shortly as 'the oath' (*e.g.* Lk. 1:73).

3. The offering of a sacrifice
Sacrifice was the universal religious rite in antiquity, but the sacrifice on the occasion of a covenant seems to have had some special features. The animal being offered was cut in two and apparently laid on the ground so that the two parties to the covenant could walk between the parts (Gn. 15:10, and *cf.* verse 17; Je. 34:18). That this was the distinctive feature of the process is indicated by the fact that the Hebrews did not normally say 'to make a covenant', but 'to cut a covenant'. Other ways of putting it are indeed found. They include 'establishing' a covenant, or

giving it, commanding it, swearing it, declaring it, and even, on occasion, making it. Obviously there was no stereotyped way of affirming that a covenant had come into existence. But there can be no doubt but that 'cutting' a covenant was the most usual as well as the most picturesque way of putting it.

4. *The witness*

There was often a witness, but this is not to be understood in our terms. We think of a witness as someone who was there and can testify to what was done. But Abraham and Abimelech had seven ewe lambs as a witness to their covenant (Gn. 21:27–30; NIV here has 'treaty' for the Hebrew *bᵉrîth*, but this is the word usually rendered 'covenant'). Jacob and Laban made a heap of stones to be their witness (Gn. 31:44–48). The witness was not an independent figure who could speak up and testify to the fact and the terms of the covenant. The witness was rather something that served to remind the participants of what they had done.

5. *The feast*

It is possible that the sacrifice offered when a covenant was made included a feast (as the peace offering did, Lv. 7:15, *etc.*). If it did not, then at least on some occasions the making of a covenant was marked by the holding of a feast. The story of the making of the covenant between Jacob and Laban ends with the words: 'So Jacob took an oath in the name of the Fear of his father Isaac. He offered a sacrifice there in the hill country and invited his relatives to a meal' (Gn. 31:53–54).

There may well have been other features. Thus, on the occasion of the covenant Jonathan made with David, Jonathan gave his friend the robe he was wearing, his tunic, his sword, his bow and his belt (1 Sa. 18:4). The exchange of such gifts is attested in similar rites in other lands and it may well have been a regular part of covenant making in Israel, even though we do not read about it often. When we are trying to work out how a covenant was made in ancient Israel we meet the difficulty that much is left unsaid in our sources. We see this clearly in the case of the dividing of the sacrifice. The dividing of the animals and the passing between the pieces is attested in the cases of Abraham and Jeremiah, two examples centuries apart, but nowhere in between. We must assume that it continued unchanged through those hundreds of years, but there is no mention of it. Other features may likewise have escaped mention in our sources. But at least in the points noted above we may feel confident that we have the main features of the making of a covenant in Israel of old.

The meaning of 'cutting' a covenant has been disputed. The reason for this action is nowhere told us and we are left to try to work it out from the nature of the whole covenant scene. Some scholars have seen in this action rather curious meanings. For example, W. Robertson Smith held that it meant that the two parties to the covenant were taken up into the mystical life of the victim. I have never been able to be quite sure what this means and I find it even harder to think that people such as Jacob or Abimelech would have embraced such an idea.

It is much more likely that they looked at the victim, cut in pieces as it was, and as they took their position in the middle of the dismembered pieces solemnly called down on themselves a like fate if they proved faithless to the serious undertaking into which they were entering. A covenant was a grave and important obligation; it should not be undertaken lightly.

That this is the meaning seems clear from the way the sacrifice is understood in a passage in Jeremiah where covenant breakers are promised punishment. God says, 'The men who have violated my covenant and have not fulfilled the terms of the covenant they made before me, I will treat like the calf they cut in two and then walked between its pieces' (Je. 34:18). This is quite clear also in the record of a covenant made in ancient Babylon in which a certain Mati'-ilu took part. The text recording proceedings speaks of the sacrificing of a goat and goes on:

> This head is not the head of the goat...it is the head of Mati'-ilu....If Mati'-ilu (breaks) this oath, as the head of this goat is cut off...so shall the head of Mati'-ilu be cut off....This loin is not the loin of the goat, it is the loin of Mati'-ilu....[1]

As part after part of the animal is identified with Mati'-ilu that worthy should have been left in no doubt about the gruesome fate that awaited him if he should break the terms of the covenant.

Covenants between men were usually between representative men, as we have seen. Thus Abraham made a covenant with

[1] A. Jeremias, *The Old Testament in the Light of the Ancient East*, vol. ii (London, 1911), p.49.

Abimelech (Gn. 21:27). The patriarch could put an army of 318 trained men into the field when it was a question of battle (Gn. 14:14), so clearly he was the head of a not unimportant clan, while Abimelech was king of Gerar (Gn. 20:2). Obviously a covenant between two such men was more than a private agreement. It carried implications for the groups of which they were the heads. Indeed, some of this is spelt out when Abimelech says to Abraham, 'God is with you in everything you do. Now swear to me here before God that you will not deal falsely with me or my children or my descendants. Show to me and the country where you are living as an alien the same kindness that I have shown to you' (Gn. 21:22–23). We are not told exactly what it was that Abimelech covenanted to do, but it is certainly implied that he would carry on with the 'kindness' he claims to have shown in the past. Even if he made no specific commitment it would still be a valid covenant. On occasion a covenant might be one-sided, with all the obligations resting on the one partner.

Other covenants between men are referred to from time to time, such as the one suggested between Nahash the Ammonite and the people of Jabesh Gilead (1 Sa. 11:1), a proposal that fell through because Nahash made it a condition that he gouge out the right eye of each of the men of the town. And David made a covenant with 'all the elders of Israel' at Hebron that he should be king (1 Ch. 11:3). There were others. But enough has been said to indicate the general meaning of covenant and to show something of its importance in the life of ancient Israel.

COVENANTS OF KINGS AND NATIONS

The covenants that God made with people were the really important covenants in the Old Testament. In recent years a good deal of attention has been given to suzerainty covenants in the ancient world, mostly those in which the Hittite kings were involved. In such covenants vassals normally pledge their allegiance to some great king, and it has been suggested that covenants of this kind may well have formed the model which the Hebrews used to help convey something of their relationship with their God. Some of the treaties discovered were between equals, as kings pledged themselves to acknowledge one another's borders, return runaway slaves and the like. More important for our present purpose were those with subordinates, when the 'kindness' of the great king is spelt out, as are the duties laid upon the vassal and the curses that will follow if the vassal breaks the treaty. Corresponding blessings for faithfulness are, of course, also listed. Such treaties are found by scholars in the Old Testament. An example of a covenant between equals might be that between Hiram and Solomon (1 Ki. 5; the actual word 'covenant' is not used here, but the relationship appears to be covenantal). And for a suzerainty covenant, that between the Israelites and the Gibeonites is often cited (Jos. 9; the word *bᵉrîth* is used several times, verses 6, 7, 11, 15, 16).

COVENANTS WITH GOD

Whether it was this sort of thing that formed the pattern or not, it is beyond dispute that in the Old Testament 'covenant' was a favourite way of referring to the relationship between God and his people. Covenants with God go back to that with Noah. When God told that patriarch that he would bring a great flood on the earth and destroy sinners, he added, 'But I will establish my covenant with you' (Gn. 6:18). After the flood had subsided God said, 'I now establish my covenant with you and with your descendants after you and with every living creature that was with you...every living creature on earth. I establish my covenant with you: Never again will all life be cut off by the waters of a flood; never again will there be a flood to destroy the earth' (Gn. 9:9–11). God proceeded to give the rainbow as 'the sign of the covenant between me and the earth' (verse 13).

In this covenant some features emerge which we will find characteristic of covenants with God and which are not necessarily found in purely human covenants. First, *the initiative is with God*. Noah is not said to have done anything in the matter. God proposed the covenant. God laid down the terms. It is unthinkable that men should negotiate with God, so a covenant with God is always a matter of accepting what God offers. Secondly, Noah is *a representative man*, so that the covenant includes others than him; in fact its terms have relevance to all life on earth. We are given no information about how the covenant was inaugurated, if there was in fact any set ceremony, but there is a reference to the rainbow as a sign or witness. A further most important feature of this covenant is that it is a covenant of *pure grace*. Noah is not asked to do anything. God simply makes a promise to him that he will never again destroy the earth with a flood.

God's covenant with Abraham is a very important one, all the more so since in the New Testament it is regarded as of continuing validity (the coming of Christ is seen as the outworking of that covenant, Lk. 1:68–73; *cf.* also Rom. 4). God promised Abraham a numberless progeny and possession of the land of Canaan (Gn. 15:5–7). When Abraham asked how he could know this, God made a covenant with him. He told the patriarch to bring certain animals and birds. Abraham was to divide the animals and arrange the halves opposite each other (the birds for some reason were not divided). In due course 'a smoking fire pot with a blazing torch appeared and passed between the pieces' (verse 17). The light would seem to symbolize the presence of God and the passing between the pieces the solemn entering into covenant. Abraham did not pass between the pieces, but then he was not undertaking any obligations. He was simply the recipient of God's good gift. In all this Abraham was a representative man. The covenant referred not only to him but also to his descendants (verse 18). They are included in the blessing on Abraham.

A little later the requirement of circumcision is laid on the patriarch and his descendants and linked with the covenant: 'This is my covenant with you and your descendants after you, the covenant you are to keep: Every male among you shall be circumcised' (Gn. 17:10). But this does not mean the abandonment of the principle that the covenant was all of grace. Circumcision was not a meritorious work, a virtuous act that earned a place within the covenant for Abraham and his progeny. It is expressly said to be 'the sign of the covenant' (verse 11). In a way similar to that of the rainbow in the covenant with Noah, it is a sign that those who receive the mark are included in the covenant made with Abraham. That covenant is consistently seen as a covenant resting on the goodness of God, not on the achievement of men. It is not a reward for faithful service but a promise proceeding from the love of God.

THE COVENANT AT SINAI

God made other covenants, such as that with Aaron and his offspring (Nu. 18:19) or that with David (2 Sa. 23:5). But perhaps the most important of all is that at Mount Sinai, a covenant with the whole nation of Israel. It is described in Exodus 24. It all began when Moses 'told the people all the LORD's words and laws', to which 'they responded with one voice, "Everything the

LORD has said we will do"' (Ex. 24:3). Early next morning Moses built an altar at the foot of the mountain and set up twelve pillars of stone to represent the twelve tribes. Then 'young Israelite men' (interestingly not priests) offered burnt offerings and peace offerings (verse 5). There seems nothing unusual about these sacrifices (except that priests are not mentioned). The blood, however, was treated in a distinctive way. Moses took half of it and put it in bowls, while the other half he dashed against the altar (the Hebrew verb denotes a much more vigorous action than NIV's 'sprinkled'). He read to the people 'the Book of the Covenant' after which they responded, 'We will do everything the LORD has said; we will obey' (verse 7).

Now Moses took the rest of the blood, the half he had put in bowls, and threw it over the people (the same vigorous verb used of throwing the other half of the blood against the altar in verse 6). He said, 'This is the blood of the covenant that the LORD has made with you in accordance with all these words' (verse 8). There is then a reference to some of the leaders seeing God and to eating and drinking, evidently the consummation of the sacrifice (verses 9–11).

This covenant was of the utmost importance. The people were now the people of God, people in covenant relationship with the one God. And God was the God of the people, in covenant relationship with this one nation in all the earth. It is scarcely an exaggeration to say that all that happened subsequently in Old Testament days is to be understood against this background. Israel stood in a special relationship to God and this governed all that the later Old Testament writers tell us. This is so even though the covenant terminology was not used by all writers. For, whether they chose to use this language or not, the idea that the nation stood in a relationship to God such as no other nation did dominates Old Testament thinking. This is well illustrated by Walther Eichrodt's treatment of the material in his *Theology of the Old Testament*. In volume 1, after a chapter on 'The Problem and the Method', he uses the word 'covenant' in every chapter heading: 'The Covenant Relationship', 'The Covenant Statutes', 'The Name of the Covenant God', 'The Nature of the Covenant God', and so on. The covenant with God dominated Israelite religion. It mattered intensely to Old Testament Israel that the nation was in covenant relationship to the one and only God. All its thinking and living revolved round this fact.

COVENANT DISTINCTIVES

In the ceremony of covenant making in Exodus 24 there are some unusual features, three in particular. The first of these is the element of personal participation. In other covenants there is a representative person who enters the covenant and by doing so takes with him all those he represents. This is what Noah did, for example, and Abraham. But in Exodus 24 we have a covenant with the nation, not with Moses. Moses has a role something like that of Master of Ceremonies. He directs what is done, but he does not enter into the covenant himself (other than as a member of the people). Twice the people took obligations on themselves (verses 3, 7). The blood was put on them, not on chosen representatives (verse 8). Moses evidently regarded this participation as important, for he is recorded as saying: 'The LORD our God made a covenant with us at Horeb. It was not with our fathers that the LORD made this covenant, but with us, with all of us who are alive here today. The LORD spoke to you face to face out of the fire on the mountain' (Dt. 5:2–4; 'Horeb' is another name for Mount Sinai).

We may fairly reflect that there is a limit to what one can do for another. While it is true that in a covenant the father stands in for his own, as Abraham did, it is also true that in the end we must all enter the covenant for ourselves or place ourselves outside its scope. It is not possible to live for ever on the spiritual capital of our ancestors. R. B. Y. Scott can say:

> The religious group which only carries on the momentum in belief and practice of an age which has passed away, and has not made its own the covenant of the fathers, will find that the covenant is no longer valid, and the living God has passed on to seek a new people for himself.[2]

A second unusual feature of this ceremony of covenant making was the putting of the blood on the people. We should probably pay the more attention to this feature because the words, 'This is the blood of the covenant' (Ex. 24:8), which accompanied the putting of the blood on the people, seem to lie behind Jesus' words, 'This is my blood of the new covenant.' As we are unfamiliar with covenant-making ceremonies and with the

[2] R. B. Y. Scott, *The Relevance of the Prophets* (New York, 1944), p.210.

manipulation of blood in the sacrifices generally, we can easily miss the point that this is a most unusual action. In fact elsewhere in the whole Old Testament blood was put on people in only two ceremonies: the consecration of a priest to his high office and the cleansing of a person who had been cured of leprosy. When Aaron and his sons were formally admitted into the office of priest a ram was killed and Moses put some of its blood on the lobe of the right ear, the thumb of the right hand and the big toe of the right foot, first of Aaron and then of his sons (Lv. 8:23–24). A similar ceremony was performed when anyone was being cleansed after being cured of leprosy (Lv. 14:14): blood was put on the lobe of the right ear, the thumb of the right hand and the big toe of the right foot; in this case there was also the requirement that the priest should sprinkle the man seven times with a mixture of water and the blood of a bird (verse 7).

Nowhere are we given an explanation of the meaning of this ceremony with the blood; but the general use of blood in connection with sacrifice points to cleansing from sin and defilement. There is no reason to doubt that when blood was put on people this was the idea. In the cases both of the priest and of the cleansed leper there is also the thought of dedication to a new life among the people of God. All this seems to form an important clue to our understanding of Exodus 24. The whole people was being cleansed from the sin and defilement of its tainted past and at the same time was being consecrated for its new role as the people of God.

The third unusual feature of this covenant was that the people took on themselves the obligation to obey God's laws. It is not said that they were asked to do this or that it was a condition of the covenant. But when Moses told them 'all the LORD's words and laws', they 'responded with one voice, "Everything the LORD has said we will do"', after which Moses wrote down what the LORD had said. After the blood had been thrown against the altar Moses read to the people 'the Book of the Covenant' and they said, 'We will do everything the LORD has said; we will obey' (Ex. 24:3–4, 7). From other passages it would seem that the Ten Commandments were especially in mind. Thus there is a passage which equates 'the tablets of stone' which Moses received on the mountain and which contained the Ten Commandments (Dt. 5:22) with 'the tablets of the covenant that the LORD had made with you' (Dt. 9:9). Again, a passage which begins with 'Hear, O Israel, the decrees and the laws...' goes on, 'The LORD our God made a covenant with us at Horeb' and shortly afterwards lists the Ten Commandments (Dt. 5:1–2, 6–21). Elsewhere we read that God commanded Moses, 'Write down these words, for in accordance with these words I have made a covenant with you and with Israel' and Moses 'wrote on the tablets the words of the covenant – the Ten Commandments' (Ex. 34:27–28). It is possible that in this last passage the 'he' who wrote is actually God, but however we resolve that question the connection of the Ten Commandments with the covenant is clear.

Curiously Exodus says nothing about what God would do. In the other covenants with God it is always what God says he will do that is the significant thing. Those covenants are in fact little more than solemn promises from God; the covenant framework simply adds solemnity. It is unusual to have a covenant with God in which God does not specifically promise anything. It is, however, implicit in Exodus 24 that God will bless the people and this is explicit in other covenant passages. Thus we read: 'I will look on you with favour and make you fruitful and increase your numbers, and I will keep my covenant with you.' This passage goes on to speak of blessings in harvest and of God's dwelling place as being among the people and adds, 'I will walk among you and be your God, and you will be my people' (Lv. 26:9–12; *cf*. Ex. 19:5–6). There can be no question but that the covenant means that Israel was given a special place in God's plan. Nor should we doubt that it foreshadowed many wonderful blessings.

The people's repeated promise to keep God's commandments remains to be considered. Some have understood this to mean that this covenant was one of works. Their idea is that Israel agreed to do certain things for God and in response God agreed to do certain things for Israel. But this is not the way Exodus 24 reads. The covenant between God and Israel proceeded from God's choice of the nation. It was God's choice that was the first and dominant factor, as is made clear in an earlier reference to the covenant: 'You yourselves have seen what I did to Egypt, and how I carried you on eagles' wings and brought you to myself. Now if you obey me fully and keep my covenant, then out of all nations you will be my treasured possession. Although the whole earth is mine, you will be for me a kingdom of priests and a holy nation' (Ex. 19:4–6). It is God's choice that is first and with that God's saving activity in delivering the people from Egypt. Obligations follow indeed ('if you obey me fully and keep my covenant'), but they are not the reason for the choice. There is nothing like 'If you do this for me, I will do that for you', either in the attitude of God or in that of the people.

Jacob's reaction to a vision he had of God is in marked contrast. That patriarch was deeply moved. He made a vow and expressed his feelings in these words:

> If God will be with me and will watch over me on this journey I am taking and will give me food to eat and clothes to wear so that I return safely to my father's house, then the LORD will be my God. This stone that I have set up as a pillar will be God's house, and of all that you give me I will give you a tenth (Gn. 28:20–22).

Jacob is certainly saying, 'If you do certain things for me, then I will do certain things for you.' But there is no equivalent attitude on the part of Israel in Exodus 24. Rather, there the people are gratefully accepting God's goodness and pledging themselves to be his servants in response.

The process has been likened to a royal wedding. When a prince marries a commoner the young man would not say to his bride after the wedding: 'My dear, you have made an excellent beginning. If you try very hard to live in the right way you will perhaps one day be admitted into the royal family.' But he could say (if he chose), 'My dear, you have become a member of the royal family. You are royalty. It is important that you live as a member of the royal family should.'

It was like that with Israel. We see the sequence in some words of Moses: 'Be silent, O Israel, and listen! You have now become the people of the LORD your God. Obey the LORD your God and follow his commands and decrees that I give you today' (Dt. 27:9–10). The people first became 'the people of the LORD'. That had already happened. It was in the past. Now ('today') came the commands and decrees. They had entered the position of privilege. Now they must live lives that befitted their new station.

That Israel was in a peculiar sense God's people and that God was Israel's God dominated Israel's thinking throughout the Old Testament period. It was not that the people felt that they could appeal to God on the grounds of the covenant. They did this occasionally, as when the Psalmist prayed, 'Have regard for your covenant, because haunts of violence fill the dark places of the land. Do not let the oppressed retreat in disgrace; may the poor and needy praise your name' (Ps. 74:20–21). But this is not frequent, probably because the Israelites were all too well aware that they had signally failed to keep up their end. You cannot appeal to God on the basis of a covenant you have broken comprehensively and often.

But if they could not plead the covenant, they could remember that God was faithful to it. Moses could say, 'Know therefore that the LORD your God is God; he is the faithful God, keeping his covenant of love to a thousand generations of those who love him and keep his commands' (Dt. 7:9). God is a faithful God. He can be relied on to keep his part of the covenant, even if Israel did not keep hers. It made a great deal of difference to all Israelite thinking.

It set Israel apart from other peoples. While the idea that God made a covenant with his people was not confined to Israel, generally speaking the little nations around Israel seem to have had the view that in some way their god was kin to them, that he was bound up with them. This led to the comforting conviction that in the last resort he was bound to come to their aid. Thus the people of Moab felt that Chemosh their god might on occasion be angry with them and punish them. But when things got serious they could rely on him to help them. He had to. In the last resort his future was bound up with theirs. If they perished so did he. And in this they were, of course, quite right. Moab has perished and where is Chemosh?

But Israel did not have this comfortable thought. Israel could point to a definite time when God entered into covenant with the nation. He had existed before that. And if he had done it once he could do it again. Israel never made the mistake of thinking that God must save the people if he was to save himself. He could say, 'be holy, because I am holy' (Lv. 11:44). They knew that being in covenant with God did not bind God to come to their aid no matter what. They knew that being in covenant with God meant rather that they must strive to be like him no matter what. The concept of covenant gave a moral emphasis to the religion of the Hebrews that was most important for the future of all mankind.

THE NEW COVENANT

But unfortunately, though Israel knew what was implied in being the people of God, Israel did not live up to that knowledge. Like the men of Ephraim, 'they did not keep God's covenant and refused to live by his law' (Ps. 78:10); 'they kept on sinning', 'their hearts were not loyal to him, they were not faithful to his covenant' (Ps. 78:32, 37). Isaiah complained, 'they have disobeyed the laws, violated the statutes and broken the everlasting covenant' (Is. 24:5), and Jeremiah, 'Both the house of Israel and the house of Judah have broken the covenant' (Je. 11:10; see also 22:9; 34:18). Ezekiel tells the people that the Lord said, 'you have despised my oath by breaking the covenant' (Ezk. 16:59). The accusation of covenant breaking is clear and it is repeated. Even though God remained faithful there was no real covenant when his covenant partner broke the covenant so consistently.

It was the case, as we have seen, that Israel was not brought into the covenant on condition that she kept the laws. But it was also the case that being the people of God involved living as the people of God, and the people did not live like that. They kept sinning and sinning and sinning. And their prophets kept telling and telling and telling them that they were placing themselves at a distance from God and cutting themselves off from his blessing. It was a hopeless situation. It was hopeless because every attempt to bring the people back and get them to keep the covenant meant trying to do something new with the same old men. Yet God was a covenant-keeping God. He said, 'I will never break my covenant with you' (Jdg. 2:1). What was to be done when a covenant-keeping God was linked to a covenant-breaking people?

The prophet Jeremiah tells of a radical new solution. He passes on this word from God:

> 'The time is coming,' declares the LORD,
>   'when I will make a new covenant
> with the house of Israel
>   and with the house of Judah.
> It will not be like the covenant
>   I made with their forefathers
> when I took them by the hand
>   to lead them out of Egypt,
> because they broke my covenant,

> though I was a husband to them,'
>> declares the LORD.
> 'This is the covenant that I will make with the
>> house of Israel
>> after that time,' declares the Lord.
> 'I will put my law in their minds
>> and write it on their hearts.
> I will be their God,
>> and they will be my people.
> No longer will a man teach his neighbour,
>> or a man his brother, saying, "Know the LORD,"
> because they will all know me,
>> from the least of them to the greatest,'
>>> declares the LORD.
> 'For I will forgive their wickedness
>> and will remember their sins no more' (Je. 31:31–34).

This means a radical break with the past. It represents a new approach to the problem of man's relationship to God. It is not that God's high standards are relaxed for one moment. God's law is to be put into their minds and written on their hearts. The moral law is being given a central place. The difference is that the law is now part of the people. It is within them, transforming them. They obey it because of what they are. This is more than the obeying of an external set of commands and ordinances. It points to a whole-hearted transformation. God's people will want to do God's will with mind and heart. Far from there being a relaxation of moral demands or moral standards, these are heightened because they are now to be part of God's people's innermost being.

This involves a knowledge of the LORD. Those who have God's law within them will not need to be told to know the LORD. They will have a personal knowledge of him and this no matter how humble they may be in the world's eyes, or for that matter how great. Neither smallness nor greatness is a disqualification. Not many people in the Old Testament are said to have actually known the LORD. In those days it was rather an aspiration, something that people might greatly long for, but which they felt they were not likely to attain. The new covenant would see a radical alteration of this situation. It would bring all God's people into a personal knowledge of him.

The new covenant would be based on forgiveness, not on a profession of readiness to keep the law of God. It is true that throughout the Old Testament there is a good deal about sin and what must be done about it; and it is true that the sacrificial system bears witness to a concern for sin, a recognition that sin is serious, that it is not to be forgiven lightly, but that God has provided a way of forgiveness. But in the making of the covenant at Sinai the emphasis was not on this. The emphasis was rather on the people's repeated declaration that they would obey God's commandments. Their failure to obey vitiated the old covenant, and this makes it very interesting that the new covenant stressed forgiveness. The new covenant would not be vitiated in the same way as the first covenant was. It makes full allowance for the weakness of sinful people. The fact that sinners can know God rests on the other fact that God has made provision for their sins and their wickedness to be put away decisively. How that will be done the prophet Jeremiah does not say. It is the fact and not the means that he sets forth. But as to the fact he is in no doubt. Forgiveness is basic to the new covenant.

The passage in Jeremiah is the most important passage for the new covenant but it is by no means the only one. Jeremiah tells us later that God will make 'an everlasting covenant with them' (Je. 32:40; so also 50:5), and he brings out the inwardness of it with God's promise, 'I will give them singleness of heart and action' (Je. 32:39). Ezekiel is another prophet who looks forward to God's 'everlasting covenant' (Ezk. 16:60; 37:26); it will be 'a covenant of peace' (Ezk. 34:25; 37:26). Isaiah makes a most important point when he says that the Servant will be 'a covenant for the people and a light for the Gentiles' (Is. 42:6). The Old Testament normally concentrates on Israel, so this linking of the Gentiles with the covenant is very significant. Isaiah also has the thought that the covenant will be everlasting (Is. 55:3; 61:8) and he has the inner strengthening idea with the thoughts of the Spirit being on the people and of God's words being in their mouths (Is. 59:21).

Such passages make it clear that the prophets did not take Israel's failure as final. They could not imagine that the covenant-making and covenant-keeping God would remain content with a broken covenant and a lost world. They looked forward confidently to a day when he would intervene decisively and deal effectively with the problem of human sin. And they interpreted that intervention in part in covenant terms – there would be a new covenant.

COVENANT AND TESTAMENT

When we turn to the New Testament we are confronted immediately with a linguistic problem: What is the precise meaning we are to give the Greek word *diathēkē*? Among the Greeks generally this is the ordinary word for a last will and testament, the document in which a man sets forth what he wants done with his property after his death. There is a little scholarly dispute about whether in one or two unusual cases the word may have another meaning, but none as to the fact that in the overwhelming number of cases it means a will, a testament. In both classical Greek and in the papyri it is used often and almost invariably, perhaps invariably, in this sense. This is the way Christians have traditionally understood the word and the title-pages of our Bibles bear witness to this understanding with their references to 'The Old Testament' and 'The New Testament'.

But when the Old Testament was translated into Greek it was this term, *diathēkē*, that was used as the rendering for the Hebrew *bᵉrîth*, 'covenant'. This is not an occasional phenomenon, for it happens 277 times. There cannot be the slightest doubt that the translators used *diathēkē* to convey the meaning 'covenant'. They passed over the usual word for covenant, *synthēkē*, and instead used the term which elsewhere was the regular word for a will.

The sixty-four thousand dollar question for interpreters of the New Testament is thus, 'In the New Testament are we to understand *diathēkē* as "testament" or as "covenant"?' Or, 'Do the New Testament writers follow the usage of Greek writings generally or that of the translators of the Old Testament?' The answer is not simple, for they seem sometimes to have followed the one and sometimes the other. Perhaps they did not make as sharp a distinction between the two concepts as we do. The basic idea in *diathēkē* is that of an authoritative disposition, and this applies equally well to a covenant in which God dictates the terms and a will in which we find the directions of a deceased person.

Perhaps we should notice that in ancient Greece a will did not have precisely the same function as with us today. Property automatically became the possession of a man's children when he died and a will was not needed. The children performed

31

important duties in connection with the burial and kept alive the memory of the deceased. But if he had no children, what then? He adopted a son and made a will directing that his property go to the adopted son. As a condition of receiving the property the son would carry out the religious and other duties laid upon him.

Such an adoption was irrevocable. An adopted son could not be repudiated. If a man had no son and adopted an heir and then later had a natural son, he could not disown the boy he had adopted. The adopted son retained his status as a son and the property was shared with the natural son. Actually the adopted son was somewhat better off than the natural son, for the natural son could be disowned and cut off from the family and his inheritance, whereas the adopted son could not. There is one diverting passage which tells of a natural son who had been disowned, then later forgiven and received back into the family. It must have been a tempestuous household, for later the father decided to disown him again. In the document we have the boy claims that his father is not entitled to do this, for he now has the status of an adopted son!

All this emphasizes the fact that among the Greeks *diathēkē* stood for something laid down with final authority. One cannot bargain with a testator to get better terms. He is dead. It is a case of 'Take it or leave it'. Now we have seen that in the Old Testament, while there are some important covenants among men where negotiation is quite proper, the most significant references to covenant and far and away the most numerous concern covenants which God makes with men. Here God lays down the terms. Man cannot negotiate with God in order to get him to change his mind and produce another agreement that better suits the human recipient of his favours. It may well be that the translators of the Old Testament felt that *synthēkē*, the ordinary word for a compact, would convey the wrong impression if used of covenants which God made. It was too much concerned with two-sidedness, with conceding as little as one must and getting as much as one can. It stood for making a deal and that the best deal that one's negotiating skills made possible. This was not what the Old Testament writers were talking about, so the translators forsook the word that might well have conveyed this meaning. Instead they used a word which indicates an authoritative laying down of the terms. And once they had made their choice on the basis of the covenants God made, they had to use it for those other covenants too.

When we turn to the New Testament it seems indisputable that sometimes *diathēkē* means a covenant and sometimes a will. It means 'covenant' in such a passage as Galatians 3:15, where Paul takes an example, as he says, 'from everyday life. Just as no-one can set aside or add to a human covenant that has been duly established, so it is in this case.' So far the words could refer either to a covenant or to a will. But Paul immediately goes on,

> The promises were spoken to Abraham and to his seed. The Scripture does not say 'and to seeds', meaning many people, but 'and to your seed', meaning one person, who is Christ. What I mean is this: The law, introduced 430 years later, does not set aside the covenant previously established by God.... (Gal. 3:16–17).

This second use of *diathēkē* shows plainly that Paul is referring to the covenant God made with Abraham. The term must mean 'covenant' here.

But we come to a different conclusion if we turn to Hebrews 9:16–17: 'In the case of a will (*diathēkē*), it is necessary to prove the death of the one who made it, because a will (*diathēkē* again) is in force only when somebody has died....' It cannot be said that a covenant is of force only when someone has died. On the contrary, it is very much concerned with the living. In this passage our term must mean a will.

It is thus clear that we must be on our guard if we would see which meaning is in mind in a given passage. The question is an important one and A. Deissmann argued forcefully for the view that in the New Testament we should always see the meaning 'will'. He said forthrightly: 'no one in the Mediterranean world in the first century A.D. would have thought of finding in the word *diathēkē* the idea of "covenant." St. Paul would not, and in fact did not.'[3] Shortly afterwards he writes, 'This one point concerns more than the merely superficial question whether we are to write "New Testament" or "New Covenant" on the title-page of the sacred volume; it becomes ultimately the great question of all religious history: a religion of grace, or a religion

[3] A. Deissmann, *Light from the Ancient East* (London, 1927), p.337.

33

of works?'[4] But though Deissmann thus holds his position strongly and reminds us that our traditional use of the terms 'Old Testament' and 'New Testament' depends on our taking the term in the sense 'will', his position cannot be sustained. In the example we noted in Galatians 3:15–17 it seems impossible exegesis to take *diathēkē* in any sense other than 'covenant'. Deissmann's point that Christianity is a religion of grace rather than of works can be taken just as well when the word is understood as 'covenant'. We must not try to twist passages to make them fit the meaning 'will'. As we shall see, there are many New Testament passages which require the meaning 'covenant'.

Before we leave Deissmann we might give a little more attention to his reference to the title-page of the Bible. We are so used to 'Old Testament' and 'New Testament' that we rarely stop to reflect that in the way we use the word 'testament' these are very curious titles for groups of writings. We would grasp the meaning better if we took the other translation and understood them as 'the Old Covenant' and 'the New Covenant'. The very title-page of the Bible bears witness to the importance of the covenant idea. The writings of Moses and David and the prophets and others are those of the old covenant. But the making of the new covenant by the death of Jesus is a radically new way to God and demands writings of its own to set it forth. Now it is clear that we do not come to God by keeping the law of Moses. We do not come to God by offering animals in sacrifice. We do not come to God by meticulously carrying out all the detailed regulations of the Old Testament. We come to God through Jesus Christ and more specifically by entering into the new covenant he established by his death.

CHRIST'S NEW COVENANT

When Jesus took the bread and broke it, speaking of it as his body, and when he took the wine and said, 'This is my blood of the new covenant', he was indeed referring to the Holy Communion and to his death, but he was also referring to the passage in Jeremiah 31. I do not see how we can possibly import the meaning 'will' into this passage. Jesus is saying that the old prophecy is being fulfilled and that the shedding of his blood is an integral part of the fulfilment. He speaks of his blood as

[4] *Ibid.*, pp.337f.

poured out for many' (Mk. 14:24), which clearly means that his blood was shed to secure the forgiveness of the many. Jesus is instituting a rite which will be carried on through the centuries in remembrance of him and he is linking it both with the forgiveness his death will bring to believers and with the new covenant to which the Old Testament writers looked forward.

We have seen that in the Old Testament the idea of covenant was of the utmost importance. No idea is more fundamental to the Old Testament than that God has in love chosen a particular people and has brought them into covenant relationship with himself. The whole life of Israel flowed from this. The laws they followed were laws given by the covenant God, and the sacrifices they offered were those laid down as part of the outworking of the covenant. Covenant dominated everything. Walther Eichrodt has said,

> the fact that every expression of the OT which is determinative for (Israel's) faith rests on the explicit or implicit assumption that a free act of God, consummated in history, has raised Israel to the rank of the People of God, in whom the nature and will of God are to be revealed. The word 'covenant', therefore, is so to speak a convenient symbol for an assurance much wider in scope and controlling the formation of the national faith at its deepest level, without which Israel would not be Israel.[5]

To speak of the making of a new covenant accordingly is not to suggest some minor modification within Judaism. It is to replace what had been seen as central with something new. The cross of Christ is right at the centre. It transforms everything. The sacrifices which were at the heart of the temple have no meaning once the sacrifice of Christ has been offered. The Jews during the New Testament period insisted on the centrality of the law and the fundamental importance of keeping the law as the way of salvation. But this insistence melts away before the insistence on grace.

Jesus, then, is instituting an observance that was to have a profound meaning for his followers through the centuries. He is pointing out that it is the fulfilment of prophecy, for Jeremiah's

---

[5] W. Eichrodt, *Theology of the Old Testament*, vol. i (London, 1961), p.14.

'new covenant' is now a reality. He is emphasizing that the forgiveness of sin flows from his death as the sacrifice that inaugurates the new covenant.

And this is absolutely revolutionary. Jesus is replacing the whole way of approach to God that his Jewish contemporaries emphasized so strongly and loved so much. He is pointing to a new and living way.

THE PEOPLE OF GOD

In other New Testament passages we find out a good deal about this new covenant. On the negative side, it is not brought about by the keeping of the law. This is quite clear in Galatians 3, where Paul points out that the law, which was so much the pride of the Jews of his day, was given 430 years after God had made his covenant with Abraham. He argues that once a covenant has been duly established no-one can alter its terms. Thus the law cannot affect the approach to God which was made plain in the case of Abraham and which in the end reaches out to all the nations of the earth (Gal. 3:15–17; *cf.* Gn. 12:3). Paul goes on to pose an antithesis: 'For if the inheritance depends on the law, then it no longer depends on a promise; but God in his grace gave it to Abraham through a promise' (verse 18). We can't have it both ways. Law and grace are mutually exclusive as ways of salvation. The conclusion is plain. The law had its place in the purposes of God, but that place was not the bringing of salvation. God has made it abundantly clear in his dealings with Abraham that the only way is the way of grace. Nothing can alter that, certainly not the law. The law was 430 years too late.

Elsewhere Paul makes it clear that 'what the law was powerless to do in that it was weakened by the sinful nature, God did by sending his own Son in the likeness of sinful man to be a sin offering' (Rom. 8:3). The law will not do. The way of salvation depends on Christ's atoning death, not on man's keeping of the law. It is clear throughout the New Testament that God's way is the way of grace and always has been. The place of the law is important, but it is not the way of salvation.

THE COVENANT WITH ABRAHAM

An interesting feature of New Testament teaching is that the covenant that God made with Abraham is consistently regarded as being on a different footing from the covenant at Sinai. The new covenant takes the place of the Sinai covenant; there is all the difference in the world between a covenant which places the written law in a central position and one which is essentially inward, one where the law is written on the heart.

But the covenant with Abraham is different. That had no reference to the keeping of law; in it God promised to bless all the people of the earth through Abraham. The Abrahamic covenant is not superseded by the new covenant but remains in full force. We have seen how Paul brought this out in his letter to the Galatians. We see its importance also in the song of Zechariah which Luke records. That aged priest praised God 'because he has come and has redeemed his people. He has raised up a horn of salvation for us in the house of his servant David' (Lk. 1:68–69). Clearly this is a reference to the coming of Christ to bring men salvation. It might conceivably be followed by a reference to the new covenant. But the song goes on to the way God has acted 'to show mercy to our fathers and to remember his holy covenant, the oath he swore to our father Abraham' (verses 72–73). The coming of Christ did not mean the end of the covenant with Abraham. On the contrary it is the way the covenant with Abraham is brought to its consummation.

Paul has an important passage about Abraham in which much the same point is made, though without specific reference to the covenant (Rom. 4). He argues that Abraham was justified by faith, not works, and that circumcision, which was, of course, the sign of the covenant (Gn. 17:10–11), was 'a seal of the right-eousness that he had by faith while he was still uncircumcised' (Rom. 4:11). This enables him to argue that Abraham is 'the father of all who believe' (*ibid.*), whether they are circumcised or not, and again that Abraham is the father of all believers (verses 16–17). Even though he does not use the covenant terminology here it is plain that Paul is thinking of Abraham as having come into right relationship with God, a right relationship which Christians in Paul's own day shared.

We should draw a similar conclusion from Paul's allegory of Sarah and Hagar, two wives of Abraham. Sarah was a free woman but Hagar a slave, and Paul takes them as representing 'two covenants' (Gal. 4:24). Hagar 'stands for Mount Sinai in Arabia and corresponds to the present city of Jerusalem, because she is in slavery with her children' (verse 25). Clearly this refers to the Judaism which Paul repudiates. It is the way of law and thus of bondage. But in contrast 'the Jerusalem that is above is free, and she is our mother'; 'brothers, we are not children of the slave woman, but of the free woman' (verses 26, 31). Again it is the way shown in the covenant with Abraham that is of permanent significance. We Christians, Paul is arguing, have come to God by Abraham's way, the way of trust. We are included in the covenant with Abraham, a covenant of grace and faith and freedom.

A BETTER COVENANT

The writer to the Hebrews is especially fond of covenant as a way of looking at Christ's saving work. In fact he uses the word *diathēkē* seventeen times, while all the rest of the writers of the New Testament manage only sixteen between them. Clearly he liked the term and found it a satisfactory and helpful way of bringing out important truths.

Repeatedly he assures his readers that the covenant Jesus made is a 'better' covenant than the old one. When Christ 'became a priest', God swore an oath that this priesthood would be 'for ever'. Our author reasons, 'Because of this oath, Jesus has become the guarantee of a better covenant' (Heb. 7:21–22). There was something firm about this covenant, backed as it was by an oath. There was nothing equivalent in the covenant on Sinai (the writer explicitly makes the point that the Aaronic priests had no divine oath behind their priesthood, verse 20).

A little later we find that the new covenant was 'founded on better promises' (Heb. 8:6). The writer does not detail what these promises were, but it is clear from his whole writing that he had especially in mind the promise of forgiveness of sin. That was written into the new covenant in Jeremiah 31:34 and it is in mind in the New Testament wherever the new covenant is mentioned. The wonderful thing about the new way is that it is all of grace. Our sins are forgiven. We do not merit our salvation in any way, but receive it as God's free gift. There is nothing better than this promise. Our author goes on to emphasize this by pointing out that 'if there had been nothing wrong with that first covenant, no place would have been sought for another' (Heb. 8:7). This leads him on to a long quotation from Jeremiah 31, which he cites as showing that God did in fact find fault. The old covenant was not satisfactory. It was replaced with a better one. We should perhaps add to this the fact that in the new covenant the blood 'speaks a better word than the blood of Abel' (Heb. 12:24). This takes us right back to the beginning of things. The implication is that the new covenant is 'better' than anything that has been since the infancy of the human race.

Paul can also argue about the superiority of the new covenant. He tells the Corinthians that it is a covenant 'not of the letter but of the Spirit; for the letter kills, but the Spirit gives life' (2 Cor. 3:6). Clearly a covenant that gives life is better than one that kills. Paul's point here is not unlike the one he makes in Galatians 4: the new covenant spells freedom over against the old which is so much involved with the keeping of specific regulations. He adds the point that the new covenant is more glorious than the old. He reminds his readers of the time Moses' face shone so that it had to be covered (Ex. 34:29–35). He is in no doubt but that the old covenant was glorious. But he points out that that glory was no more than temporary ('fading', 2 Cor. 3:7), which means that it was inferior to the glory that does not fade away, the glory that arises from 'the ministry of the Spirit' (verse 8). He goes on to detail other ways in which the new covenant is more glorious, but they all boil down to this, that the new covenant brings an effectual and lasting salvation, whereas the old ends in nothing but condemnation.

That the superiority of the new is to be seen in the forgiveness it brings, in contrast to the old and its demands which men could not fulfil, comes out in a number of places. It is instructive to notice the way the writer to the Hebrews uses the quotation from Jeremiah 31 which foretells the establishing of the new covenant. In chapter 8 he quotes it at some length, beginning with the promise of the new covenant and not stopping until he reaches the words about forgiveness (Heb. 8:8–12). Later he refers to the same prophecy of Jeremiah, but quotes it much more shortly. The second time he cites the words about the making of a covenant and the writing of God's law in people's hearts and minds. 'Then he adds: "Their sins and lawless acts I will remember no more"' (Heb. 10:16–17). He mentions just those two things: the inwardness of the new covenant and the forgiveness of sins it brings about. He omits everything else. Plainly it is the inwardness of the new covenant and especially its provision for effectual forgiveness of sins that matter to him. The new covenant does not merely tell us about forgiveness. It brings it.

Once our author makes the point that even pious people who

lived under the first covenant had their sins forgiven only through what Christ has done. 'Christ is the mediator of a new covenant,' he writes, 'that those who are called may receive the promised eternal inheritance—now that he has died as a ransom to set them free from the sins committed under the first covenant' (Heb. 9:15). Pious people of old approached God by way of the sacrifices. But 'it is impossible for the blood of bulls and goats to take away sins' (Heb. 10:4). All that the sacrifices effected was a 'reminder of sins' (verse 3). What really took those sins away once and for all was the sacrificial death of Jesus. The offering of animal sacrifice was the way God mediated forgiveness in the days of the first covenant, but it was the death of Christ, not that of the animals, that really delivered people from their sins. There is no other way of dealing with sin and obviously this makes the new covenant superior not only to the old one, but to any other that might conceivably be devised. It is God's way of putting away our sin and it puts sin away once and for all.

Sometimes there is the thought that in the new covenant people are consecrated or set apart for God. Thus we read of 'the blood of the covenant that sanctified' the Christian (Heb. 10:29). This writer does not use the 'sanctify' words in quite the same sense as does Paul. With Paul they refer to the process of becoming holy, the progressive growth in grace. But in Hebrews it is rather the initial act of being set apart to be God's. We should probably see this also in the passage about Abel to which we have already referred. Our author speaks of coming 'to Jesus the mediator of a new covenant, and to the sprinkled blood that speaks a better word than the blood of Abel' (Heb. 12:24). The sprinkling of blood points to cleansing and consecration. Abel's blood cried to God for vengeance (Gn. 4:10), but the blood of Jesus brings forgiveness and consecration to the service of God. The forgiven belong to God. This may be seen also in the opening greeting in 1 Peter where election is 'for obedience to Jesus Christ and sprinkling by his blood' (1 Pet. 1:2). The sprinkling of blood is linked with obedience and it thus points to that setting apart to be God's that we have just seen in Hebrews.

One further thing we should certainly notice. In his great benediction at the end of the letter the writer to the Hebrews says, 'May the God of peace, who through the blood of the eternal covenant brought back from the dead our Lord Jesus, that great Shepherd of the sheep . . .' (Heb. 13:20). With this we should

40

notice his references to Christ as having suffered 'once for all' (*e.g.* Heb. 9:12). The main point in the argument right through this letter is that the new way that Christ made open to God by his death is God's final way. There were preliminary indications of various kinds in the Old Testament, but all that they did was to prepare the way for the coming of Jesus. In him is God's final word. His death for sin, Son of God as he is, puts sin away finally and definitely. 'There is no longer any sacrifice for sin' (Heb. 10:18). The old way was superseded by what Christ did, but his followers need not fear that the way he established will ever be replaced while the world stands. There is an utter finality about the new covenant. It is eternal. To the end of the earth and to the end of time there is no other way.

To see the death of Jesus as establishing a new covenant, then, is to see it as a radical re-shaping of all religion. It is the offering of the sacrifice that not only establishes a covenant but does so by taking sin away. This is clear in the record of Jesus' words in Matthew: 'This is my blood of the (new) covenant, which is poured out for many for the forgiveness of sins' (Mt. 26:28). This being so, there is no need for the multiplicity of regulations governing approach to God which were so characteristic of Judaism and against which Paul made such vigorous protest. The way to God is now seen to be through Christ and through him alone. 'Salvation is found in no-one else, for there is no other name under heaven given to men by which we must be saved' (Acts 4:12).

As Paul saw so clearly, this gives us a freedom that is not found elsewhere. We are not bound to approach God by this or that liturgical path, or by keeping this or that series of regulations. We come boldly in the name of Christ. All else falls away. Nothing else matters. Of course, being a follower of Christ is a whole-hearted and full-time affair. But it is this because this is involved in the living out of what it means to belong to Christ.

Every Christian enters the covenant by faith, and here the references to the covenant with Abraham as of continuing force are important. Abraham is the classic example of faith for the New Testament writers and to be involved in the covenant with Abraham means to live by faith as that patriarch did. Not all the descendants of Abraham were caught up in his covenant with God, and Paul specifically makes the point that in the sense that matters Abraham's children are those who believe, whether they are his physical descendants or not, whether they are circumcised or not. And, of course, a consideration of the place of faith in the covenant calls us to consider the reality of our faith. Without faith, there is no membership in the covenant.

The Holy Communion is a constant reminder of the place of the covenant. Every time we eat the bread and drink the wine in that service we 'proclaim the Lord's death until he comes' (1 Cor. 11:26). We proclaim to others and to ourselves our deep conviction that the Lord's death is central. It is by that death alone that our sins are put away and that we are brought into right relationship with God. Our participation is a pledge that we, whose covenant with God has been established at such cost, will live in a manner befitting the covenant.

As we saw in Hebrews and as it is at least implied throughout the New Testament, the new covenant is God's final way. The covenant is eternal. There is no way of improving on an eternal covenant. Jesus is 'the guarantee of a better covenant'.

For further study

1. Consider the covenant with Abraham (Gn. 15; 17:1–7, 19–21; Lk. 1:67–75; Rom. 4). What may we learn from these passages about the Christian way?
2. Compare the passages about the old covenant (Ex. 24:1–8) and the new covenant (Je. 31:31–34). What do they teach us about the new and living way?
3. What light do the passages that speak of the institution of the Lord's Supper shed on the new covenant? (See Mt. 26:26–29; Mk. 14:22–25; Lk. 22:14–20; but especially 1 Cor. 11:23–34.)
4. The epistle to the Hebrews speaks of the new covenant as 'a better covenant' (Heb. 7:22). From your reading of the whole letter, in what ways is it 'better'?
5. What changes should you make in your own life as a result of your close study of the new covenant?

2
Sacrifice

Sacrifice is a term we use quite often, but in a very different sense from that which the ancients gave it. We dimly realize that once there were people who literally offered animals in sacrifice to their gods and we perhaps reflect that there are still some who do just that. But when we use the word it is almost always in a metaphorical sense. We are not talking about any offering of animals. We are talking about some act we do at cost to ourselves and for the benefit of others (or sometimes for some future good for ourselves). Thus we may speak of the sacrifices some parents make to give their children a good education. Ancients like me remember that during the years of the Second World War we were frequently called upon to make sacrifices to assist our country. That meant forgoing comfort and pay rises and it involved making do with inferior substitutes instead of insisting on the superior article; on occasion it meant going without something altogether. Or we may speak of the sacrifices an athlete makes in training. For the greater good set before him in the future he forgoes present ease and leisure. All such usages bring out the idea of a deprivation of one kind or another. For us sacrifice means cost.

The idea of cost or personal deprivation is certainly involved in the way the people of the Bible used the expression. But they normally had a more specific idea in mind. They thought of the sacrifices offered up in the temple. There was a great variety in the forms of sacrifice and modern scholars usually find it impossible to put all sacrifice under any one heading as though to say, 'Sacrifice is this' or 'Sacrifice is that'. There is no one idea in sacrifice, no common source for all the varieties. Some of the Old

Testament sacrifices were offerings of cereals or of liquids (wine mostly), but this class of offering does not feature prominently in the New Testament. There the references are mostly to the animal sacrifices and of these the Old Testament knows four main types: the burnt offering, the peace offering (which NIV renders 'fellowship offering'), the sin offering and the guilt offering. These are not often mentioned by name in the New Testament, though sometimes specific sacrifices are used as descriptions of the offering of Christ. Thus, according to NIV, Paul speaks of God as 'sending his own Son in the likeness of sinful man to be a sin offering' (Rom. 8:3) and most would agree that the translation can be justified. Hebrews quotes from Psalm 40 a passage which includes the words, 'with burnt offerings and sin offerings you were not pleased' (Heb. 10:6; *cf.* verse 8). A scribe agreed with Jesus that 'to love your neighbour as yourself is more important than all burnt offerings and sacrifices' (Mk. 12:33). The Passover sacrifice is spoken of once (1 Cor. 5:7) and, while the term 'Day of Atonement' is not actually mentioned, the Day of Atonement sacrifices are clearly in mind on at least one occasion (Heb. 9:7).

But this kind of specific reference is rare. It is more usual to have a general reference, such as when we read that 'Christ loved us and gave himself up for us as a fragrant offering and sacrifice to God' (Eph. 5:2). Again, Christ 'has appeared once for all at the end of the ages to do away with sin by the sacrifice of himself' (Heb. 9:26). We can scarcely doubt that sacrifice is in mind when we read the words of John the Baptist, 'Look, the Lamb of God, who takes away the sin of the world!' (Jn. 1:29) or those of the Seer of Revelation: 'Then I saw a Lamb, looking as if it had been slain' (Rev. 5:6). We should also see sacrifice behind many of the passages which refer to blood, such as 'To him who loves us and has freed us from our sins by his blood' (Rev. 1:5).

There cannot be the slightest doubt that sometimes the men of the New Testament used 'sacrifice' as a helpful category when they wanted to bring out something of what Christ's death meant. It thus becomes important for us to find out, if we can, what this kind of language meant to those who wrote it and those who first read it. This means, in the first instance, that we must examine what the Old Testament says about sacrifices and about the blood that was shed in them.

We immediately come across a difficulty, because of the number and the complexity of the references to sacrifice in the books of the Old Testament. This is especially true of Leviticus, which has detailed regulations for most of the sacrifices. Often they mean little to people like us who have never seen an animal sacrifice, and in any case the sheer bulk of the regulations makes it easy for us to get bogged down in the multiplicity of the rules and the occasions. On a first reading it is bewildering. But it may help put some order into this apparent chaos if we notice that, despite the obvious differences between the sacrifices, there is an impressive similarity in broad general outline. When any of the four great animal sacrifices was being offered we may discern five or six stages (see the table on p. 46).

1. The 'bringing near'

The first stage was when the worshipper 'drew near' the animal he proposed to offer. To us this seems no more than the necessary preliminary to a sacrifice and an obvious one at that. How could a sacrifice be offered unless the worshipper brought the animal near? But to the Hebrews this was seen as a significant action, so much so that the causal form of the verb 'to draw near', *i.e.* that form of the verb that means 'to make to draw near' or 'to bring near', became a technical expression with the meaning 'to sacrifice'. It was not necessary to say to what one drew near or what it was that one drew near. The verb 'to make to draw near' was enough to convey the idea of sacrifice.

There were of course some implications. When a worshipper made an animal draw near he had the intention of worshipping. He wanted to honour God, to get rid of his sin, to live in fellowship with God and man. He came obediently, bringing the prescribed offering. For most sacrifices the young of one of the domestic animals was specified (ox, sheep or goat, in some cases pigeons; some animals were excluded such as the horse or the donkey). It must be ceremonially clean and, with a partial exception in the case of certain freewill offerings (Lv. 22:23), it must be without blemish, perfect of its kind.

2. The laying on of hands

The worshipper laid his hand on the head of the animal (Lv. 1:4, *etc.*). The Hebrew verb means something like leaning on the animal. It was a firm contact, not a casual touch. The meaning of this is disputed. Some hold that it meant that the worshipper was identifying himself with the offering. If this is the way of it,

45

THE ANIMAL SACRIFICES IN LEVITICUS
(figures refer to chapter and verse in Leviticus)

	Burnt	Peace	Sin	Guilt
1. The worshipper 'brings near'	male from flock or herd: bull, sheep or goat; dove or pigeon (1:5, 10, 14)	domestic animal, male or female (3:1, 6, 12)	for priest or people, young bull (4:3, 13f.); for leader, male goat (4:22f.); for citizen, female goat (4:27f.) or lamb (4:32)	ram plus silver (5:15)
2. The worshipper lays his hand on the head of the prescribed victim				
3. The worshipper himself kills the prescribed victim				
4. The priest puts the blood	against the altar on all sides (1:5,11); drains blood of birds on side of altar (1:15)	against the altar on all sides (3:2, 8)	for priest or the community, seven times before the curtain, on horns of incense altar, at base of main altar (4:6f., 17f.); for individual, on horns and at base of main altar (4:25, 30)	against the altar on all sides (7:2)
5. The priest burns on the altar	the whole animal or bird (1:9, 13, 17)	specified parts (3:3f., 9f., 14f.)	as for peace offerings (4:8–10)	specified parts (7:3f.)
6. Disposal of the rest of the carcase	— (the hide to the priest, 7:8)	parts to the priest (7:31–34); the rest eaten by worshippers (7:15–21)	for priest or community, burnt outside the camp (4:11f., 21); for individuals, eaten by priestly males (6:25f., 29)	eaten by priestly males (7:6)

the action said, 'This is *my* sacrifice. This is the animal *I* am offering.' It certainly did this at least. But others think that the action was a symbolic transferral of the sins of the worshipper to the animal, so that when it died it was taking the punishment due to the worshipper for his sins. It was being treated as the sins it bore deserved. They hold that this is the obvious symbolism and that it is supported by the fact that in later times at least there are passages which tell us that, as the worshipper laid his hands on the animal, he confessed his sins. It is not easy to see what the laying on of hands means if there is no symbolic transfer to the animal which was to die of the sins being confessed.

3. *The killing of the animal*

The animal was killed by the worshipper. If the offering was a bird the priest would perform this action (Lv. 1:14–15; 5:7–8, *etc.*), but this was probably on account of the small size of the victim. The next stage was the manipulation of the blood, and with a little bird there may have been a problem in having one person do the killing and another collect and use the blood. But for

Probable Plan of the Tabernacle

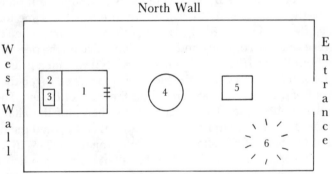

1. The holy place in the tent of meeting
2. The most holy place in the tent of meeting
3. The sacred ark
4. The laver
5. The bronze altar of sacrifice
6. Probable site of ash heap

animals it was certainly the worshipper who performed the act of killing (Lv. 1:3–5; 3:1–2, *etc.*). In this way he gave symbolic expression to his recognition that his sin merited the severest punishment. He himself performed the act which set forth the truth that he deserved death.

4. *The manipulation of the blood*

So far the actions have been the same whatever the sacrifice. It did not matter whether it was a burnt offering, a peace offering, a sin offering or a guilt offering. In all cases stages 1–3 were identical. Differences emerge with stage 4. Here everything depends on which sacrifice is being offered.

And it is here that the work of the priest begins. Up to now it has been the worshipper who did everything. But at stage 4 it is the priest who collects the blood and proceeds to use it. At least in the later temple he collected it in a conical vessel. This shape made it impossible for him to set it down and this meant that the priest must move without delay to the prescribed actions so that the blood had no chance to settle and coagulate.

If the sacrifice was a burnt offering the priest was required to 'bring the blood and sprinkle it against the altar on all sides' (Lv. 1:5, 11); if a bird was offered its blood was 'drained out on the side of the altar' (Lv. 1:15). The procedure was the same for a peace offering (Lv. 3:2, 8, 13). The big differences came when the sacrifice was a sin offering and here it depended on the person(s) for whom the sacrifice was being offered. If it was for a priest or for the whole congregation the blood was sprinkled seven times in front of the curtain that marked off the Holy of Holies. Then the priest put some of the blood on the horns of the altar of incense (a small altar in front of the curtain) and poured the rest of it at the base of the altar of burnt offering (Lv. 4:5–7, 16–18). When the sacrifice was offered on behalf of a sinning ruler or a wayward member of the community, there was no sevenfold sprinkling in front of the curtain. The blood was put on the horns and poured out at the base of the altar of burnt offering (Lv. 4:25, 30, 34). Where the offering was a bird part of the blood was sprinkled 'against the side of the altar; the rest of the blood must be drained out at the base of the altar' (Lv. 5:9).

It is not completely clear what was done in the case of a guilt offering. We read that its blood 'is to be sprinkled against the altar on all sides' (Lv. 7:2), which is exactly the provision made for the burnt and peace offerings. This would lead us to think that the blood was treated in the same way in these three offerings. But in Leviticus 5 there seems to be no great difference between the guilt and the sin offering and some hold that the same ritual was observed for both. In support of this it may be pointed out that there is one law for them both (Lv. 7:7). Some scholars hold that the guilt offering had more to do with offences against one's neighbour and the sin offering with those against God. They point out that a monetary compensation goes with some at any rate of the guilt offerings (Lv. 6:5). But there is also a monetary compensation when the sin is against God (Lv. 5:14–16), so this does not prove much. The fact is that we do not have enough information to be dogmatic. But for our present purpose that does not matter. We simply note that the solemnity of the sin offering was heightened by an elaborate blood ritual and that this must have had the effect of making it plain that sin could not be taken lightly.

5. *The burning on the altar*

Some part of the animal was always burnt on the altar, this apparently being regarded as God's portion as it ascended heavenwards in the smoke rising from the altar fire. It was 'an aroma pleasing to the LORD' (Lv. 1:9, 13, 19). In the case of the burnt offering the whole animal was consumed in the altar fire, so that stage 5 completed that sacrifice. In the case of the other three, certain prescribed parts were burnt on the altar, mostly the internal fat. No difference appears to have been made between one of these sacrifices and the others. The sin offering is specifically said to involve the same parts as the peace offering (Lv. 4:8–10, 26, 31, 35), while the description of the relevant parts in the guilt offering seems to match that of the peace offering (Lv. 7:3–5; *cf.* 3:3–5).

6. *The disposal of the rest of the carcase*

As we have seen, there was no stage 6 in the burnt offering. The whole carcase had been burnt up in stage 5, though we should notice that the destruction was not quite total – the hide of the animal belonged to the officiating priest (Lv. 7:8). If the sin offering was being made for a priest or for the congregation prescribed parts were burnt on the altar, then the remainder of the animal was taken to a clean place 'outside the camp' and there burnt up, hide, flesh, head, legs, inner parts, offal – all are specified (Lv. 4:11–12, 19–20). If, however, the offering was being made for a non-priestly individual the flesh was to be eaten by the officiating priest (Lv. 6:25–26) and other priests (verse 29). A further regulation links the guilt offering with the sin offering: 'They belong to the priest who makes atonement with them. The priest who offers a burnt offering for anyone may keep its hide for himself' (Lv. 7:7–8). This last sentence looks like a regulation about the burnt offering tacked on to rules about the guilt offering, but it may be held to show that the hide was a regular priestly perquisite in all sacrifices. If not, we do not know what happened to the hide in the other offerings.

The big difference was with the peace offerings. The usual parts were burnt on the altar, as we have noticed. Then prescribed parts were set aside for the officiating priest, namely the breast and the right thigh (Lv. 7:31–34). The rest of the animal was eaten by the worshippers (Lv. 7:15–21). This made the offering of such a sacrifice a very joyful occasion. People would come together in festive mood and enjoy a good meal as the consummation of the act of sacrifice. This kind of sacrifice was offered on great occasions, often in conjunction with burnt offerings. Thus we find the combination when the covenant was renewed under Joshua with the conquest of Canaan nicely under way (Jos. 8:31) and peace offerings were made when Saul's kingship was confirmed (1 Sa. 11:15). The dedication of the Temple was an obvious occasion for holy joy and Solomon offered a large number of peace offerings (1 Ki. 8:63). But these offerings might also be offered in times of difficulty, for example when the Israelites 'sat weeping before the LORD' after a defeat in battle (Jdg. 20:26; 21:4). A curious example is that of the woman 'dressed like a prostitute and with crafty intent' (Pr. 7:10) who seduced the simple young man, saying among other things 'I have peace offerings at home' (verse 14). Clearly, in such a case, the peace offering was little more than a conventional religious symbol, the real thing being the enjoyment of the meat meal.

ADVANTAGES AND DEFECTS

Such in broad outline was the sacrificial system. It had some clear advantages. Nobody who came thoughtfully to God by the way of sacrifice could be in any doubt but that sin was a serious matter. It could not be put aside by a light-hearted wave of the hand but required the shedding of blood. And it was not fuzzy and indefinite. Worshippers knew what they had to do. It held out to them the prospect of fellowship with God. People were not left to wonder whether and how they could approach him. They had a clear-cut, definite path by which they could approach with assurance. The striking ritual, when duly carried out by people who came with proper internal dispositions, must have been a valuable expression of religious feeling. The devotion of the worshippers would have been stirred and stimulated. An essential element in the sacrificial approach was the element of cost. David could say to Araunah, 'I will not sacrifice to the LORD my God burnt offerings that cost me nothing' (2 Sa. 24:24). No-one who came to God by the way of offering the best in his flock would put a low value on the privilege of such an approach. He would realize, as many of us today do not, that the service of God must cost us something.

But if there were important values in the sacrificial system there were also some demerits. The very externality of the system made it possible for people to overlook the spiritual truths that sacrifice so splendidly enshrined. We can scarcely regard the lady of Proverbs 7 as a shining example of spiritual excellence, though she had evidently gone through the motions of offering sacrifice. The prophets made a frequent target of those who offered the sacrifices punctiliously but who passed over weightier matters like upright dealings with their fellows and genuine worship of God. In every age people have found it easier to perform outward actions than to live pure lives.

Many scholars hold that there is a serious defect in the whole system, in that the sins covered by the sacrifices were of the less serious kind, mostly sins of inadvertence and transgressions of ritual taboos. They point out that for sins done 'with a high hand' ('defiantly', NIV) there was no sacrifice (Nu. 15:30). We should be clear that the whole sacrificial system was meant for people in covenant relationship with God, perhaps we might say for those in a state of grace. But sins that put them outside the covenant put them outside the sphere of the sacrifices also. Thus the sins of Eli's sons and his failure to restrain them were so serious that 'The guilt of Eli's house will never be atoned for by sacrifice or offering' (1 Sa. 3:14).

There were certainly limitations on the type of offence for which sacrifice might be offered. But it is surely going too far to say that the only sins for which it availed were sins of inadvertence and ritual defilement. There is not the slightest reason for thinking that the only sins covered were those specifically mentioned in Leviticus. The sins listed there can be no more than examples. It is impossible to hold that for centuries a whole nation carried on a sacrificial system as costly and elaborate as that in Leviticus while firmly believing that it availed for nothing more than a few comparatively minor offences while their real sins, those that deeply troubled their consciences, went unprovided for. Certainly in rabbinic times, when specific offences are mentioned, sacrifice was held to avail for serious sins and there is every reason for holding that this was the case from the very first.

The Old Testament never tells us in set terms why sacrifice was held to do away with sin. It was enough that it was so. We are told many times that sacrifice was offered 'to make atonement' or the like, and, as we have already noticed, the term 'blood' was often used. In the actual offering of the sacrifices the manipulation of the blood of the animal was a most important feature, especially in the sin offering. In modern discussions it is often held that it is the blood that gives us the clue to what sacrifice meant. It will repay us to devote attention to this aspect of our subject.

THE BLOOD

The word 'blood' is used in the Old Testament 362 times in all, so it is not exactly rare. On 103 occasions it refers to the blood of sacrifices, ninety-four being sacrifices in the Levitical system we have just been looking at. There are also half a dozen occasions when blood is mentioned in connection with the first Passover, while the other three refer to heathen sacrifices.

But far and away the most frequent use of the term is to indicate death with violence, a use which is found 203 times. For example we read, 'Whoever sheds the blood of man, by man shall his blood be shed' (Gn. 9:6), where the first occurrence of the word plainly points to murder and second equally plainly to execution. There are some subdivisions of this category, such as when we read of 'innocent blood'. There may be references to shedding innocent blood (which Manasseh did, 2 Ki. 24:4), or the idea may be found without the verb, as when Jeremiah told his persecutors that if they killed him they would 'bring innocent blood' on themselves (Je. 26:15; NIV inserts 'the guilt of' before 'innocent blood', but this is not in the Hebrew; it is enough to say simply 'innocent blood'). A dozen times there are references to one's blood being on oneself (*e.g.* Jos. 2:19), while five times there are references to the blood of animals which are done to death, as when Joseph's brothers killed a goat and dipped his robe of many colours in the blood (Gn. 37:31).

BLOOD AND LIFE

But the passages which have featured in recent discussions are those which connect life and blood. There are seven of these, of which perhaps the most striking is Leviticus 17:11: 'For the life of a creature is in the blood, and I have given it to you to make atonement for yourselves on the altar; it is the blood that makes atonement for one's life.' Most would understand the last part of the verse differently, as in the translation of RSV: 'it is the blood that makes atonement, by reason of the life.' This understanding of the Hebrew signifies that it is because of the connection of life and blood that blood makes atonement. This is held to be reinforced by the prohibition of eating meat with the blood still in it. The passage in Leviticus goes on, 'None of you may eat blood, nor may an alien living among you eat blood.' It then provides that, when an Israelite hunts 'any animal or bird that may be eaten', he is to drain out the blood and cover it with earth 'because the life of every creature is its blood. That is why I have said to the Israelites, "You must not eat the blood of any creature, because the life of every creature is its blood; anyone who eats it must be cut off"' (Lv. 17:12–24).

Such passages certainly show that the Israelites saw life and blood as closely connected and that they treated blood with great respect. This may be strengthened by noticing occasional metaphorical statements, such as that made on the occasion when three of David's mighty men broke through the ranks of the Philistines to bring their leader some water from the well near the gate of Bethlehem. David had longed for a drink from this well; but when the mighty men brought it at the risk of their lives he counted it too precious to drink. He poured it out as an offering to God, exclaiming, 'Is it not the blood of men who went at the risk of their lives?' (2 Sa. 23:17). But we must bear in mind that this is a metaphorical use. David is not suggesting that to drink the water would be literally to drink the blood or the lives of the men in question.

Then there are passages which put 'life' and 'blood' in parallel in such a way as to indicate (it is said) that there is not much difference between them. Thus we read, 'for your lifeblood I will surely demand an accounting...from each man, too, I will demand an accounting for the life of his fellow man' (Gn. 9:5). Or again, 'From oppression and violence he redeems their life; and precious is their blood in his sight' (Ps. 72:14, RSV; NIV translates the expression that means 'redeems their life' as 'will rescue them'). But not too much should be deduced from passages like this. In the first example, while the words 'life' and 'blood' are used, the plain meaning is murder. If anyone murders another then God will hold him responsible. The passage lends no support to any view that rejects the link of blood with death. As for Psalm 72, there is certainly a parallelism between 'life' in the first clause and 'blood' in the second. But the meaning appears to be given by the very similar words in Psalm 116:15, 'Precious in the sight of the LORD is the death of his saints.' 'Blood' is to be given its normal meaning in Psalm 72:14 and 'redeeming the life' in parallel will mean 'saving from death'.

The men of the Old Testament certainly saw life as specially linked with blood. Obviously, when the blood was taken from the body of an animal or man, so was the life. Some scholars have put a great deal of emphasis on this and have gone so far as to argue that, for the Hebrew, 'blood' spoke of life, not of death. Thus F. C. N. Hicks could write:

> The blood, in fact, needs to be dissociated from the idea of death. To us, with our modern associations, it is merely the evidence, the revolting evidence, of slaughter and destruction. To the men of the ancient world it was not revolting, but precious. It was life, once prisoned and misused, now released.[1]

Similarly Vincent Taylor says, 'The victim is slain in order that its life, in the form of blood, may be released... the bestowal of life is the fundamental idea in sacrificial worship.'[2]

On this view blood and death have little to do with one another. It is life, not death, that blood signifies. When the priest stood by his altar with a basin full of blood it was not really

[1] F. C. N. Hicks, *The Fullness of Sacrifice* (London, 1946), p.242.
[2] Vincent Taylor, *Jesus and His Sacrifice* (London, 1939), pp.54–55.

blood: it was a basin full of life. It was the animal's hard luck that
the priest could not get his basin full of life without the animal
dying. But its death was no significant part of the ritual. It was
the release of its life that mattered.

BLOOD AND DEATH

For all its popularity in some circles, however, this view is
difficult to maintain on the evidence of the Old Testament. We
have already seen that the Old Testament writers use the term
'blood' 203 times out of its 362 occurrences to denote violent
death. Moreover, the use of the term for the blood of the sacrifices
tends to be concentrated in Exodus-Leviticus, where it occurs
seventy-eight times (nineteen in Exodus and fifty-nine in Leviticus), leaving only twenty-five references in all the rest of the Old
Testament. But the use of 'blood' for violent death is not specially
concentrated anywhere; it is widely spread throughout the whole
Old Testament. It is simply not true, as Hicks says it is, that we
must dissociate blood from the idea of death if we are to understand the Old Testament. The opposite is the case. With the
exception of two books, right through the Old Testament the
idea most commonly suggested by 'blood' is death by violence.

Actually the passages which link 'blood' and 'life' support this
view too. It is only by taking a few passages very literally and
ignoring the majority that the equation Hicks and Taylor seek
can be made out. Careful examination of the 'life is in the blood'
passages actually shows that the meaning is 'life given up in
death' and not simply 'life'. We have already noticed that in the
words, 'for your lifeblood I will surely demand an accounting...
from each man, too, I will demand an accounting for the life of
his fellow man' (Gn. 9:5) what is in mind is murder, however
close we may find the linguistic link between 'life' and 'blood'.
The passage is telling us that anyone who kills another will be
held responsible for the murder. It is nonsense to claim that such
a passage speaks to us of life released and not death.

The blood of the sacrifices seems to mean much the same. We
have seen that in Leviticus 17:11 the blood is closely connected
with atonement and this is the case in other places also. But this
should not be exaggerated. Atonement is not usually specifically
linked with blood; the priest is simply required to manipulate
the blood in such and such a way. A dozen times, however, there
is a connection in the style of Leviticus 17:11. For example, we

read of a bull and a goat 'whose blood was brought into the Most Holy Place to make atonement' (Lv. 16:27). Passages like this are seized upon as proving that atonement is made, not by death, but by the offering of life.

But consider this very similar passage where murder is being discussed: 'Bloodshed pollutes the land, and atonement cannot be made for the land on which blood has been shed, except by the blood of the one who shed it' (Nu. 35:33). The words about atonement are the same as those used in describing the effect of the sacrifices. But there is no question about the meaning of 'blood' in the following phrase. 'The blood of the one who shed it' means the execution of the murderer. It is death and not life to which 'blood' points in this passage and in others like it.

Those who link blood and life do not usually notice that the Hebrew word *nephesh,* translated 'life' in Leviticus 17:11 and other passages, does not mean exactly what the English word 'life' means. It often has a meaning like 'life given up in death'. It is found in passages which speak of 'taking away', 'losing', 'destroying', or 'giving up' life, while thirty times it refers to those trying to murder someone as 'seeking his *nephesh*' (*e.g.* Ex. 4:19; Ps. 35:4). This is not so very different from the English use, but other uses are quite unlike anything we say. Thus the Hebrew might speak of 'lying in wait for the *nephesh*' or 'laying a snare for the *nephesh*' when murder is being planned (*e.g.* 1 Sa. 28:9; Pr. 1:18). Or we might notice the prayer of the sailors as they prepared to throw Jonah into the sea, 'let us not perish for this man's *nephesh*' (Jon. 1:14, RSV; NIV inserts 'taking' before 'this man's *nephesh*', but this is not in the Hebrew). They are referring to his death. Similarly Joab got the wise woman from Tekoa to speak to King David about people who wanted to put a man to death 'for the *nephesh* of his brother whom he killed' (2 Sa. 14:7).

Then there is a string of passages where *nephesh* is actually translated 'dead' or the like. Thus there is the injunction, 'Do not cut your bodies for the dead' (Lv. 19:28). Again, there is an interesting sequence in Isaiah where the LORD makes the *nephesh* of the Servant 'a guilt offering', and the passage goes on to say that the Servant 'poured out his *nephesh* unto death' (Is. 53:10–12). The guilt offering and death are closely linked.

I am not suggesting that *nephesh* should not normally be taken to mean 'life'. It does mean life. But we should not overlook these links with death. A word which may be used in this fashion can scarcely be taken as unambiguous proof that it means 'life' rather than 'death' when it refers to blood that has been taken out of a body.

We should also bear in mind that the Hebrews put a strong emphasis on the link of life with the body. It is regularly pointed out that they thought of life after death not in terms of the immortality of the soul but of the resurrection of the body. For them 'life' and 'the body' went together. If they found it difficult to think of human life as continuing after the body had died, why should we hold that they thought of the life of a slain animal as persisting in the basin the priest held? Such a conception seems quite out of keeping with the normal Hebrew way of looking at life and death.

In any case there are many passages which leave no doubt that the sacrificed animal or bird was thought of as dead when its blood was used. To take an example more or less at random, when the priest was conducting the ceremony for the cleansing of a house that had been unclean because of some infection variously translated as 'a fretting leprosy' (AV), 'a malignant leprosy' (RSV), 'a destructive mildew' (NIV), he was 'to take the cedar wood, the hyssop, the scarlet yarn and the live bird, dip them into the blood of the dead bird...' (Lv. 14:51). Here we have a clear reference to 'blood' in a sacrificial and cleansing context, and there can be no doubt but that it is death that is in mind. The bird whose blood it is is expressly called 'the dead bird'.

ATONEMENT APART FROM WORSHIP

Those who hold to the 'blood'='life' equation maintain that the death of the victim has little or no significance when a sacrifice is offered. What matters, they say, is the release of life. Atonement is secured when life is surrendered, released, set free for a new function. But we should not overlook the fact that sometimes atonement is attempted or accomplished quite apart from the ritual of the tabernacle or temple. Examination of such passages should tell us something about the way the Hebrews understood atonement and whether it was normally connected with life or not.

Sometimes atonement was brought about with money. At the time the census was taken each of the Israelites was to pay the

LORD 'a ransom for his life at the time he is counted' (Ex. 30:12). The money is expressly said to be 'atonement money' (verse 16) and twice it is said in set terms to make atonement (verses 15, 16). There are other such examples where there is no question of life or death and which accordingly do not help our inquiry very much. Except that both the payment of money and the killing of an animal may perhaps be thought of as kinds of price.

There are some passages, however, in which there is no question but that atonement is seen as due to death. Thus on the occasion when the Israelites made the golden calf and worshipped it, Moses impressed on them the fact that they had sinned greatly: 'You have committed a great sin.' But he wanted to put things right. He said, 'But now I will go up to the LORD; perhaps I can make atonement for your sin.' Then he went to the LORD, asking that they be forgiven. He added, 'but if not, then blot me out of the book you have written' (Ex. 32:30–32). His method of seeking atonement was to ask that he himself be blotted out. He offered his death to atone for their sin.

Another time atonement was looked for during the wilderness wanderings. Some Moabite women had seduced Israelite men and led them to join in immoral conduct and the worship of idols. Phinehas took resolute action in killing an Israelite, Zimri, and the Moabite woman with whom he was having intercourse, a certain Cozbi, the daughter of a Moabite tribal chief. It is recorded of Phinehas that 'he was zealous for the honour of his God and made atonement for the Israelites' (Nu. 25:13). Again atonement is by way of death, in this case the death of two of the principal sinners against God.

A third example is the procedure for dealing with a murder by a person or persons unknown. The elders of the nearest town were to take a heifer that had never been worked, bring her to a valley that had never been ploughed and planted and where there was a flowing stream. They were to break the heifer's neck and wash their hands over its body saying, '"Our hands did not shed this blood, nor did our eyes see it done. Accept this atonement for your people Israel...."' And the bloodshed will be atoned for' (Dt. 21:1–8). The death of the heifer atoned for any sin that might be thought to rest on the town. In this passage the word 'blood' is mentioned four times in verses 7–9 and the verb *kipper*, 'to make atonement', twice, but atonement is not connected with blood in any of these instances. It is the death of the heifer by means of a broken neck and not any life released in blood that brings atonement.

A fourth incident is that in which there was a famine during the reign of David and it was revealed to the king that this was due to the fact that King Saul had put certain Gibeonites to death (2 Sa. 21:1). The Gibeonites should have been inviolate as far as Israel was concerned in terms of the agreement recorded in Joshua 9, but evidently Saul had violated the agreement on some unrecorded occasion. Now David summoned the Gibeonites and asked, 'How shall I make amends...?' where the Hebrew means 'How shall I make atonement...?' (verse 3). The Gibeonites replied that they did not look for silver or gold and that they had no right to put anyone to death. When David pressed them further they said, 'let seven of (Saul's) male descendants be given to us to be killed' (verse 6). It is a gruesome story and we need not think that the God of Israel approved of the execution of seven innocent descendants of the earlier king. For us the significant thing is the fact that both the Gibeonites and David accepted without question that the way to make atonement was to bring about death.

There is then quite a bit of evidence that in ancient Israel it was accepted that atonement could be brought about by the death of the relevant victim, and this quite apart from any sacrifice in the temple. It is not necessary for us to agree with the ideas of Moses about the value of his own death, nor with the Gibeonites in their estimate of the importance of executing some of Saul's descendants, before we can see what they thought atonement meant and how it could be secured. Of course the fact that death was a suitable means of securing atonement apart from the sacrifices does not prove that this was the way the sacrifices secured it. But at least it raises a question about the argument from the equation of blood and life. If atonement is secured by releasing life, we are justified in arguing, then why should atonement outside the sacrifices be repeatedly sought not by any release of life but by the infliction of death? Since the sacrifices involved the deaths of animals, should we not see these deaths as significant?

ATONEMENT IN THE TEMPLE

Where atonement is held to be secured by some activity within the framework of Israel's worship, the most common way of putting it is to refer quite generally to the whole sacrifice as effective. A typical example is the provision in Ezekiel's vision whereby the prince 'will provide the sin offerings, grain offerings, burnt offerings and fellowship offerings to make atonement for the house of Israel' (Ezk. 45:17). This does not locate atonement in any one part of a sacrifice, nor for that matter in any one sacrifice. The general impression left by a number of such passages is that it is the whole act of sacrifice rather than any one ritual detail that is important. Indeed, in the example quoted it is not even any one sacrifice that is singled out. Atonement is linked quite generally with them all. While it is true that sometimes it is said that the blood is connected with atonement (as in Lv. 17:11), this is far from universal.

Indeed sometimes the making of atonement is connected specifically with some other part of the sacrificial process. For example, we read that the worshipper 'is to lay his hand on the head of the burnt offering, and it will be accepted on his behalf to make atonement for him' (Lv. 1:4). In similar fashion it is said, 'He shall burn all the fat on the altar as he burned the fat of the fellowship offering. In this way the priest will make atonement for the man's sin' (Lv. 4:26; so also verses 31, 35). It is possible that such references to the fat, coming as they do at the end of the rite in each case, may be meant to summarize the whole. But as they stand they look very much like statements that it is the burning of the fat that secures atonement. Certainly they do not link atonement specifically with the blood.

The fat is always regarded as specially important: 'All the fat is the LORD's' (Lv. 3:16). The eating of fat and of blood are prohibited in the same terms and indeed sometimes in the same expression: 'You must not eat any fat or any blood' (Lv. 3:17). The manipulation of the blood is, of course, an essential part of sacrifice, but then the burning of the fat on the altar is no less essential. Outside worship we see much the same attitude. 'The blood of the slain' and 'the fat of the mighty' (so rather than 'flesh' of NIV) are linked in David's elegant lament over Saul and Jonathan (2 Sa. 1:22). If we are to think of blood as a symbol of life, fat would seem to be no less so. But, of course, in both cases it is death rather than life that is in mind. Both blood and fat are mentioned in Isaiah's denunciation of the people for their wrong attitude to sacrifice (Is. 1:11; *cf*. 34:6). Clearly fat is very important for an understanding of the efficacy of sacrifice. And equally clearly there is no reason for equating fat with life.

Now and then there is language which seems to show that atonement was held to be brought about in the sacrifices by means other than the release of life in the blood. Thus when Aaron and his sons were solemnly set apart as priests of the LORD they were instructed 'to eat these offerings by which atonement was made' (Ex. 29:33). The reference is to some bread and to the meat of a ram from which, of course, all the blood had been drained. There is definite reference to atonement where blood is excluded and where there is nothing else that might symbolize life. There is another reference to eating that which made atonement in the incident following the deaths of Nadab and Abihu (Lv. 10:17), in this case a query as to why it had not been eaten. In both passages it is the dead body that is in question and it is not easy to see how this could be brought into a symbol of life. In each case it is plainly the death of the victim that is the important thing.

So is it in some metaphorical passages which use the imagery of sacrifice as a symbol for slaughter. Thus Jeremiah speaks of a day of vengeance: 'The sword will devour till it is satisfied, till it has quenched its thirst with blood. For the Lord, the LORD Almighty, will offer sacrifice...' (Je. 46:10). There are some grim words of Zephaniah: 'The LORD has prepared a sacrifice; he has consecrated those he has invited. On the day of the LORD's sacrifice I will punish the princes...' (Zp. 1:7–8). In passages like these it is plain that sacrifice means death. The prophets are speaking of the slaughter of evil men and speaking of it as sacrifice to make their point more vividly. On the view that sacrifice is essentially the release of life for higher purposes such passages are meaningless. Clearly their force arises from the fact that the prophets see sacrifice in terms of death and thus as a suitable metaphor when it is the death of the Lord's opponents which they have in mind.

We should possibly add references to the institution of the Passover, where blood was the means of averting destruction. It was to be put on the lintels and doorposts so that the destroying angel would pass over them (Ex. 12:7, 13, 22–23). It is true that this first Passover was not quite the same as a normal liturgical sacrifice. But it has cultic overtones and it led into the annual Passover sacrifice. And in this use of blood once again there seems no place for understanding the imagery as pointing to life.

It is the death of the atoning victim that is in mind (even though the offering is not said in set terms to make atonement).

The evidence that the Hebrews understood blood to symbolize life or that they identified the two is thus not as abundant or as clear as would be needed to establish the point. It depends on taking certain passages linking life and blood very literally and seeing in them the explanation of all the others.

But this ignores the fact that the Hebrews were fond of using 'blood' in vivid metaphorical ways. Thus David complained that Joab shed the blood of war in peace and put the blood on his belt and in his shoes (1 Ki. 2:5). If blood=life, what are we to make of this? Again, the Psalmist speaks of the righteous as bathing their feet in the blood of the wicked (Ps. 58:10; *cf.* Ps. 68:23). Job exclaimed, 'O earth, do not cover my blood' (Jb. 16:18) and Isaiah passed on the word of the LORD, 'Your hands are full of blood' (Is. 1:15). There are some well-known words in Joel which speak of God showing wonders in heaven and on earth, 'blood and fire and billows of smoke' and which go on to speak of the moon being turned to blood (Joel 2:30–31). Examples could be multiplied. The Hebrews tended to use the term 'blood' in picturesque metaphors, more particularly as a vivid way of referring to death.

When a sacrifice was offered we should see it as a killing of the animal in place of the worshipper and the manipulation of the blood as the ritual presentation to God of the evidence that a death has taken place to atone for sin. When the New Testament writers refer to the death of Christ as a sacrifice, we should not understand them to be making some far-fetched identification of his blood with his life. Rather they are solemnly referring to the significance of his death.

BLOOD IN THE NEW TESTAMENT

The term blood is not used as often in the New Testament as it is in the Old (it is found ninety-eight times). But, as in the Old, the most frequent single classification is that which refers to violent death. Thus Paul tells us the words of his prayer on one occasion, recalling 'when the blood of your martyr Stephen was shed...' (Acts 22:20). Now Stephen was killed by stoning, a form of death in which the actual amount of blood shed was small. Clearly the shedding of blood is being taken as equivalent to death by violence. We see the same thing in another prayer, that of the martyrs in Revelation: 'How long, Sovereign Lord, holy and true, until you judge the inhabitants of the earth and avenge our blood?' (Rev. 6:10). They are described as 'those who had been slain because of the word of God and the testimony they had maintained' (verse 9) and the reference to their blood must be held to cover all forms of death by violence. It makes no sense to say that only those whose deaths had been brought about by the actual, physical shedding of blood are in mind. It means all those put to death because of their faithfulness, no matter what the method of their execution. So with 'the blood of Abel' and 'the blood of Zechariah' (Lk. 11:51). These expressions are very similar to 'the blood of Christ' (Eph. 2:13) and show that this should be taken to mean 'the death of Christ'.

A dozen times 'blood' is used of the blood in the Jewish sacrifices. These need scarcely detain us, for they add nothing to what we saw in our treatment of the Old Testament. They simply show that the former way of speaking continued on in New Testament days.

The references to the blood of Christ often show clearly that it is his death that is in mind. For example, Paul speaks of 'the blood of his cross' (Col. 1:20; NIV paraphrases), where the meaning is surely 'his death on the cross'. Crucifixion (like stoning) was a form of execution in which little blood was shed, so there cannot be any emphasis on blood as such. It is simply a way of referring to death. So is it with the expression 'justified by his blood' (Rom. 5:9), which in the context cannot be so very different from 'reconciled... through the death of his Son' in the following verse (though, of course, 'justified' and 'reconciled' are different ways of looking at atonement; it is 'blood' and 'death' which are much the same).

THE SACRIFICE OF CHRIST

The usage of 'blood' in the New Testament, then, does not lend support to the view that it points to life. We are not to think that when the New Testament writers used the word they referred to life set free from the bondage of the body and available for new and greater purposes. They meant that Christ had died. And if they used the expression in a way that recalls the sacrifices and the blood shed in them, then they meant that the death of Jesus is to be seen as a sacrifice which accomplishes in reality what the old sacrifices pointed to but could not do.

Explicit sacrificial language is used in a variety of ways. There are two words to be considered, 'sacrifice' (*thysia*) and 'offering' (*prosphora*), which sometimes occur together as in the 'Sacrifice and offering' cited in Hebrews 10:5. Mostly when the sacrifices of the old way are considered the thought is that they could not bring the worshippers forgiveness. As the writer to the Hebrews put it, 'it is impossible for the blood of bulls and goats to take away sins' (Heb. 10:4); they 'were not able to clear the conscience of the worshipper' (Heb. 9:9).

By contrast, the sacrifice that Jesus made is effective. It was a sacrifice offered in love: 'Christ loved us and gave himself up for us as a fragrant offering and sacrifice to God' (Eph. 5:2). We should notice further that there can be emphasis on the actual physical sacrifice Christ offered. Thus the writer to the Hebrews points out, in a passage in which he dismisses burnt offerings and sin offerings and stresses the importance of doing the will of God, that 'by that will, we have been made holy through the sacrifice of the body of Jesus Christ once for all' (Heb. 10:10). The will is important and we should not overlook the contrast between Christ's willing sacrifice of himself and the uncomprehending, involuntary sacrifices that necessarily occurred when animals were offered. But we must not go on to the extreme of saying that all that matters is the yielded will, that Christ saved us by being perfectly submissive to the will of God. There is truth in that, but what Hebrews is saying is that the will of God in question meant 'the sacrifice of the body of Jesus Christ'. What happened on Calvary mattered. The yielded will was important; but so was the broken body.

The writer is ready to concede a certain effectiveness to the Levitical sacrifices in their own sphere. But when we are thinking of the reality of heaven, he holds, it is necessary to be purified 'with better sacrifices than these' (Heb. 9:23). Animal sacrifice can never produce a purification valid in heaven. But Christ's sacrifice can. 'He has appeared once for all at the end of the ages to do away with sin by the sacrifice of himself' (Heb. 9:26). 'The sacrifice of himself' means an infinitely better sacrifice than any that was possible under the Levitical system.

That is one point that this author emphasizes. Another is the finality of Christ's atoning sacrifice. Repeatedly he tells us that Christ offered himself 'once and for all' or the like. Believers have been made holy 'through the sacrifice of the body of Jesus Christ once for all' (Heb. 10:10); he 'offered for all time one sacrifice for sins' (verse 12); 'by one sacrifice he has made perfect for ever those who are being made holy' (verse 14). And he removes decisively the possibility of any further offering by saying that, when sins have been forgiven (as they have been through what Christ has done), 'there is no longer any sacrifice for sin' (Heb 10:18). The utter finality of Christ's sacrifice is an important truth.

SPIRITUAL SACRIFICES

There are other references to sacrifice. The New Testament Christians liked to use this imagery to bring out important aspects of the service they render God as their response to the great salvation God has brought about through the sacrifice of his Son. To see Christ as having offered the perfect sacrifice that brings us salvation is not to enter a realm of cheap grace. It does not mean that we offer no sacrifice. It means that our sacrifice is of a different order. It is not atoning, but a costly response to a sacrifice that is atoning.

The way of salvation is a way of sacrifice. That means basically that it is the sacrifice of Christ that takes away sins once and for all. But it also means that those for whom the sacrifice was offered live sacrificially. They offer their bodies 'as living sacrifices, holy and pleasing to God' (Rom. 12:1). Paul speaks of himself as being made a sacrifice in the service of other Christians (Phil. 2:17) and he refers to the gifts the Philippian Christians sent him as 'a fragrant offering, an acceptable sacrifice, pleasing to God' (Phil. 4:18). The writer to the Hebrews refers to 'a sacrifice of praise – the fruit of lips that confess his name' and he speaks of doing good and sharing with others as sacrifices with which God is well pleased (Heb. 13:15–16). Peter is another who sees Christians as offering 'spiritual sacrifices acceptable to God through Jesus Christ' (1 Pet. 2:5). Clearly there is an important element of sacrifice in the service that Christians are expected to render to God.

THE ONE ATONING SACRIFICE

But in the New Testament, when the sacrificial terminology is used, it is mostly to emphasize what Christ has done. The sacrifice that matters is the death of Jesus on Calvary's cross. This was not a sacrifice in the literal sense any more than the redemption that

it about is a literal redemption. But just as redemption
re us vividly some aspects of our salvation, so is it with
. The people of New Testament days were people who
od by their altars and watched while the priests collected
od of animals offered in sacrifice on their behalf. They had
seen them use that blood in the prescribed fashion. They had
witnessed parts or all of their designated victims ascend in the
flames of the altar. With a somewhat different idea of fragrance
from ours they had recognized this as a sweet-smelling odour.

And through it all, as the writer to the Hebrews makes
especially clear, they must have been assailed by doubts. Sacrifice
was a splendidly solemn way of dealing with sins. It stirred the
emotions and gave the worshipper something to do. But did it
really take away sins? Could any thinking person believe that the
death of some poor animal, a bull perhaps, or a goat or a lamb,
would put him in the right with a God who was holy and just?

But the sacrifice of Christ was a different matter. All the old
and familiar imagery helped them to understand what Christ's
death was about. They could appreciate references to blood as
cleansing and to death as a means of putting away sins. And
what was no more than dimly hinted at in the case of the animals
they could see perfectly accomplished in Christ.

No more than any of the other ways of looking at the cross does
this one tell us the whole story. But it is an important chapter. It
brings out the meaning of the cross in its own distinctive way.
We may say that it puts emphasis on these things at least.

1. *Sin is defiling*
In an ancient sanctuary everything was arranged to put emphasis
on the holiness of God. Even ceremonial faults were seen as
defiling and sin was much more so. Sin stained the worshipper
and made him unclean. Sin meant that he was not fit to approach
the holy God.

2. *Purification*
When a sacrifice was offered the worshipper was cleansed.
Whether it was a ceremonial defilement or a moral lapse, the
offering of sacrifice was seen as purging the sin so that the
worshipper was now in a state of purification. His sin was
completely removed.

3. The death of the victim counts

In a sacrifice the blood must be manipulated in prescribed ways and part or all of the animal must be burnt on the altar. All this speaks of the necessity for death, nothing less, if sin is to be put away. Sin is not some trifle, to be airily dismissed with no effort. Sin means death (Ezk. 18:4; Rom. 6:23) and nothing less suffices to take it away.

4. Salvation is at cost

David showed an insight into the meaning of sacrifice when he said to Araunah, 'I will not sacrifice to the LORD my God burnt offerings that cost me nothing' (2 Sa. 24:24). The use of the terminology of sacrifice means that the way of forgiveness is costly. It is not until we come to the death of Jesus on the cross that we can see the full meaning of costliness. But inherent in the concept is that forgiveness comes only at cost.

5. Spiritual sacrifices

The New Testament writers look for a response to the sacrifice of Christ. The believer must offer himself as a living sacrifice, which certainly means that his whole way of life is to be different because of what Christ has done for him. The sacrifice of Christ means that the way of salvation is free; but it does not mean that it is cheap.

But the really important thing is that Christ has made the perfect sacrifice, and 'there is no longer any sacrifice for sin'.

For further study

1. From Leviticus 1–7; Psalm 51; Hebrews 7:11 – 10:18, list the advantages and defects you discern in the sacrificial system of the Old Testament. What lessons does this system teach for your own spiritual life?
2. What do we learn about the nature of sacrifice from the passages that connect 'life' and 'blood'? (Use a concordance.)
3. Make a list of passages referring to the sacrifices Christians are expected to offer. (Find them by looking up New Testament references to 'sacrifice' in a concordance.) What do they tell us about the nature of the Christian life?
4. What can we learn from the epistle to the Hebrews about the sacrifice of Christ?

3
The Day of Atonement

Approach to God was a tricky business in the days of Moses and Aaron. On the one hand it was the greatest of blessings and nobody wanted to be without God's promised presence. In the wilderness period God had said, 'My Presence will go with you' (Ex. 33:14) and Moses regarded that presence as essential. Without it he did not want to move: 'If your Presence does not go with us, do not send us up from here' (Ex. 33:15). But God did grant his presence and spoke of 'their camp, where I dwell among them' (Nu. 5:3). The presence of God might even be referred to casually, as something that might almost be taken for granted, as when 'Moses took the staff from the LORD's presence' (Nu. 20:9).

But on the other hand God was awe-inspiring and powerful. To approach him in the wrong way might be disaster. That is the point of the story of Nadab and Abihu. They 'offered unauthorised fire before the LORD, contrary to his command' (Lv. 10:1). The result was that 'fire came out from the presence of the LORD and consumed them, and they died before the LORD' (verse 2). Just exactly what their offence was is not clear. But the offering of incense was carefully regulated (Ex. 30:7–9) and clearly these two young men had chosen to impose their way of doing things rather than accept what God had commanded. This was all the more serious in that they had just gone through the solemn ceremony of being made priests, at the culmination of which 'the glory of the LORD appeared to all the people. Fire came out from the presence of the LORD and consumed the burnt offering and the fat portions on the altar' (Lv. 9:23–24). This above all times was a time for sticking closely to what God had commanded. These men had a position of high privilege, and those who stand close to the Lord must above all people be responsive to the commands of the Lord. Nadab and Abihu were not, and their fate was an impressive warning to all that God must be approached carefully.

But that did not mean that there was no approach to God. Right through the literature that tells of the wilderness wanderings there runs the thought that God willed to be among his people and to be known by them. But approach must be made in the right way. Men must not think that God might be presumed on or that they could rush into his presence any time they wanted and just as they were. So we read: 'The LORD said to Moses: "Tell your brother Aaron not to come whenever he chooses into the Most Holy Place behind the curtain in front of the atonement cover on the ark, or else he will die, because I appear in the cloud over the atonement cover"' (Lv. 16:2; 'Most Holy Place' and 'atonement cover' are NIV's translations of expressions traditionally rendered 'Holy of Holies' and 'mercy seat'). Not even the high priest is entitled to presume on the presence of God. The little room that was in a special sense the place of God's presence was not to be entered lightly. Anyone who presumed to enter in the wrong way and at the wrong time must expect to die, as the fate of Nadab and Abihu showed. God is majestic and powerful – and remote. This must never be forgotten.

But on just one day in the year approach was permitted. It must be done in the right way and with the proper preparation and even then only one man entered the Holy of Holies. But it might be done. It was done in connection with the putting away of the nation's sins, which added to the importance and the solemnity of the occasion.

It was a day of fasting, which in itself was significant. In the Jewish liturgical year there were several feasts but just one great fasting day, the Day of Atonement. On this most solemn day the people remembered the greatness and the majesty of God and the pickle they had landed themselves in by the sins they had committed. So they engaged in picturesque and unusual liturgical action in order that those sins might be put away. They had, of course, a regular sacrificial system in which animals were offered on the altar every day. Some of the sacrifices expressed homage to God and some expressed fellowship or thanksgiving, but many were directed towards atoning for sin. But clearly they were not adequate. They did not cover all eventualities and even after they had been offered in the correct manner the people had the uncomfortable feeling that God might still be displeased with something not atoned for.

So, on the tenth day of the seventh month, there came this solemn time of fasting and penitence. Special rites, used only on this day, brought home the seriousness of sin and the importance of dealing with it. This was the day of the 'scapegoat' (='escape-goat'), the animal that carried the sins of the people away as it was lost in the wilderness. And it was the one day in all the year when the high priest entered the Holy of Holies. Obviously the day was very special.

THE CEREMONIES OF THE DAY OF ATONEMENT

The high priest began the day by bathing himself (Lv. 16:4). This in itself was distinctive, because on other days he was required in the exercise of his ministry to do no more than wash his hands and his feet (Ex. 30:19–21). But this was a very special day and there was a whole-heartedness about the approach to cleansing (as about everything else). After bathing, the high priest put on plain white linen clothing, which symbolized holiness and suited the humble approach that characterized the day better than the gorgeous robes of his office did. Then he collected the animals that would be used for the main sacrifices. For himself and his household he took a young bull for a sin offering and a ram for a burnt offering; for the Israelite community he took two male goats for a sin offering and a ram for a burnt offering (Lv. 16:3, 5). Other sacrifices would be offered that day (Nu. 29:7–11), but these were the important ones.

The high priest began with the bull and offered it 'for his own sin offering to make atonement for himself and his household' (Lv. 16:6). And now, early in the day, came the first moment of excitement and tingling tension.

The high priest entered the Holy of Holies.

He took a censer full of burning coals from off the altar and two handfuls of incense and went behind the curtain into that little dark room that was the Holy of Holies (verse 12). He promptly put the incense on the coals and such a plentiful supply as two handfuls would guarantee a thick cloud of smoke to cover the mercy seat 'so that he will not die' (verse 13). This was apparently done to hide the mercy seat, the symbol of the presence of God, from human gaze rather than to cover the priest and shield him from the divine wrath. The effect was to retain the concept of a God who had mystery about him, but also to keep the high priest safe. Thus protected he proceeded to bring the blood of the bull into the Holy of Holies. There he sprinkled it once against the face of the mercy seat and then seven times in front of it (verse 14).

After the offering of the bull the high priest cast lots over the two goats, 'one lot for the LORD and the other for the scapegoat' (Hebrew, 'for Azazel'; verse 8). The one 'for the LORD' he proceeded to offer as a sin offering for the people. When it came to the use of the blood of this animal there came the second thrilling moment – the high priest went into the Holy of Holies for the second time and did with this blood what he had done with that for his own sin offering: 'In this way he will make atonement for the Most Holy Place because of the uncleanness and rebellion of the Israelites, whatever their sins have been.' The regulation goes on, 'He is to do the same for the Tent of Meeting, which is among them in the midst of their uncleanness' (verse 16).

The point of this is that the circumstances of everyday life made it easy for people to contract forms of ceremonial defilement, while rebellion against the Lord was endemic among the Israelites (as among all men). All this meant that they had defiled the place where they came to worship and this part of the day's ceremonies was directed to removing the uncleanness. This is probably in mind also when the high priest came 'to the altar that is before the LORD' and put some of the blood of both animals on all the horns of the altar and sprinkled it on the altar seven times (verses 18–19). Leviticus does not say specifically which altar this was; most commentators today hold it to be the altar of burnt offering, though the Rabbis thought it was the incense altar.

Now the high priest and the place of worship were both ceremonially clean. Attention moved to what we at any rate would regard as more serious, all the sins of the people. The high priest laid both his hands on the head of the remaining goat and confessed 'all the wickedness and rebellion of the Israelites – all their sins'. We saw in the last chapter that there is some dispute about the laying on of hands in the ordinary run of sacrifices, but there is none about this one. We read specifically that the high priest shall 'put them [*i.e.* the sins] on the goat's head'. Thereafter 'He shall send the goat away into the desert in the care of a man appointed for the task. The goat will carry on itself all their sins to a solitary place; and the man shall release it in the desert' (verses 21–22).

This was the great, central activity of the day. The nation's sins had been solemnly confessed and dealt with in accordance with God's command. They were no longer laid to the charge of the people.

Now sin and defilement had been dealt with. The high priest took off the simple linen garments in which he had officiated as he led the people in those purifying and cleansing rites. He put on his glorious robes and offered burnt offerings for himself and the people (the rams of verses 3, 5), offerings which expressed the homage of the people of God and their representative. It was at this point also that he burnt the fat of the sin offering. The carcases of both the bull and the goat were taken outside the camp and burnt up in their entirety (verse 27).

Such were the events of the day according to Leviticus 16. Apart from this chapter we have little information about the day. But any time it is mentioned it is a day of special solemnity. People must not do any work on it and they must 'deny themselves', *i.e.* fast, 'from the evening of the ninth day of the month until the following evening' (Lv. 23:32). Anyone who did not observe this fast 'must be cut off from his people', while the Sabbath obligation is enforced in that the Lord will 'destroy from among his people anyone who does any work on that day' (Lv. 23:29–30). Quite apart from the unusual offerings we have already noticed, special sacrifices were offered to mark the annual observance (Nu. 29:7–11). The making of atonement on the horns of the altar of incense is spoken of briefly in Exodus 30:10 (*cf.* Lv. 16:18), but this adds little to what Leviticus 16 tells us. It simply underlines the truth that the Day of Atonement had wide-ranging importance for the whole of the Jewish worship. There is one more reference: when the year of jubilee came, it was ushered in with the blowing of the trumpet everywhere throughout the land on the Day of Atonement (Lv. 25:9).

THE SIGNIFICANCE OF THE DAY OF ATONEMENT

All this shows that the day was one of special importance and solemnity. The careful performance of rites which took place once a year only must have impressed on the worshippers the truths that sin matters and that something must be done about it if it is not to separate people from God. That it was prescribed at all seems a tacit admission that the sacrificial system did not remove all sin, though this conclusion does not seem to have been drawn in Old Testament days. But the writer to the Hebrews drew it. He makes a good deal of the fact that the Day of Atonement shows that the sacrifices normally offered could not remove sin (Heb. 9:7–9), and indeed he goes further and says that even the Day of Atonement could not do this (Heb. 10:1–4).

There are two specially noteworthy features of the observance of this day. The first, of course, is that on this day and on this day alone in all the year there was admission to the Holy of Holies. It was perhaps not much to crow about, for it was a very restricted admission. Only the high priest could enter and he only after taking the most stringent precautions. But at least it did hold out the hope of access into the very presence of God, if only by a representative.

The other is the placing of the sins of the people on the scapegoat. There is dispute about the meaning of the expression 'for Azazel' ('scapegoat' in NIV and other translations). Some scholars hold that this was the name of a demon, perhaps even of Satan himself, so that evil was, so to speak, being sent back where it belonged. Others think that it means 'complete destruction' (the sins are no more), while a third view is that it signifies 'rocky precipice' (at least in later times the goat was finally pushed over a precipice). With the information available to us it is impossible to be certain. What is clear is that the people saw their sins completely removed. The sins were laid on the goat, and taken into the wilderness so that they saw them no more.

The day was a great national occasion and many scholars hold that, in accordance with this, it was the sins of the nation as a whole rather than those of individuals that were primarily in mind. This is not unreasonable. But certainly in later times it was held that the sins of individuals were covered by the observances of this day and it is not at all improbable that this idea was there from the first. The ceremonies witnessed to a conviction that the normal offering of sacrifices did not cover all the sins people committed. Something more was needed, a point which will be taken up and given emphasis in the New Testament.

THE RABBIS[1] AND THE DAY OF ATONEMENT

Leviticus 16 does not give us a complete guide to the ceremonies of the Day of Atonement. The main outline is clear and we may well argue that everything that is needed is said here. But it would not be possible to go through all the ritual with nothing more to guide us than the directions given in this chapter and the gaps might conceivably be filled in more ways than one. To cite one small example, the high priest is directed to take a censer full of burning coals into the Holy of Holies together with incense with which to make a cloud of smoke (Lv. 16:12). But there is no direction about taking it out. Did censers pile up in the Holy of Holies from year to year? Did the high priest remove last year's censer when he took this year's in? Or did he take his censer out at a later point in the day's activities? There is no indication. The main points are quite clear and there would have been no difficulty in filling in the gaps by customary procedures. All that I am saying is that there were gaps.

In the rabbinic writings there is a good deal of information which shows us how the gaps were filled in in later times. There is, of course, no way of knowing whether this was the way things were done in the Old Testament period, but the Rabbis show us the procedure during New Testament times. This will be the Day of Atonement as the New Testament writers knew it. In general the effects of the additions the Rabbis made to the Old Testament material is to emphasize the solemnity of the day. There are many statements which put it on the level of the Sabbath and some which regard it as more solemn still. Other regulations are aimed at securing punctilious attention to the correct performance of every detail of the ceremonial. The importance the Rabbis attached to the Day of Atonement may be gauged from the fact that in the Mishnah an entire tractate is devoted to this one day

Proceedings began seven days before the day of the fast itself. At that time the high priest was taken from his house to the temple, so that he could more easily be shielded from accidental uncleanness. If he contracted uncleanness he would be debarred

---

[1] During the early centuries of our era there were many scholarly Jewish Rabbis. They taught orally, but about the end of the second century their teaching was committed to writing in a compilation called the *Mishnah* (which means 'Instruction'). From this and later Jewish writings we get valuable information about the ideas and practices of the Jews during the New Testament period.

from officiating on the great day and then where would Israel be? Just in case the worst came to the worst, a deputy was appointed to officiate in his stead if for any reason he was unable to proceed. He might contract a seven-day defilement. Or he might die! In fact the high priest never was disqualified and this was accounted one of the ten wonders about the temple (Aboth 5:5; this is one of the tractates of the Mishnah). According to one scrupulous Rabbi another wife was put on standby lest his wife should die before the offering of sacrifice. His reasoning was that the high priest was required to offer a sin offering not only for himself but also for 'his household' (Lv. 16:6), and the absolute minimum for a household is a wife. However this learned view was rejected by the majority on the common-sense grounds that 'If so there would be no end to the matter' (Yoma 1:1; to be consistent there would have to be a standby for the standby wife and so on, and where would the process end?).

Throughout the seven days the high priest was to perform the priestly duties of presenting the blood, burning the incense, trimming the lamps and the like, apparently to keep his hand in in priestly ceremonial actions so that all would go smoothly on the day. In the same spirit, on the night before the great day the animals to be used in the sacrifices were brought before him so that he would be familiar with them. On the third and seventh days he was sprinkled with the ashes of a heifer in case he had unwittingly contracted some uncleanness which neither he nor anyone else knew anything about. An interesting provision is that he was to be continually instructed in the correct ritual and urged to recite it himself 'lest thou hast forgotten or lest thou hast never learnt' (Yoma 1:3). On the eve of the Day of Atonement he was solemnly adjured not to change any of the things his mentors had said to him (Yoma 1:5). This appears to be a reference to a dispute between the Sadducees and the Pharisees. The former held that the incense should be lit outside the curtain, but the Pharisees abhorred this dreadful action and maintained that it should be lit only inside the curtain.

On the evening before the great day the high priest had a light meal (a heavy one would encourage sleep and he was not going to get any). A bevy of priests saw to it that he was kept awake all night (according to Maimonides, 'lest any impurity might affect him'). He spent the time reading and expounding Scripture or else hearing someone else engage in these pious practices.

When it was morning he immersed himself in water. On this day all told he immersed himself five times; he immersed himself every time he changed his robes. In addition he washed his hands and his feet ten times. This first immersion was in the temple court in a place separated from the public gaze by a linen sheet (all his other immersions were 'in the Temple by the Parwah Chamber', Yoma 3:3; this was to the south of the Court of the Priests). After his immersion he put on his golden robes and offered the daily burnt offering.

Now the special offerings of the day began. The high priest immersed himself a second time, then changed into the simple white linen that characterized him on that day. He laid his hands on the bull and confessed his sins and those of his household. A noteworthy feature of this confession was that in his prayer he used the sacred name of God, that name indicated by 'LORD' (as spelt in many translations) and which scholars think was something like 'Yahweh'. Normally this name was never pronounced for fear it would be used wrongly and thus someone would be breaking the command not to take it in vain. People used a reverential substitute like 'Lord' or 'The Holy One'. But on this day the high priest used 'LORD' ten times.

The lots used to decide the fate of the two goats were originally wooden, but later golden ones were used. One was marked 'For the LORD' and the other 'For Azazel'. They were placed in a casket which the high priest shook. Then he put in both hands and pulled them out, one in each hand. He put the lots on the heads of the goats and said, 'A Sin-offering to the LORD', apparently making no distinction between the two animals. He tied a cord of crimson wool on the head of the goat for Azazel and a similar cord about the throat of the goat that was to be slaughtered (Yoma 4:1–2).

Now he came to the bull a second time and laid both hands on the animal. His confession differed from the one he used on the first occasion in that this time he associated with him in the sins he was confessing not only his own household but also 'the children of Aaron, thy holy people'. He slaughtered the bull and gave the blood in a basin to a man who had the responsibility of stirring it to make sure that it did not congeal.

IN THE HOLY OF HOLIES

The high priest then took coals from the altar in a censer of gold and he put two handfuls of incense into a ladle. These he took into the Holy of Holies, the censer in his right hand and the ladle in his left. The Mishnah says that there were two curtains guarding the entrance with the space of a cubit between them. The outer curtain was looped back on the south side and the inner one on the north. The high priest could thus pass between them with both hands full. In the Holy of Holies he set the censer down between the two poles used to carry the ark (Yoma 5:1). After the ark was taken away the custom was to set it down on a stone called 'Shetiyah' ('Foundation'), a stone three finger-breadths high. Then he heaped the incense on the coals so that the whole place was filled with smoke.

He came out and prayed in the Holy Place, but briefly 'lest he put Israel in terror'. The people understood that it was dangerous to go into the Holy of Holies and they would be anxious if the high priest did not reappear quite quickly. Now he took the blood and returned with it to the Holy of Holies. There he sprinkled it once upwards and seven times downwards counting as he did so, 'One, one and one, one and two....' This he did, not as though he were trying to sprinkle upwards or downwards but 'as though he were wielding a whip' (Yoma 5:3). Josephus, the first-century Jewish historian, says that the sprinkling was done 'toward the ceiling seven times, and likewise on the floor'[2] but there does not seem to be support for this view.

Next he slaughtered the goat that had been marked 'for the LORD'. He collected its blood and did with it what he had done with that of the bull. That completed his work inside the curtain, but he had more to do outside it. He began with the blood of the bull and sprinkled it on the outer side of the curtain with an eightfold sprinkling, counting as he had done before. He set down the blood of the bull, took the blood of the goat and sprinkled it in the same way on the outer side of the curtain. He proceeded to pour the blood of the bull into that of the goat, then to pour the mixed blood into the container that had previously held the blood of the bull (apparently to ensure a thorough mixing). The next bit of the ritual is rather complicated. He took some of the mixture, sprinkled the horns of the golden altar of incense with it, sprinkled some of it on that altar and poured the rest of it at the western base of the altar of burnt offering. He

[2] Josephus, *Jewish Antiquities*, Book iii, 242–243.

must have kept some of the blood back, for he went on to sprinkle the outer altar and finally to pour the residue at the southern base of that altar. A curious note informs us that the two streams of blood joined in the channel and flowed into the Kidron, where it was sold to the gardeners as manure (Yoma 5:6), an interesting blend of piety and practicality.

THE SCAPEGOAT

Now came the turn of the scapegoat. The high priest laid his two hands on the animal and made confession of 'the iniquities and transgressions and sins which thy people, the House of Israel, have committed and transgressed and sinned before thee' (Yoma 6:2). The goat was then led away. Theoretically any man could perform this duty, but it became the custom to have a member of one of the priestly families do it. Ten booths were established along the way to the ravine at intervals of half a Sabbath-day's journey, each being under the charge of eminent citizens of Jerusalem who would invite the man leading the goat to have food or water. Then they would escort him to the next booth and go back again to their own, the return journey thus not exceeding the limit prescribed for the Sabbath.

Nobody went with the man from the last booth. They simply stood and watched while he divided the scarlet cord into two pieces. He tied one piece to the rock and the other to the goat's horns. Then from behind he pushed the goat over the precipice. It rolled over and over and was broken in pieces before it had gone half-way down (Yoma 6:6). Having thus made quite sure that the animal would not come back, the man returned to the last booth and remained there until nightfall (when another day began).

Meantime the high priest completed his work on the animals slaughtered earlier. He cut off the sacrificial portions and burnt them on the altar. He put the remainder of the carcases on carrying poles, so that they could be taken out to the place of burning. Presumably he delivered them to the men who would carry them there, but this is not said.

The arrival of the scapegoat at the wilderness was signalled all the way back to Jerusalem by the waving of towels. One of the Rabbis, R. Ishmael, thought that this was not really needed. He maintained that a cord of scarlet wool was tied to the door of the sanctuary and that when the scapegoat reached the wilderness the wool turned white in accordance with the words of the LORD through the prophet Isaiah, 'Though your sins are like scarlet, they shall be as white as snow' (Is. 1:18). According to the Talmud this sign ceased forty years before the destruction of the temple (Yoma 39b; 'Talmud' means 'Teaching' and is the name given to a later and fuller collection of rabbinic teaching than the Mishnah; 'Yoma' is the title of one of its divisions.)

Be that as it may, when the signal was received the high priest went to the court of the women and began to read from the Law, the prescribed passages being Leviticus 16 and 23:26–32, after which he recited from memory Numbers 29:7–11. He concluded this part of the day's activities with some prayers. He could do the reading and praying either in the linen garments or in his own white robe. While he was doing this the carcases of the animals were being burnt up.

THE NOTE OF JOY

The penitential part of the day was over. The high priest underwent another immersion and changed into his golden robes. Majesty and splendour were now the order of the day rather than the penitence and simplicity that had marked the earlier observances. The high priest offered his ram (Lv. 16:3) and that of the people (Lv. 16:5) and seven male year-old lambs (Nu. 29:8).

It will be recalled that the high priest had left the censer in the Holy of Holies. He had put it down on the stone called Shetiyah, together with the incense ladle, and there they had remained. At this point he went back for them. First he had to change into the simple linen robes (preceded of course by another immersion!). Thus arrayed he went back into the Holy of Holies, retrieved the censer and ladle and came back out (Yoma 7:4).

He had one final immersion and changed back into his golden robes. This was the correct vesture in which to burn the afternoon incense and to trim the lamps. That completed his duties for the day and he was free to go home. There he made a feast for his friends 'for that he was come forth safely from the Sanctuary' (Yoma 7:4). It had been a dangerous adventure. It was well to rejoice at its safe conclusion.

In another tractate we read of a further expression of joy at the end of the Day of Atonement: 'the daughters of Jerusalem used to go forth in white raiments; and these were borrowed, that none should be abashed which had them not.... And the daughters of

Jerusalem went forth to dance in the vineyards' (Taanith 4:8). The day was a solemn one, with a concentration on the serious business of the nation's sins. But at the end of the day, when atonement had been made and the high priest had survived his entrances into the Holy of Holies, the dominant notes were those of relief and joy.

THE REMOVAL OF SIN

During the New Testament period Judaism attached great importance to the correct performance of the prescribed ritual on the Day of Atonement. All the additions to the regulations of the Old Testament seem to be designed to ensure that all was done in proper order and that the worshippers were left in no doubt about the seriousness of their sin and about the importance of taking God's way of getting rid of it.

But we should not think that the ritual was held to be valid of itself, as though all that was needed was to go through the right actions and recite the right words. Repentance and restitution were seen as necessary and they were insisted on in strong terms.

If a man said, 'I will sin and repent, and sin again and repent', he will be given no chance to repent. (If he said,) 'I will sin and the Day of Atonement will effect atonement', then the Day of Atonement effects no atonement. For transgressions that are between man and God the Day of Atonement effects atonement, but for transgressions that are between a man and his fellow the Day of Atonement effects atonement only if he has appeased his fellow (Yoma 8:9).

The Day of Atonement is clearly regarded as important, but only if there are the right internal dispositions and if the person has done what he can to undo the effects of his sin. Sometimes it is suggested that in fact it was the attitude that was all important and that the rites were no more than a piece of pageantry, a series of dramatic symbols. The reality was the prayer and the fasting. Now and then a rabbinical statement can be found to support this position, for example, 'Though no sacrifices be offered, the day in itself effects atonement.'[3] But this kind of thing appears to be a rationalization from a time subsequent to the destruction of

[3] Cited from *The Jewish Encyclopedia*, vol. ii, p.286.

the temple. When sacrifice was no longer possible people looked for some other way.

But there is no evidence that while the temple was still functioning any responsible Jews held that the sacrifice did not matter. To read through the tractate Yoma is to enter an atmosphere where every ritual detail is ordained by God and must be performed accordingly with scrupulous care. We see this, for example, in the requirement that everything must be done in exactly the right order; otherwise it did not count. If the high priest became confused and did some things in an incorrect order, he had to go back to the place where the original mistake occurred and start again from that point (Yoma 5:7). The ritual must not be varied in any way. There can be no doubt but that repentance was rated very highly and its absence made the rite void (though occasionally we find the view that the Day of Atonement availed for all Israelites except those who cut themselves off from Israel). But there is nothing to indicate that while the temple was still standing responsible people held that repentance was enough without the performance of the divinely ordained ceremonies. All must be performed as God had directed.

Precisely what it was that effected atonement is not completely clear. There is a saying of R. Simeon:

> As the blood of the goat that is sprinkled within (the Holy of Holies) makes atonement for the Israelites, so does the blood of the bullock make atonement for the priests; and as the confession of sin recited over the scapegoat makes atonement for the Israelites, so does the confession of sin recited over the bullock make atonement for the priests (Shebuoth 1:7).

Here atonement is associated both with the blood and with confession, and with three different animals, the bull, the goat for the sin offering and the scapegoat. The Rabbis do not seem to have tied atonement to any one part of the day's activities and we are probably right in seeing it as due to the whole of the observance rather than specifically to any one moment.

But when the right internal attitude is joined to the due performance of the ritual of the Day of Atonement, it is plain that the Judaism of the New Testament period saw the nation's sins as removed. This is strikingly brought out in the scenes of rejoicing that brought the day to its close. Linked with this of course was the fact that the high priest had emerged unscathed from the Holy of Holies. Purification from sin and access to God were both prominent in the ceremonial of this day.

Some Old Testament scholars raise questions about the kind of sin that the whole sacrificial system was held to remove. They hold that only inadvertent sins and ritual defilements were in view. Even the Day of Atonement, they maintain, was concerned with this kind of thing, with the involuntary defilements that people contracted through the year and with which they consequently defiled their place of worship. On this view the Day of Atonement was directed towards making the temple ceremonially clean once more. I am more than doubtful whether there is satisfactory evidence for such a position, but whatever the truth about the way the day was viewed in the Old Testament period there is none about its scope as the Rabbis saw it.

> For uncleanness that befalls the Temple and its Hallowed Things through wantonness, atonement is made by the goat whose blood is sprinkled within (the Holy of Holies) and by the Day of Atonement; for all other transgressions spoken of in the Law, venial or grave, wanton or unwitting, conscious or unconscious, sins of omission or of commission, sins punishable by Extirpation or by death at the hands of the court, the scapegoat makes atonement (Shebuoth 1:6).

The day was a wonderful provision of God. Properly observed, the Rabbis held, it availed for all the sins of all the people.

THE DAY OF ATONEMENT IN THE NEW TESTAMENT

The Day of Atonement receives serious treatment in the epistle to the Hebrews, though elsewhere it does not attract much attention from the New Testament writers. It is referred to simply as 'the Fast' in Acts 27:9, but this is no more than a note of time and there is no treatment of what the day signified. It is arguable that the idea of the day, though not the exact term, lies behind a few passages (notably 2 Cor. 5:21; Gal. 3:13). But this is not a rich harvest and we must turn to Hebrews for a clear and meaningful treatment of the significance of the day. As in the Old Testament and in the rabbinic writings there is a twofold emphasis – the day points to access and to cleansing.

Just as is the case in Leviticus 16, the writer to the Hebrews introduces his treatment with a reference to access to the presence of God. He speaks of the tabernacle furnishings and points out that the high priest was the only person permitted to enter the Holy of Holies and he on one occasion only in the whole year. He draws a conclusion: 'The Holy Spirit was showing by this that the way into the Most Holy Place had not yet been disclosed as long as the first tabernacle was still standing' (Heb. 9:8). The line of approach is not 'This is the way the sins of Israel are remitted' but rather, 'This is the way the high priest may enter the Holy of Holies.' Of course there is a connection. Indeed, there is a double connection, for in the first place it is sin that inhibits access and thus must be dealt with if access is to be obtained, and in the second place the purpose of the access into the Holy of Holies on this day was that sin should be dealt with.

It is probably this connection with sin that motivates the emphasis on blood. The high priest entered the sacred place 'only once a year, and never without blood' (Heb. 9:7). It was an adventure for the high priest to enter the Holy of Holies and one whose outcome could not be foreseen. Thus it was essential that his entrance be attended by every precaution, and a most important precaution was the presentation of the blood of a sacrificial victim. Only with the blood could the people's representative be cleansed from his sin and be accepted as fit to approach the presence of God.

The writer to the Hebrews bears this in mind. He points out that Christ entered the heavenly Holy Place not 'by means of the blood of goats and calves; but he entered the Most Holy Place once for all by his own blood, having obtained eternal redemption' (Heb. 9:12). The contrast between the blood of Christ and the blood of animals is important, for 'it is impossible for the blood of bulls and goats to take away sins' (Heb. 10:4). Just as it was impossible for animal blood to take away sin, so it was impossible for it to secure access. Christ's blood is different. It really opens up the way into the presence of God.

Our author contrasts the limited nature of the access secured by the high priest with that secured by Christ in two ways. First, the high priest dealt only with an earthly tabernacle or temple, but Christ with 'the greater and more perfect tabernacle that is not man-made, that is to say, not a part of this creation' (Heb. 9:11). Putting it another way, he says, 'Christ did not enter a man-made sanctuary that was only a copy of the true one; he

83

entered heaven itself, now to appear for us in God's presence' (Heb. 9:24). The access with which the high priest concerned himself was to the tiny dark room in the temple which was a symbol of the presence of God. The access with which Christ was concerned was access into the very presence of God in heaven.

The second contrast concerns people. The high priest could do no more than enter the Holy of Holies himself. He could not take anyone with him. And he could enter only on the one day in the year. The fullest exercise of his ministry with all the solemnity at his command obtained only a very limited access: access on one day for him only. The people must forever be content with access by proxy. But in Hebrews there is emphasis on two wonderful truths: Christ secured access into the very presence of God in heaven (as we have just seen, Heb. 9:11–12, 24) and access not for himself only but for all his people as well. Our writer exhorts us:

> Therefore, brothers, since we have confidence to enter the Most Holy Place by the blood of Jesus, by a new and living way opened for us through the curtain, that is, his body, and since we have a great priest over the house of God, let us draw near to God with a sincere heart in full assurance of faith... (Heb. 10:19–22).

Because Christ's blood was shed, all who believe in him have access into the very holiest of all, a truth incidentally which was given expression in another way when the Synoptists tell us that at the moment of Jesus' death the curtain in the temple 'was torn in two from top to bottom' (Mt. 27:51; Mk. 15:38; Lk. 23:45). The Day of Atonement ceremonies bring home to Christians the fact that because of what Christ has done they find the way into the very presence of God open before them.

PUTTING AWAY SIN

We turn now to the other idea so prominent in the Day of Atonement activities, purification from sin. There is no question that this was a prominent thought in the Old Testament observances of the day, though it is not easy to be sure of exactly what was thought to bring about atonement. The high priest confessed the people's sins as he laid his hands on the head of the scapegoat and 'put them on the goat's head'. As a result, 'The goat will carry on itself all their sins to a solitary place' (Lv. 16:21–22). This seems clear enough, but there is a difficulty in that the high priest has already offered the other goat as a sin offering (which, of course, is expiatory), after which we read that he had 'made atonement for himself, his household and the whole community of Israel' (Lv. 16:17). Nor can we solve the difficulty by appealing to Jewish tradition, for the Mishnah makes no difference in the confessions made over the two goats. In general it gives no indication that atonement was affected by one part of the day's activities rather than another.

There seems merit in the suggestion that the two goats were really one sacrifice, a suggestion which is supported by the requirements that they should be as nearly as possible identical and that they should even have been purchased at the same time. If this view be accepted we have the thought that the one offering of the two goats secures access into the Holiest and also takes away sin. A complicating factor is the further confession over the bull and the requirement of repentance. Perhaps our safest course is to hold that the whole of the day's activities were needed to secure the blessings and that no attempt was made to differentiate sharply between the various parts of the comprehensive whole.

However this problem be resolved, there is no doubt about the fact that the Day of Atonement was seen as the occasion when sin was put away. Josephus speaks of the scapegoat as 'being intended to avert and serve as an expiation for the sins of the whole people',[4] a view which would have been accepted by most Jews of his day. But the author to the Hebrews takes up this very point. He vigorously repudiates the view that the ceremonies of the Day of Atonement take away sin. 'Those sacrifices', he says, 'are an annual reminder of sins, because it is impossible for the blood of bulls and goats to take away sins' (Heb. 10:3–4); they are no more than 'external regulations applying until the time of the new order' (Heb. 9:10); 'sprinkled on those who are ceremonially unclean' the blood and the ashes may 'sanctify them so that they are outwardly clean' (Heb. 9:13), but more they cannot do. The very fact that they continue to be offered year after year shows our author that they cannot perfect the worshippers who make use of them. If they could, would they not have done their job and then cease to have been offered (Heb. 10:2)?

But what the animal sacrifices in general and those on the Day

4 Josephus, *Jewish Antiquities*, Book iii, 241.

of Atonement in particular could not do, that Jesus has perfectly accomplished. Jesus 'entered the Most Holy Place once for all by his own blood, having obtained eternal redemption' (Heb. 9:12). There can be no improvement on 'eternal redemption'. Jesus did not 'enter heaven to offer himself again and again, the way the high priest enters the Most Holy Place every year' (Heb. 9:25). Repeatedly our author stresses the fact that Jesus offered himself once and for all (Heb. 7:27; 9:12,26,28; 10:10,12,14,18). The finality of his sacrifice is impressive over against the annual repetition of the high priest's work on the Day of Atonement.

There is also a contrast between the high priest and Jesus. The former must offer for his own sins (Heb. 7:27; 9:7). But Jesus is 'holy, blameless, pure, set apart from sinners, exalted above the heavens' (Heb. 7:26). Such a high priest does not need to offer sacrifice for himself. His sinlessness indeed is an integral part of the perfection of his offering.

Perhaps we should notice a point at which the two are alike. In the Levitical system all the sacrifices, including those of the Day of Atonement, were regarded as being of divine origin. When the high priest entered the Holy of Holies, or put the people's sins on the head of the scapegoat and sent them away into the wilderness, he was doing what God in his mercy commanded to be done. There is no hint that any magic is being applied or any attempt being made to coerce God. There are no pagan ideas of appeasement of an offended deity. Atonement is of divine origin and sin is put away only because God wills it and has ordained means whereby it can be accomplished. We see this in the work of Christ. The epistle to the Hebrews opens with a majestic sentence which stresses that God has always taken the initiative in his dealings with his people and that this divine initiative comes to its climax in the work of Christ. The writer never loses sight of the fact that salvation is all of God. Specifically, when he thinks of the atonement of Christ in terms of the Day of Atonement ceremonies he quotes Psalm 40 and applies it to him who came to do the will of the Father, 'And by that will, we have been made holy through the sacrifice of the body of Jesus Christ once for all' (Heb. 10:10). All is of grace, for all is of God.

The Day of Atonement, then, has its place in the New Testament picture of Christ's saving work. It contributes to the idea of the new and living way two thoughts: access and forgiveness.

1. Access

Our sins separate us from God (Is. 59:2). We have no way of remedying the situation. But Christ has opened for his people the way into the very presence of God. This does not mean an occasional access. Christians live day by day in the assurance that the way into the presence of God is open wide. They need the mediation of no earthly priest. Indeed, now all of life is lived in God's presence. This is a most important truth for the average Christian. The average person is just that – average. He or she has no great importance in the eyes of the world. Indeed that is one of life's frustrations. When an injustice is done to us we have no access to the great ones who might put things right. We are continually pushed around by low-grade bureaucrats and kept in our place by office receptionists. It is possible to spend hours awaiting the pleasure of some subordinate official.

This is part of life and if anything can be done about it I do not know what it is. But believers have access where it really counts. Christ's fulfilment of the Day of Atonement ceremonies has opened up the way into the very presence of God for the humblest of his people. Nothing on earth can take away what this means in terms of prayer and of companionship.

2. Forgiveness

The imagery of the scapegoat, fulfilled in Christ's perfect bearing of sins, means that sins are really forgiven. The blood of animal sacrifices could never cope with the problems of man, made in God's image as he is. But the blood of Christ can and does. Our Day of Atonement was the day of the cross. Jesus 'suffered outside the city gate to make the people holy through his own blood' (Heb. 13:12).

For further study
1. How was approach to God restricted and safeguarded in Old Testament times? What do we learn about God from this?
2. The writer to the Hebrews uses the ceremonies of the Day of Atonement to teach important lessons about the work of Christ. Make a list of the contrasts and the resemblances he finds.
3. What light does the scapegoat shed on the work of Christ as sin-bearer?

4
The Passover

It cannot be said that the New Testament writers see the Passover as a dominating concept when they seek to interpret the cross. If they are thinking in sacrificial terms they prefer a general reference. But there are exceptions. Paul says explicitly, 'Christ our Passover was sacrificed' (1 Cor. 5:7; NIV has 'our Passover lamb', but there are objections to this translation, as will be brought out later). All four Gospels have relevant sections. The Synoptists place the institution of the Holy Communion at a Passover meal, which means at the least that the continuing remembrance of the death of Jesus is done in such a way that Passover associations are present. John seems to place the death of Jesus at the time the Passover victims were sacrificed and to regard that death as in some sense a Passover sacrifice. Nor should we overlook the fact that the exodus is recalled a number of times in the New Testament and, of course, the exodus was introduced by the Passover. It is clear that for the first Christians there were some aspects of Christ's saving work that were best brought out by thinking of the Passover.

THE PASSOVER IN THE OLD TESTAMENT

Modern Old Testament scholars ask hard questions about the Passover. What was its original form? How did it relate to the feast of unleavened bread? What is the connection with the full moon? And with the offering of the first-born? And with the coming of spring? Should it be seen as a spring festival? These and other such questions have their importance, but for our present purpose they may be ignored. They are not the questions and not even the kind of questions that the first Christians asked.

If we are to see what the New Testament writers had in mind when they applied Passover imagery to the work of Christ, we must see what it was that first-century people thought about the Passover. That means that we must take the Old Testament narrative as it stands. For the first Christians the Old Testament story was the divinely given account of the way their God had delivered their ancestors from Egypt and made them into a nation. So we proceed to look at the account.

The Israelites were in bitter bondage in Egypt. Nine plagues had come and gone on the Egyptians but none of them had procured the release the oppressed people looked for so longingly. God had repeatedly sent the message to Pharaoh, 'Let my people go' (Ex. 5:1; 8:1,20; 9:1,13; 10:3), but Pharaoh had not let them go. Now came the prophecy of a tenth and more grievous plague than any of the nine: 'Every firstborn son in Egypt will die.' In this plague God will protect his own people: 'among the Israelites not a dog will bark at any man or animal.' This will make it clear that God is acting to help his people: 'You will know that the LORD makes a distinction between Egypt and Israel' (Ex. 11:5,7).

The deliverance of the Israelites was not to be automatic. They must do as God directed and identify themselves as those obedient to his commands. On the tenth day of the month Abib each household or group of households must select a lamb or kid, the number being regulated so that the animal would be sufficient for the group for one meal (Ex. 12:3–4). The kid or lamb was to be a year-old male and without blemish. Then on the fourteenth day of the month the chosen animal was to be killed 'between the evenings'. The meaning of the expression is not immediately obvious and it can be understood in more ways than one (NIV understands it as 'at twilight'). In the first century this was understood to mean the time between the sun's commencing to decline (say about 3 p.m. on our time) and its actual disappearance. Some of the blood of the animal was to be put 'on the sides and tops of the door-frames of the houses' where the Israelites were to eat the meal (Ex. 12:7). The animal was to be roasted whole and eaten that night, together with bitter herbs and bread made without yeast. The whole of the animal was to be eaten and if any of it remained until the morning it was to be burnt up. It was to be eaten 'with your cloak tucked into your belt, your sandals on your feet and your staff in your hand' (Ex. 12:11). 'Eat it in haste', the instruction proceeds; 'it is the LORD's Passover' (Ex. 12:11).

The placing of the blood was important and the reason for it is now given: 'The blood will be a sign for you on the houses where you are; and when I see the blood, I will pass over you. No destructive plague will touch you when I strike Egypt' (Ex. 12:13). The Israelites did as they were told (Ex. 12:28) and escaped the destruction which overtook the Egyptians. The death of the first-born was the last straw for the Egyptians. They wanted no more plagues. So they urged the Israelites to get out of the country. The Israelites needed no second bidding. They left in haste; they 'took their dough before the yeast was added, and carried it on their shoulders in kneading troughs wrapped in clothing' (Ex. 12:34).

Such were the events. The Israelites were instructed that they must keep this feast for ever as a memorial of the deliverance God had given them (Ex. 12:14–15). Not only were they to observe the one night of deliverance, but they were to eat bread made without yeast (=unleavened bread) for seven days. The Old Testament often refers to 'the feast of unleavened bread' which includes the Passover as well as the seven days following. This feast was to be an Israelite observance; no uncircumcised person was to eat of it (Ex. 12:43–49).

A GREAT OCCASION

The Passover became a most important part of the Jewish year. It commemorated not simply a deliverance, but that deliverance which made a nation out of the slave rabble into which the descendants of the great patriarchs had degenerated in Egypt. They had been but seventy in number when they went into Egypt (Ex. 1:5), but when they were delivered they were a multitude. In a very real sense the Passover commemorated the birth of a nation and that nation the people of God. To mark the greatness of the occasion the calendar was changed. The month in which it occurred was henceforth to be the beginning of the year (Ex. 12:2).

Passover was one of the three times in the year when all male Israelites were to appear before the LORD (Ex. 23:14–17; Dt. 16:16; 'the Feast of Unleavened Bread' in such passages means, of course, the Passover and the seven days following). We cannot be sure of how regularly it was observed in early days, but there are references to its observance in the wilderness (Nu. 9:1–5), in the Promised Land (Jos. 5:10), under Solomon (2 Ch. 8:13; *cf.*

1 Ki. 9:25), on a great occasion under Hezekiah (2 Ch. 30:1–27) and another under Josiah (2 Ki. 23:21–23; 2 Ch. 35:1–19), and by the exiles who returned from Babylon (Ezr. 6:19–22). Clearly it was a most important festival, even though there were times when it was not observed as it should have been (2 Ch. 30:5).

Passover was an annual reminder to the Israelites of the greatest deliverance recorded in their sacred books. To some modern scholars it seems that the number of Hebrews who were in Egypt was very small and that those who escaped were no more than a tiny handful. But that was not the way it appeared to men of the first century as they read their Bibles. To them it was crystal clear that God had once intervened in history to give his people a wonderful deliverance from the hand of a powerful oppressor. God had compelled the strongest power in the world to let his people go. He had made Pharaoh set the people free when Pharaoh's fixed intention had been to keep them as slaves.

The later books of the Old Testament look back to the exodus and regard it as the greatest of all deliverances, the classic example of what God could do to set his people free. Literature like the Psalms contains many references to those exciting days and there is an illuminating passage in which Jeremiah, centuries after the exodus, speaks about this deliverance. Actually he is not engaging in historical reminiscence but trying to bring out the magnitude of the disaster that he foresaw was about to overtake the people. He makes his point by telling his hearers that their plight will be so serious that to get them out of it will require a deliverance greater than that which brought their ancestors out of Egypt!

'So then, the days are coming,' declares the LORD, 'when people will no longer say, "As surely as the LORD lives, who brought the Israelites up out of Egypt," but they will say, "As surely as the LORD lives, who brought the descendants of Israel up out of the land of the north and out of all the countries where he had banished them." Then they will live in their own land' (Je. 23:7–8).

Nothing could illustrate more strikingly the fact that for Israel the definitive deliverance was the series of events which made up the exodus and which were commemorated every year when the Passover was celebrated. That was the standard by which all other deliverances would be judged.

The Passover, then, was primarily the commemoration of a great deliverance. Some have so stressed this that they have denied that it should rightly be thought of as a sacrifice. They see 'sacrifice' as a term to be used of rites directed at removing sin or expressing homage to God or the like and they do not see anything of the sort in the Passover. But this is surely to go too far. The Passover is spoken of as 'the LORD's offering' (Nu. 9:7,13) and the verb 'to sacrifice' is used of it (Dt. 16:2,4,5,6). Indeed, on occasion it is called 'the Passover sacrifice' or 'the sacrifice from the Passover Feast' (Ex. 12:27; 34:25). The fact that initially it was a family observance in private houses without the mediation of a priest does not alter this, nor does the fact that in later times it was eaten in the homes of the people rather than in the courts of a temple or shrine.

There is no real reason for doubting that the Passover was seen as a genuine sacrifice, all the more so since in due course the slaughter of the lamb or kid took place at the temple with the priest handling the blood. It is likely, therefore, that there was some idea of forgiveness of sin associated with it. It seems that in time all sacrifice was held to be atoning at least in one aspect and this would be true of the Passover as of all the others. It may be significant, moreover, that when Ezekiel refers to the Passover he has the prince provide a sin offering every day throughout the seven days of the feast (Ezk. 45:21–23). Some draw attention to the importance of the use of blood in the original Passover and suggest accordingly that the idea of cleansing from sin was there from the first. This may be going too far, but it is not easy to deny that there was such an idea in later times.

Be that as it may, there is no denying that the fundamental idea in the Passover is that of deliverance. The day had its solemn side and spiritually minded people always bear in mind their unworthiness and their need of forgiveness and cleansing when they approach the Lord. We must not overlook this. But the main thought in the annual observance was certainly deliverance. The Passover reminded worshippers that God is mighty, that he had once intervened to deliver his people from a strong enemy (and could do so again if need be), and that from that deliverance there had emerged the nation that was in a special sense the people of God.

THE PASSOVER IN RABBINIC LITERATURE

The rabbinic writings give a good deal of attention to the Passover (for example, the Mishnah devotes a whole tractate to it). These enable us to build up a fairly complete picture of the way the feast was observed in the New Testament period. It is clear that it was a great occasion. Josephus says that in the year AD 66 there were 255,600 animals sacrificed at this feast and that 2,700,000 worshippers participated in it.[1] All agree these figures are greatly exaggerated, but even when we allow for this it is plain that the feast was very popular and that large numbers went up to Jerusalem to celebrate it. Jews came from all over the known world for it, so Jerusalem was invariably crowded at this time of the year.

The ancient rites were scrupulously observed. A distinction, however, was made between that first Passover in Egypt and subsequent commemorations, and this led to a few differences. For example, the victim was no longer selected on the tenth day of the month, nor was blood put on the door-posts and lintel (Pesahim 9:5). The first Passover was eaten in haste as people made ready to move smartly as soon as permission was given, but in later times people reclined at ease and ate in leisure as befitted free men. A slave eats standing, but even the meanest in Israel was forbidden to eat the Passover 'unless he sits down to table' (Pesahim 10:1). Such contrasts underlined the blessings that flowed from God's action on behalf of his people. God had made them free.

The festal character of the day was marked with some unusual activities. Thus Passover was one of the few occasions in the year when the flute was played before the altar (Arakhin 2:3). It was the one occasion in the year when the Holy Place was whitened and one of only two when the altar was whitened (Tabernacles was the other; Middoth 3:4).

Preparation for the Passover started well in advance. Bridges and roads were repaired a month before so that pilgrims could make the journey to Jerusalem unhindered. Jerusalem was the only place where the sacrifice could be eaten (Zebahim 5:8; Kelim 1:8). Graves were whitewashed to guard against people contracting defilement unwittingly. Stringent tests were applied to determine uncleanness where there was any doubt (Oholoth

---

[1] Josephus, *The Jewish War*, Book vi, 424–425; in Book ii, 280 he puts the number at 3,000,000.

18:4). This was a most important festival and no uncleanness could be tolerated on such an occasion.

A fascinating example of the lengths to which rabbinic precautions could go concerns a man who had a boil and wanted treatment for it at this time. If a physician cut it off, then the moment it was severed from the body it became dead tissue. Contact with it would render anyone unclean and physician or patient or both were almost certain to be disqualified from keeping the feast. So the procedure was that the physician cut enough to leave the boil hanging by a thread. It was still part of the man's body and thus living and therefore not defiling. The patient then stuck it on a thorn and pulled away from it smartly, thus severing it from his body. In this way neither of them touched the defiling tissue and both were able to keep the feast (Kerithoth 3:8)!

The citizens of Jerusalem were under an obligation to make their homes available to pilgrims and that without charge. However, it was good manners for a man to leave behind for his host his empty wine pitcher and the skin of the animal he had sacrificed (Talmud, Yoma 12a; Megillah 26a). No matter how many people came up to Jerusalem there was always room for them, this being accounted one of the ten wonders of the temple period (Aboth 5:5).

PREPARING FOR THE MEAL

On the evening of 14th Nisan (the day began at sunset, so this was the beginning of that day) the head of each household made a solemn search for yeast, in silence and by candlelight. All yeast found was promptly put away by burning it or by crumbling and scattering it to the wind or by throwing it into the sea (Pesahim 2:1). It was still legal to put yeast away on the following morning, the exact time for its complete destruction being indicated by the removal of the second of two defiled cakes which were placed on the temple porch (Pesahim 1:5).

The evening sacrifice in the temple was put forward an hour to make time for the offering of the large number of Passover victims. The temple court was filled with worshippers and their victims and the gates closed. After this group had offered they went out, the process was repeated for a second group and repeated yet again for a third group. The Levites sang the Hallel (Psalms 113–118) for each group, but they did not finish it with the third group because the number was smaller. The actual slaughtering of the kid or the lamb was done in each case by the representative of the company for whom the animal was offered and for this purpose he might even be a slave (Pesahim 8:2). The blood was caught in a basin and passed down a line of priests with the last one throwing it in one jet at the altar. Prescribed parts were burnt on the altar. Each animal must be offered for a specific company which might include women, slaves or minors but must not be composed exclusively of such (Pesahim 8:7).

In modern times it is widely thought that the victim was a lamb and 'the paschal lamb' or 'the Passover lamb' has become an accepted phrase. This is misleading because, of course, a kid was quite acceptable (Pesahim 8:2; Menahoth 7:6). The term used in the original institution might mean either a lamb or a kid (see footnote in NIV on Ex. 12:3). There is the record of a solemn discussion as to whether sheep were superior to goats and the conclusion is reached that the two are equal (Kerithoth 6:9). It is curious (and inaccurate) that references to 'the Passover lamb' persist.

When the temple ritual was concluded the worshipper took his slain animal away to be roasted, but he must not take it outside Jerusalem (Makkoth 3:3). It was roasted whole, a spit of pomegranate wood being inserted at the mouth and passing through to the vent. Care was taken both in the roasting and subsequently in the eating that no bone be broken.

THE FEAST

At the meal the animal was, of course, the principal dish and it had to be consumed in its entirety. Each member of the company was required to eat at the very least a piece the size of an olive. If any part of the animal was not eaten (and this included bones, sinews and the like) it was to be burnt next day. Other necessary constituents of the meal were bitter herbs and bread made without yeast. An interesting provision is that there should be four cups of red wine for each member of the company, even if they had to be provided from the paupers' fund (Pesahim 10:1). This does not mean that the meal was a drunken revel. The Rabbis detested drunkenness and they required the wine to be heavily diluted, the normal proportions being three parts of water to one of wine. An incidental reference to a kettle in the context of mixing the four cups seems to show that warm water was used.

Justification for the four cups was found in the four expressions used to describe the deliverance from Egypt (Ex. 6:6–7). As an aid to the enjoyment of the meal it was provided that all should fast from the time of the evening sacrifice.

The meal began with the appropriate blessings (*i.e.* thanksgivings), that of the festival and that of the wine, after which the first cup of wine was drunk. Then the herbs, the bread and the roasted animal were brought before the head of the company. It seems that the food was not eaten straight away. Instead a second cup of wine was poured out and then the son of the house asked his father why there were such unusual happenings that night. This was the father's cue to explain the significance of it all and it was required of him that he include the whole section beginning at Deuteronomy 26:5 (Pesahim 10:4). Rabban Gamaliel laid it down that three things must be included in this explanation if the man was to fulfil his obligation:

> Passover, unleavened bread, and bitter herbs: 'Passover' – because God passed over the houses of our fathers in Egypt; 'unleavened bread' – because our fathers were redeemed from Egypt; 'bitter herbs' – because the Egyptians embittered the lives of our fathers in Egypt (Pesahim 10:5).

This part of the evening concluded with the singing of the Hallel (Psalms 113–118) as far as the end of Psalm 113 according to the house of Shammai or as far as the end of Psalm 114 as the house of Hillel would have it. This was followed by a thanksgiving for redemption.

The second cup of wine was drunk. Hands were washed and one of the two unleavened cakes was broken followed by the giving of thanks. Pieces of the broken bread with bitter herbs between them were dipped in haroseth (a compound of dates, raisins, *etc.* with vinegar) and handed to the members of the company. This brings us to the main part of the meal: the lamb or kid was eaten.

Now came the third cup of wine and over it the president said the blessing for the meal. This appears to be 'the cup of blessing' to which Paul refers (1 Cor. 10:16) and the name makes it likely that it was at this point in the meal that Jesus instituted the Holy Communion. Now came the fourth cup and the singing of the rest of the Hallel. The whole ends with two short prayers called 'the Benediction over song' (Pesahim 10:7).

It is provided that there must not be an *epikoman*, but unfortunately nobody now knows what the word meant. It derives from two Greek words with a meaning like 'after meal'. This has been understood to signify that there must be no dessert. Alternatively, it may mean that there must be no revelry at the close of the meal (which could reduce the solemn commemoration into little more than an ordinary convivial gathering). It must all be over by midnight, a conclusion reached from the words of Scripture, 'That same night they are to eat the meat' (Ex. 12:8). Actually the passage goes on to provide only that it must not be left until morning (verse 10), but 'the sages' prescribed midnight for duties that must be performed before day 'to keep a man far from transgression' (Berakoth 1:1).

THE SIGNIFICANCE OF PASSOVER

The Rabbis tell us a good deal about the proper way to keep the Passover and they dwell on the joyfulness of the whole festival. But they are not inclined to go deeply into the meaning of what was done. There are, however, some indications which help us understand the meaning of it all as they saw it.

In part the Passover was seen as bringing about forgiveness of sins. This was far from being the most prominent feature of the observance, but it seems that the Passover, in common with all the sacrifices, had this as part of its aim. Thus we read, 'God said to Israel: "I am now occupied in judging souls, and I will tell you how I will have pity on you, through the blood of the Passover and the blood of circumcision, and I will forgive you"' (Exodus Rabbah xv.12). In line with this Josephus tells us that the Israelites 'in readiness to start, sacrificed, purified the houses with the blood...'.[2] It seems that the use of blood always gave rise to thoughts of expiation of sin, so it is not surprising that the blood shed at Passover should share in this aspect of sacrifice.

But the note of deliverance is much more prominent. There are many references to the Passover as redeeming or delivering Israel from Egypt. Thus 'On account of two kinds of blood were Israel redeemed from Egypt – the blood of the Passover and the blood of circumcision' (Exodus Rabbah xvii.3). The paschal victim is here seen as a ransom; it was the payment of a price that set the

[2] Josephus, *Jewish Antiquities*, Book ii, 312.

people free. This produced a mood of exultation:

> Therefore are we bound to give thanks, to praise, to glorify, to
> honour, to exalt, to extol, and to bless him who wrought all
> these wonders for our fathers and for us. He brought us out
> from bondage to freedom, from sorrow to gladness, and from
> mourning to a Festival-day, and from darkness to great light,
> and from servitude to redemption; so let us say before him the
> *Hallelujah* (Pesahim 10:5).

Such a note of joy is common and it is probably true to say that it
is the most frequent note struck in rabbinic references to the
Passover. This festival commemorated the greatest deliverance
in the nation's history and accordingly the emphasis was on the
fact that everyone should rejoice before the Lord. But we should
not overlook those other aspects of forgiveness and redemption.

Passover was a time when the idea of community was very
prominent. Jews gathered from all the world to keep the feast, a
fact which was significant in itself. Passover was not a purely
individual affair to be observed according to individual taste.
While the most important part of the celebration took place in
homes with small companies of people, the occasion was corporate, not individual. The Mishnah forbids the slaughtering of
the sacrifice for one person (Pesahim 8:7). There is, it is true, an
alternative opinion that permits it, but according to the Talmud
this is allowable only if the man can eat it all (Pesahim 91a). As a
lamb or a kid is in question this effectively prohibits it. Josephus,
too, says that feasting alone is not permitted.[3] Passover was a
time for the collective joy of the nation, not the private happiness
of individuals.

At the first Passover, that in Egypt, the company was a family
or a group of families, but in later times a family grouping was
not regarded as necessary. But there must be a company, and
often it is held that ten persons was the minimum. Josephus, for
example, says this,[4] but there are references to companies of five
(*e.g.* Mishnah, Pesahim 9:10), though such small groups were
probably exceptional. Ten was a more acceptable figure. It is
sometimes said that the maximum number was twenty, but the
Mishnah can speak of a company of a hundred (Pesahim 8:7).

---

[3] Josephus, *The Jewish War*, Book vi, 423.
[4] *Ibid.*

However, as the feast took place for the most part in private houses, twenty would have been a much more usual figure. It is interesting that even when the people no longer met in families the groups remained small. Probably the circumstances of the original Passover were better kept in mind with small numbers.

The gathering at the temple when the sacrifice was offered gave the necessary emphasis to national unity. This was important, for, as we have seen, the Passover marked the birth of the nation. This comes out in passages like that in a Jewish exposition of the book of Numbers, called Sifre Numbers, which tells us that the people were redeemed in order that they might belong to God (on Nu. 15:37–41). When God gave them commandments in the wilderness, the writer says, the Israelites complained. But God replied that they were his slaves: 'For this reason have I redeemed you, that I might give decrees and you should keep them.' Here the thought is plainly expressed that Israel was not redeemed for the people's own personal convenience but in order that they might be the servants of God. The redemption from Egypt was the redemption of a community which was to be in a unique sense bound to God as the people of God.

Active participation in the observance was important. On many occasions we read of the requirement that everyone must eat at least an olive's bulk of the sacrifice. Participation must also be an intelligent participation, as is shown by the explanation the father gives his son early in the celebration: 'according to the understanding of the son his father instructs him' (Pesahim 10:4). There is also something of an identification with the original generation, for 'In every generation a man must so regard himself as if he came forth himself out of Egypt', a requirement backed up with a reference to Exodus 13:8 (Pesahim 10:5; though we should notice that the words are absent from some manuscripts).

Passover was certainly a time when the Jews looked back. They looked back to the deliverance from Egypt and in due time the idea appeared that many of the great events recorded in the Old Testament took place at Passover time. Thus it is not surprising that the celebration came to take on a Messianic aspect. Jews looked forward to the time when God would send his Messiah and what more natural than that this should be especially looked for at Passover? The idea that Elijah would come at Passover certainly appeared in due course, as also the view that the Messiah would come at this feast. This view is attested in the

Jewish exposition called Exodus Rabbah (section xviii. 12) and the writer is so sure of it that he says that if anyone appears at a time other than Passover and claims that he is the Messiah, he is to be rejected. The time of his appearance is a sufficient refutation of his claim. How much of this goes back to New Testament times is uncertain. But none of it is out of harmony with the ideas of the Jews of that period and in particular the very nature of the feast was such as almost to compel Messianic ideas among those who looked for the Redeemer.

THE PASSOVER IN THE NEW TESTAMENT

There are several references to the Passover in the New Testament which are not relevant to our inquiry. They simply tell us that such and such a happening took place near Passover or the like. They do not relate to Christ's atoning work nor to the way Christians should live. But there are certainly some that are relevant.

We begin with the fact that there are links between the Passover and the Holy Communion, that meal which centres on Christ's death. The Last Supper is called a Passover meal in all three Synoptic Gospels (Mt. 26:17–18; Mk. 14:14–16; Lk. 22:11–15). There is a problem in that John's Gospel places the death of Jesus at the time the Passover victims were being slain. No explanation has won universal acceptance, but the most probable solution is that there were different calendars in use at the time. Jesus and his disciples apparently followed an unofficial calendar and held their Passover meal on the day before that appointed in the official calendar. That would explain why there is no mention of a lamb or kid, the central feature in the Passover meal, in the account of the Last Supper. The temple authorities would not have allowed the offering of a Passover sacrifice on what they held to be the wrong day. John's account goes along with the official calendar. Both link Jesus' death in one way or another with the Passover.

This is reinforced by the fact that in all the Gospels it is clear that Jesus chose the time of his death. John tells us that Jesus said, 'I lay down my life – only to take it up again. No-one takes it from me, but I lay it down of my own accord' (Jn. 10:17–18). Jesus need not have gone to Jerusalem at the time. He need not have allowed Judas's treachery to reach its consummation; he could have disclosed it to the other disciples and they could have prevented Judas from going to the high priests just then. He need not have gone to the Garden of Gethsemane at the time he did. It is plain that he chose to die at just this time, with the Passover in everyone's mind. He does not give the reason for this. But the principal themes of Passover were very well known.

On the last night of his life Jesus inaugurated a service, the Holy Communion, which we may profitably compare with the Passover. There are of course significant differences. The central feature of the Passover, the sacrificed animal, is quite absent from the Christian service. Three of the four cups of wine are likewise missing and the one that is there is shared. The Passover was no ordinary occasion, but a great annual festival when worshippers gathered from all over the world to the one central place. Holy Communion from the first seems to have been the normal weekly service of believers in their local assemblies; it was not a gathering of the world-wide church. Again, the Passover commemorated a past deliverance. The Lord's Supper certainly does this, but it does more. The very title 'Holy Communion' points to a present activity (*cf.* the Book of Common Prayer, 'feed on him in thy heart by faith with thanksgiving'), while the words 'you proclaim the Lord's death until he comes' (1 Cor. 11:26) are forward-looking.

But there are important resemblances. In both there is the solemn liturgical use of bread and wine. In both there is the solemn commemoration of the past. In both there is a living hope for the future. We may fairly say that the institution of the Holy Communion, in the way in which it was done at Passover time, directs our attention to certain important aspects of our Lord's saving work. It has us looking back to God's great act at Calvary and it has us looking forward to the time when Christ will come again to bring his saving work to its consummation. And it brings out something of the communal nature of the Christian way, for it is a service which looks for the participation of the whole local group of believers.

Some have seen a reference to the Passover in the words of John the Baptist, 'Look, the Lamb of God!' (Jn. 1:29, 36), but this seems unlikely. Nor should we put much emphasis on the expression, 'the Jewish Passover Feast' (Jn. 6:4), as do some who suggest that the words imply a contrast with a 'Christian Passover Feast'. But this is surely to read too much into the expression. Are we to think that 'the Jewish Feast of Tabernacles' (Jn. 7:2) implies a Christian Feast of Tabernacles? And where does the process stop? The early Christians were not slavish imitators of the Jews and they did not pattern their observances on the Jewish liturgical year. Such allusions appear to exist only in the minds of those who put them forward. There is no real evidence.

More significant is the fact that John puts the death of Jesus at the time the Passover victims were being slain in the temple. This is no more than approximate, but we must bear in mind that people did not normally estimate time in those days as precisely as we do. John tells us that Pilate sat on the judgment seat to sentence Jesus at 'about the sixth hour' (Jn. 19:14). The evening sacrifice was offered in the temple on the day the Passover victims were killed at half after the eighth hour or, if it was the eve of a Sabbath, at half after the seventh hour. Allowing for the time it would take to get Jesus from the Praetorium to Golgotha it seems that John is saying that Jesus was hanging on the cross at the time the sacrificial victims were being killed in the temple.

This is supported by the fact that John sees a fulfilment of Scripture in that no bone of Jesus was broken. This is really quite surprising. In the first place the legs of the two who were crucified with Jesus were broken and if that happened to them, it would have been expected that it would happen to him. Then in the second place, his side was pierced with a spear, a most unusual procedure (Jn. 19:31–36). To have Jesus' bones unbroken through both happenings is quite unexpected. John does not say which Old Testament passage or passages he had in mind, but most agree that he was thinking of the requirement that no bone of the Passover sacrifice was to be broken (Ex. 12:46; Nu. 9:12; some think of Ps. 34:20, but this seems much less suitable). In as theological a writer as John it is difficult to escape the impression that the truth that is being conveyed is that in his death Jesus fulfilled all that the Jews looked for, but did not find, in the Passover. Jesus' death gave what the Passover pointed to but could not give. The Passover foreshadowed the great deliverance that God would bring about and for which his deliverance in ancient times formed the model. In Jesus, and specifically in his death, that great deliverance was accomplished.

Paul specifically identifies Christ's sacrifice with the Passover when he writes 'Christ, our Passover' (1 Cor. 5:7; NIV adds 'lamb', but this is not in the Greek and is misleading: there is no lamb imagery here). Paul has been rebuking the Corinthians for their failure to discipline erring members. Specifically they had not taken decisive action in the case of a church member who had been guilty of a repulsive kind of immorality (1 Cor. 5:1–2). Paul insists that immorality is not to be tolerated in a Christian community. 'Don't you know', he asks, 'that a little yeast works through the whole batch of dough?' He firmly instructs them, 'Get rid of the old yeast that you may be a new batch without yeast – as you really are' (verses 6–7).

This leads on to the thought that Christ, our Passover, has already been sacrificed. Paul is taking yeast as a symbol of evil. It will be recalled that in the Jewish Passover observance there was a ceremonial search for yeast to ensure that it was all destroyed well before the sacrifice was offered. Paul's point is that for Christians the Passover sacrifice is the sacrifice of Christ, a sacrifice which is already past. Believers should long since have abandoned evil. It is a vivid reminder that Christ's death to deliver us means among other things that we put all evil away with decision. The death of Christ for sinners means their death to sin: they have been crucified with Christ (Gal. 2:20), they are to reckon themselves as dead to sin (Rom. 6:11). The believer is forgiven, but not only this: he has victory over evil. The Passover with its emphasis on deliverance is an apt symbol for this aspect of atonement and the Christian way.

The original Passover delivered the Israelites from destruction and introduced them into a new life in which things Egyptian had no place. They were no longer slaves to the oppressor. They were free. So with the Christians. The death of Christ was the decisive intervention which delivered them from destruction and from sin and introduced them to a new way of life. And in that new way they were free from the slavery to sin that had hitherto characterized them, as it does all people.

It is possible that we should see another reference to the Passover in the description of Christ as 'a lamb without blemish or defect' (1 Pet. 1:19), following, as it does, a reference to redemption in the previous verse. But the Passover victim might as easily be a kid as a lamb and, further, lambs were offered in sacrifice other than that at Passover time. The connection cannot be said to have been established. The most we can say is that the Passover would fit the words. We cannot say with assurance that it is this that is in mind. In any case the passage scarcely adds to what we have seen elsewhere. It underlines the thought of deliverance by the blood of Jesus, a major thought in the use of Passover imagery.

From all this it is plain that the New Testament writers do not make the Passover their major category when they are interpreting the death of Jesus. There is no getting around Paul's reference in 1 Corinthians 5:7, but some maintain that all the other passages could be explained otherwise than as pointing to the Passover. Possibly. But it is more than doubtful whether they should be so explained and whether we can neglect the Passover when we try to understand the new and living way of the Christians. Apart from Paul's specific reference we should bear in mind at least these three things:

1. Jesus chose to die at Passover time.

2. The Synoptists place Jesus' death after he and the Twelve had eaten the Passover, but they link that Passover meal with the Holy Communion, an ongoing remembrance of Jesus' saving death.

3. John chose to write in such a way as to bring out the truth that Jesus' death took place at the time the Passover victims were being killed in the temple. This surely means that he saw the death of Jesus as the true Passover sacrifice.

At the time Jesus died attention in Jerusalem was concentrated on the Passover and it is more than difficult to contend that this had no significance for the Christians.

Passover may not be the leading New Testament category by which to interpret the atonement, but it is certainly one of the subordinate strands in New Testament thinking. What the Passover sacrifice signified for the Jews, that and more Christ's sacrifice has done for the Christians. It emphasizes the thought of deliverance, deliverance from a powerful enemy. Because Jesus died as a Passover sacrifice those who trust in him are no longer subject to the forces of evil. They have been delivered. They are free.

And Passover reminds us that we are members one of another. Passover was a corporate observance, a feast to be celebrated in the company of others. Both in the Old Testament and in contemporary Judaism the Passover was to be observed in companies. The observance stressed the truth that God's salvation is not a purely individual experience. The deliverance from Egypt marked the birth of a nation, the emergence of the people of God. The deliverance on the cross marked the emergence of the true Israel, the people of God in more than a merely national sense. Now the people of God are plainly seen as all those who have been delivered by Christ, from whatever nation they may come. They are no longer slaves to sin. They belong to God and to one another in the fellowship of the redeemed people of God, for 'Christ our passover is sacrificed for us' (1 Cor. 5:7, AV).

For further study

1. Outline the principal features of the original Passover observance. What do they tell us about God's deliverance of his people?
2. Among the Jews the Passover was not a private observance, but a community occasion. Are there similar community occasions in Christianity?
3. What do you see as the central meaning of the Passover
   (a) in its original observance;
   (b) for the Rabbis;
   (c) for the modern Christian?

5
Redemption

One of the notes that runs through the New Testament is that of freedom. It meant a good deal to those who first espoused the Christian way that it brought them liberation. In this it speaks to our generation, for we should like to be free. We are constantly reminded that there are limitations on our freedom. Our psychologists often give the impression that we are all trapped in an intricate web of complexes and inhibitions, so that freedom is an illusion. Others, more sociologically minded, see us as the slaves of our class, upbringing, physical constitution, and generally the circumstances of life. The structures of society are held to spell injustice and to limit our freedom. While all nations these days give lip-service to the importance of human rights, yet in a depressingly large number of states freedom is a fragile thing and apt to be terminated by the physical imprisonment of those who do not conform. Freedom is elusive. But it is a subject of continuing interest and importance.

Not least is this the case for Christians. Conventional Christianity tends to settle down into a rigidly defined way of life. Anyone who trangresses accepted taboos is apt to be looked on as no more than nominally Christian. Hard and fast patterns tend to be laid down. Even the radically minded are not immune. They tend to see their 'free' way as the only Christian way and they are highly critical of stuffy conservatives. It is easy for all of us to prate of our freedom while we settle into a restricted existence which is really a slavery of our own manufacture.

It is all the more interesting that first-century Christians, who knew what literal slavery was and some of whom were literally slaves, insisted that in Christ people are free. 'It is for freedom

that Christ has set us free,' Paul wrote (Gal. 5:1) and
church appears to have exulted in living out the impli␣
such words.

One of the ways the Christians spoke of freedom was ␣
concept of redemption. This is a concept we may easily misinter-
pret, partly at any rate because it has become such an important
religious term. Indeed, for us it is almost entirely a religious
word, but for the people of the first century it was not so. We use
the term now and then in non-religious contexts, as when we
speak of the redemption of a bond or the like. But this is comparatively rare. Almost always when we hear the word 'redemption' we understand the speaker to be expounding some religious
theme. 'Redeemer' means 'Jesus Christ'. The whole word-family
is at home in a religious setting.

But for the New Testament writers the important thing was
that the whole word-group was not religious. It was secular. A
man did not have to be a devotee of any particular religion to pick
up what was meant when he heard someone using the terminology. Redemption was part of the language of ordinary people
in their ordinary everyday life. Christians could use it knowing
that it was a vivid picture-word, a word which everyone could
understand and which, properly used, conveyed forcefully one
important aspect of Christian teaching. It was the fact that it was
not a religious word which gave it its usefulness and its wide
intelligibility.

A further point is that we tend to use the word in a more
general sense than did the people of antiquity. In a good deal of
modern writing redemption means much the same as 'deliverance'. It does not matter greatly how the deliverance is effected.
But in antiquity the word was specific. It meant not simply
deliverance, but deliverance in a particular way. We shall see
this if we look at the way the term was used.

THE GREEK BACKGROUND

The term as used in the all-pervasive Greek culture of antiquity
had its origin in the practices of warfare. When people went to
war in ancient times they lacked the refinements of our modern
civilization. They had no atom bombs, no poison gas, no germ
warfare. But in their own humble way they did what they could
to make life uncomfortable for one another. One of their happy
little customs was that, when battle was over, the victors some-

107

times rode round the battlefield rounding up as many of the vanquished as they could. Then they took them off as slaves. It meant a tidy profit and an increase in the spoils of war, though I guess the new slaves did not like it much.

Anyway, when they got them back home and looked them over, they sometimes found there were important people included in their haul. These were men of rank, men who counted for a good deal in their own country, but whose upbringing and manner of life made them not particularly suitable for hard menial labour and the kind of work that was the common lot of slaves. But if they were not much good as slaves, they were valued in their own homeland.

Then the victors let it be known back in the land of the vanquished that they were ready to release such-and-such captives, always, of course, on receipt of a consideration. The home folk would pass round the helmet (or whatever other way they had of raising funds) and, when they had the required amount, send it over to the land of the victors and buy back their brothers. This is the process that the ancients called 'redemption'. They used the verb 'redeem' of it and anyone who carried it out was a 'redeemer'. The sum of money was called the 'ransom'.

You see the meaning? There were people whose rightful place was back there in the homeland, alongside their brothers. But by a cruel accident of war they had fallen into the power of a strong enemy. They could not break free. Left to themselves they would remain in captivity for the rest of their lives. If they were to be set free, money must be paid. For them to be restored to the place where they belonged they must be bought out of their captivity.

This buying of prisoners of war out of their captivity was the basic idea in redemption. But the redemption words came to be used of other forms of freeing people. They were sometimes used, for example, of setting slaves free. We usually think of slaves as slaves for life, and so, of course, most of them were. But it was possible for a slave to be set free. Sometimes his master would set him free, simply because he liked him and wanted to do him good. Or a well-wisher might buy him and let him go. But there was one process which was specially significant for our purpose. Scholars call it *sacral manumission*. It worked like this.

A slave who desperately wanted to be free could save the price of his freedom. It would be a long and difficult process, because by definition his labour belonged to his owner. But if he was determined he could save up the odd coins that came his way and steadily build up his little hoard until he had the sum that was needed.

Then he would go to the temple of some god and pay the money into the temple treasury. His owner would come along and go through the solemn rigmarole of selling him to the god, the money, of course, being the slave's own hard-earned savings. Usually there would be the inclusion of some words such as 'for freedom' in the document setting out the details, and this would make it quite clear that the slave was being set free and not being bought by the temple authorities as a menial drudge to do the lowly services required to keep the temple going. They would carve into the wall an account of proceedings. And if anyone at any time questioned the former slave's right to be regarded as a free man, he could take him along to the temple and point to the inscription that for all time set forth the fact that he was free. Quite a few such inscriptions survive which, of course, is what enables us to know what went on. Here is an example of such an inscription, dated 200–100 BC:

> Date. Apollo the Pythian bought from Sosibius of Amphissa, for freedom, a female slave, whose name is Nicaea, by race a Roman, with a price of three minae of silver and a half-mina. Former seller according to the law: Eumnastus of Amphissa. The price he hath received. The purchase, however, Nicaea hath committed unto Apollo, for freedom. Names of witnesses follow.[1]

Nicaea had saved the three and a half minae of silver that was her price, paid it into the treasury of the god Apollo, and had been 'sold' to the god 'for freedom'. Technically she now belonged to Apollo and there may have been a few pious obligations laid on her to remind her of the fact. But as far as men were concerned she was free. The price had been paid. She was no longer a slave.

Perhaps we should notice one more thing about the Greek background. While the New Testament writers are clearly making use of a well-known concept and for the most part using the common vocabulary, there is a slight difference in the word for 'redemption'. Where Greek speakers generally used the word *lytrōsis*, the New Testament writers tend to use the compound

[1] Cited from A. Deissmann, *Light from the Ancient East* (London, 1927), p.323.

apolytrōsis. It is not easy to see a difference in meaning between the two terms. In this general period there seems to have been a liking for compound words. People loved to use longer, more sonorous terms instead of simple, ordinary words. It may be the use of *apolytrōsis* by the New Testament writers is no more than another example of this tendency. But it may be more. They use *apolytrōsis* ten times altogether and all the other words from the root a total of nine times. Now I cannot claim to have read all the extant Greek literature by a long way, but with the resources open to me I have been able to find only ten examples of *apolytrōsis* in all the Greek writings. It is a rare word, so that the New Testament usage stands out. It seems to me that the New Testament writers chose to use an unusual and distinctive word because they wanted to bring out the truth that the redemption Christ brought about in dying for sinners was no ordinary redemption, not just one more redemption among others. It was sufficiently like other redemptions for the word to be very suitable, but sufficiently different for the distinctive word to be appropriate.

THE JEWISH BACKGROUND

But the early Christians were not Greeks (though they used the Greek language for their writings), but Jews. They had our Old Testament for their sacred Scripture and they read about redemption there. The presumption is that they used the term in much the same way as they found it in their Bible. At least we should study it there. They tended to use the translation of the Old Testament into Greek, the translation called the Septuagint. A comparison of this translation with the original Hebrew shows that the redemption words translate words from three different word-groups in the Hebrew. It will repay us to look at the way these word-groups were used.

The first of these Hebrew roots is *g'l*. This has to do with the family and it is a broad term to cover all sorts of things that help to further the life and fortunes of the family. It points to the things people do when they are acting in the interests of those to whom they are related. C. Ryder Smith thought it a pity that English does not have a verb like 'to kinsman', for that would give an excellent equivalent of the verb from this word-group. Since we do not have such a word we must make do with other terms. But whichever one we choose, the basic idea is that of promoting the interests, the welfare of the family.

Since a family does many things, this covers a wide range of activities. An interesting use is that in the book of Ruth, where it is used of the duty a kinsman had of looking after the family fortunes when a man died without children. It was regarded as a terrible thing that a man should have no-one to carry on his family name, and the Law provided that the brother of the dead man should marry the widow and that the first child of this marriage should be regarded as the child of the dead man. In this way his name would be carried on and would not die out from Israel (Dt. 25:5–6). If there was no brother the duty fell to the next of kin. Ruth was a childless widow who came under the provisions of this law. Boaz recognized her need and he was quite prepared to carry out the duty of a relation. But he pointed out that there was in fact a closer relative than he. That man had the first claim on the woman and it was not until he waived that claim that Boaz could go ahead and marry Ruth (Ru. 4:1–12).

But this was not the only duty that might fall to the lot of a kinsman. When a murder took place the whole family of the murdered man was injured. The next of kin was required to put this right. He was to take the initiative and execute the murderer, in which capacity he was 'the avenger of blood' (Nu. 35:19, *etc.*). The shed blood defiled the land and it was only when the 'avenger of blood' executed the murderer that the land was cleansed. Now in English 'avenger of blood' does not seem to have much to do with 'kinsman', nor does either expression have much in common with 'redeemer', but they are all translations of the one Hebrew word. It denotes a man who acted in any one of a number of ways to forward the welfare of the family.

The Old Testament mentions some of the other ways. A member of a family might become very poor and sell himself into slavery as a means of settling his debt (Lv. 25:47). But the purchaser did not have the right to hold such a slave for life. That slave was entitled to be redeemed (Lv. 25:48–49). The new owner could not refuse to sell him to his next of kin, as he could refuse to sell him to someone from the general public. There was a right of redemption. One of the man's brothers, or his uncle, or his cousin or anyone from the family could put up the money and the slave must be redeemed. Indeed, if he himself could raise the price he was entitled to redeem himself.

But, of course, if a man became poor and needed money, the

last thing he would sell was himself. He would sell his property first. If matters subsequently improved he had, generally speaking, the right to redeem. There were some limitations to be kept in mind. For example, a house in a walled city must be redeemed within a year (Lv. 25:29–30). This restriction did not apply to a house in a village, a settlement with no walls about it. For purposes of redemption such a situation was reckoned as being like a field and there was no time-limit (Lv. 25:31). But apart from a few such restrictions the impoverished person had the right to redeem. The former owner, or for that matter some other member of his family, could come up with the money and the property must be sold to him. It was important that each family retain its basic property from generation to generation and the process of redemption provided a means whereby times of temporary financial stringency would not have permanent consequences in the loss of land and homes.

There is an example of the exercise of this right in the time of Jeremiah. The word of the LORD came to Jeremiah and told him to buy his cousin's field in Anathoth, 'because as nearest relative it is your right and duty to buy it' (Je. 32:7; the Hebrew means more exactly 'the right of redemption is yours'). Jeremiah obeyed the direction and he goes on to tell us how he weighed out the money, signed the deed, sealed it and generally complied with the legal requirements (Je. 32:9–12).

For our purpose the interesting thing about all this is that, while *g'l* might denote all sorts of activities in the interests of the family, when the Old Testament was being translated into Greek the redemption words were used only when it was a question of paying money to secure release. This might be release of persons or of property. But the price-paying idea was fundamental. If no price was paid then the translators used some other word. We see this, for example, in their treatment of the 'avenger of blood' in Numbers 35. No money was paid; the kinsman simply executed the murderer. This is not redemption. It came within the wide-ranging scope of the Hebrew term, but it did not fit into the Greek category of redemption. That meant the paying of a price to secure release. As this was not involved the translators did not use any of the redemption words for the 'avenger of blood'.

THE LORD, THE REDEEMER

Sometimes God is said to redeem and this presents us with a

little problem, for it is unthinkable that God should make a payment to anyone in all his creation. Until now, every use of the redemption words we have looked at has conveyed the thought that a release is secured and that by the method of making a payment. But we also read that God said to the oppressed Israelites in Egypt: 'I will free you from being slaves to them and will redeem you with an outstretched arm and with mighty acts of judgment' (Ex. 6:6). Then when the deliverance in question has been accomplished we find Moses and the Israelites singing: 'In your unfailing love you will lead the people you have redeemed' (Ex. 15:13).

Clearly God made no payment to the Egyptians to secure the deliverance of his people. But we should not overlook the reference to the 'outstretched arm' (Ex. 6:6) or the words, 'You stretched out your right hand' (Ex. 15:12). By contrast, there are passages in which God is seen as so great and the people of the earth as so little that the greatest of men are as nothing before God. Thus we read, 'Surely the nations are like a drop in a bucket; they are regarded as dust on the scales; he weighs the islands as though they were fine dust' (Is. 40:15). One drop does not count for much in a bucket. The dust which a trader does not bother to wipe off his scales before weighing is very fine dust indeed. In this way the prophet brings out the greatness of God and the impossibility of any power on earth resisting his will.

But this kind of language is not used when the idea of redemption is in mind. Then it is rather the 'stretched out arm' that is emphasized. Thus the Psalmist can sing, 'You are the God who performs miracles; you display your power among the peoples. With your mighty arm you redeemed your people . . .' (Ps. 77:14–15). And among the proverbs we read, 'Do not move an ancient boundary stone or encroach on the fields of the fatherless, for their Defender [more exactly, 'Redeemer'] is strong' (Pr. 23:10–11). Jeremiah speaks of a time when 'The people of Israel are oppressed, and the people of Judah as well. All their captors hold them fast, refusing to let them go.' The situation is hopeless. The enemy is too strong. But then, 'Yet their Redeemer is strong; the LORD Almighty is his name. He will vigorously defend their cause so that he may bring rest to their land, but unrest to those who live in Babylon' (Je. 50:33–34).

In passages like these there is an emphasis on the power of God, a power that he puts forward on behalf of his people. Being as great as he is, he could rescue them with effortless ease. But because he loves his people he puts forth his power. He saves them at cost. It is this that gives the use of the redemption terminology its point. Bishop Westcott could write: 'It cannot be said that God paid to the Egyptian oppressor any price for the redemption of His people. On the other hand the idea of the exertion of a mighty force, the idea that the "redemption" costs much, is everywhere present. The force may be represented by Divine might, or love, or self-sacrifice, which become finally identical.'[2] The term may be used metaphorically but the metaphor retains its point. The idea of price-paying is not out of mind.

REDEMPTION AND GRACE

The second Hebrew word-group translated in the Septuagint by the redemption words is *pdh*. Here there is no element of family obligation as in *g'l*, or indeed of any obligation at all. Where this root is used people may redeem or not, at least in most cases. In other words there is an element of grace involved. The person or thing might be left in the state of captivity. But the other chooses to redeem.

We see something of its force in its application to the animals of the domestic herd. The principle is laid down in Exodus 13:12: 'you are to give over to the LORD the first offspring of every womb. All the first-born males of your livestock belong to the LORD.' That meant that the first-born offspring of all the domestic animals should be offered in sacrifice. But there were some animals which were not deemed suitable for use in sacrifice, the donkey for example. The first-born donkey according to this law belonged to God, not to the human owner. But it could not be offered on the altar. Such an animal must be redeemed or destroyed; the human owner must not benefit from it. 'Redeem with a lamb every first-born donkey,' ran the regulation, 'but if you do not redeem it, break its neck' (Ex. 13:13). Human sacrifice was also forbidden, but in this case there was no alternative to redemption. The passage goes on to give the firm instruction, 'Redeem every firstborn among your sons.'

This had an interesting application when the Israelites were delivered from the land of Egypt. In their captivity in that land there seems no doubt that such regulations, if they existed, could

[2] B. F. Westcott, *The Epistle to the Hebrews* (London, 1892), p.296.

not be carried out. And, of course, in the form in which we have them, the regulations were given only after the Israelites had been brought out of the land of their captivity. There were then a great number of Israelite first-born sons who had never been redeemed. What was to be done about them? 'The LORD said to Moses, "Count all the firstborn Israelite males who are a month old or more and make a list of their names. Take the Levites for me in place of all the firstborn of the Israelites, and the livestock of the Levites in place of all the firstborn of the livestock of the Israelites"' (Nu. 3:40–41). The Levites were to belong to the LORD. They were to do his service in the sanctuary and elsewhere and in this way they became the ransom price, the price that delivered the first-born throughout the nation. Actually the number of first-born came to 22,273 (Nu. 3:43) and the total of the Levites was only 22,000 (verse 39). To provide for the excess a price was paid in money, five shekels for each first-born over and above the number of Levites. This amount was paid over to Aaron and his sons (verses 46–48), presumably to be used in the service of God in some way.

It is explicitly provided that 'you must not redeem the first-born of an ox, a sheep or a goat; they are holy' (Nu. 18:17). They are animals required for sacrifice on the altar. The worshipper had no choice there. Nor had he with human offspring. As we have seen, the first-born of men must be redeemed (*cf.* also Nu. 18:15). The same applied to the first offspring of unclean animals. They could not be offered on the altar, but they did not belong to the human 'owner', so they must be redeemed (Nu. 18:15). This had its relevance to the situation in which a man might make a vow that he would offer an animal in sacrifice to the LORD. He could not in this way dedicate the first-born of the cow or the sheep, because these animals already belonged to the LORD (Lv. 27:26). But he could dedicate other sacrificial animals (Lv. 27:9). The practice of redemption gave him a way of making an offering out of one of the unclean animals. He could not offer it in sacrifice, but he could dedicate it to the LORD, then redeem it at its set value plus one fifth (Lv. 27:11–13). 'If he does not redeem it, it is to be sold at its set value' (Lv. 27:27). Presumably the money was then put into the temple treasury.

With this verb, as with *g'l*, passages occur in which God is said to redeem Israel. And again, as with *g'l*, there is often the thought of the exertion of a mighty power which God puts forth because he loves his people. Nehemiah could pray about Israel, 'They are your servants and your people whom you redeemed by your great strength and your mighty hand' (Ne. 1:10). Similarly the Psalmist refers to 'the day he redeemed them from the oppressor, the day he displayed his miraculous signs in Egypt, his wonders in the region of Zoan' (Ps. 78:42–43; he proceeds to dwell on some of those powerful signs). And there is that passage in David's prayer in which the king asks, 'And who is like your people Israel – the one nation on earth that God went out to redeem as a people for himself, and to make a name for himself, and to perform great and awesome wonders by driving out nations and their gods from before your people, whom you redeemed from Egypt?' (2 Sa. 7:23). As with the other word-group, it is plain from such passages that the basic idea of cost is present. God puts forth a mighty effort to save those he loves. His deliverance is at cost.

The other thing we must notice when this word-group is used is that there is no thought of obligation. I suppose that we cannot say that even the use of *g'l* means that God has no freedom. The Old Testament writers always think of God as omnipotent and free. He does what he wills. But *g'l* has the notion of family about it, and it might be expected that God, the mighty Father, the great Kinsman, would act for his own. Not so with *pdh*. Where this verb is used there is no suspicion of obligation of any sort. It brings out the other thought that God's deliverance is always a matter of grace. Sinners can never say, 'God *must* save me. He is obliged to do something for me.' There is no necessity laid upon God. He saves freely. He saves because he is a loving God. Where this word-group is used, grace and redemption go together.

RANSOM

The third word-group is that connected with the root *kpr*. This differs from the others in that in them the verb is the most prominent member of the word-group (though nouns do occur), whereas with this one we find the noun 'ransom' (*kōpher*) characteristically. It means the money that anyone pays to be delivered.

It is used, for example, in the case of a man who owned a dangerous bull. If the animal gored someone and the person died, the animal must be killed. But if the owner knew that the bull 'has had the habit of goring', and if he has been warned about this, he is responsible for seeing to it that the dangerous bull is kept locked up. Then if he is careless and lets the animal get out and it gores someone so that that person dies, the owner is in trouble: 'the bull must be stoned and the owner also must be put to death' (Ex. 21:28–29). The man knew that the animal was dangerous. He knew that he was responsible for keeping it penned up. He had not done this, and someone had died. That was his fault. He must pay the penalty.

But this might be thought a trifle hard. It is quite a different case from wilful murder. There is no malice aforethought. The man has been guilty of carelessness, criminal carelessness if you like, but he is not a murderer. So it is provided that, 'if payment [more literally, ransom] is demanded of him, he may redeem his life by paying whatever is demanded' (verse 30). He pays the ransom and he goes free. The death sentence no longer hangs over him.

The word is used also of what happens at the census: 'When you take a census of the Israelites to count them, each one must pay the LORD a ransom for his life at the time he is counted. Then no plague will come on them when you number them' (Ex. 30:12). Unless Yahweh's command was obeyed there would be plague among the people. The ransom is paid in the place of the life that would otherwise be forfeit.

In another place the term is used in a prayer that a man be saved from death: 'Spare him from going down to the pit; I have found a ransom for him' (Jb. 33:24). Or, as the proverb has it, 'A man's riches may ransom his life' (Pr. 13:8). On all such occasions it is clear that the term conveys the idea of payment for deliverance. Sometimes the word is used metaphorically, but the basic idea is clear. The *kōpher* is a sum of money paid for release.

Once the word is used of God's activity, when he says, 'I give Egypt for your ransom, Cush and Seba in your stead. Since you are precious and honoured in my sight, and because I love you, I will give men in exchange for you, and people in exchange for your life' (Is. 43:3–4). Clearly there is a metaphorical element here but equally clearly the term conveys the thought of price. God's people are delivered at cost.

Our study of the use of the redemption terminology in the Old Testament then leads us to the conclusion that it is concerned with release on payment of a price. It is not used of simple release. For that other terms were available and were in use. The idea of the payment of a price (the 'ransom') is basic to all the redemption words. Now and then there is a metaphorical use and, especially when the words are used of God's activity, the actual price paid cannot be stressed. But there is always the thought of deliverance at cost. Sometimes it is deliverance from slavery and sometimes from a sentence of death. But both inside and outside the Bible that is the usage. As far as I am able I have searched the literature of antiquity and my conclusion is that redemption, apart from some metaphorical uses which depend on the normal usage, always denotes deliverance from a state of captivity (the prisoner of war), or from slavery, or from a death sentence. And always it is deliverance in a particular way, by the payment of a price. The idea of the payment of a price is fundamental to redemption.

Now and then we see something of the original flavour of the word in the way we use the term in modern times. The usage of the pawnshop is an example. I must confess that I have no first-hand knowledge of the subject, but some of my friends who have been unfortunate tell me that the process goes something like this. You take along your treasured possession and 'uncle' decides what he will let you have for it. The possession is handed over and the cash goes in the reverse direction, together with a pawn-ticket.

Then a most interesting situation develops. The keeper of the pawnshop cannot dispose of what you have left with him. It is yours, not his, and he is required to keep it safely. Of course, if you do nothing about it, in time you forfeit your right to it and he may legitimately sell it. I am not talking about its ultimate fate, but about the intermediate period. During that time it is yours. He cannot dispose of it. But for all the good it is to you it might well be his. For you to have beneficial possession of what you own you must go along to the shop with your pawn-ticket, the money you borrowed and the interest on it, and buy back – redeem – your possession. It is yours. But to benefit from it you must buy it back.

We see something of the original meaning also in our descriptions of sporting practices. Perhaps there is a cricketer who is having a lean time. His bat will no longer do wonders and there is every chance that he will be dropped from the team. Then, just when everyone is beginning to think, 'He is past it; his day is done' he comes to light with a brilliant century and all the sports writers chorus, 'Jones redeemed himself with his magnificent display!' Notice the way they use our verb. They do not use it of a player who in his first test-match does well. He had no reputation to lose and thus had nothing to redeem. Nor do they use it of one at the height of his career who simply adds another to his long list of successes. His place is secure and he needs no redemption. No; they apply it to one who is in a bad way. His reputation is as good as gone. Then, so to speak, he buys it back with his unexpected success.

SLAVES OF SIN

How does all this help when all we want to do is to understand the New Testament? To answer that we must go back to the very beginning of the Bible. We read in Genesis 1 of God's creation of all that there is, mankind included. That means that we all belong to God. We are his by right of creation. He made us in his own image, made us for himself. And nothing we ever do can alter that. We may turn away from God, we may live our lives in selfish concern for our own interests, we may deny that God even exists. But we cannot alter the fact that because he made us we are his.

Then in Genesis 2 we read of life in the Garden of Eden. Our first parents lived there in fellowship with God, their Maker. But into that picture there came sin, and that meant a radical alteration of a lot of things. To get its basic significance I think it is easiest to turn to John 8. There we read of Jesus having a discussion with some Jews. 'If you hold to my teaching,' he said, 'you are really my disciples. Then you will know the truth, and the truth will set you free' (Jn. 8:31–32). That last word seems to have riled them. You know how it is. Sometimes when you are in a discussion your opponent's use of a particular word rouses you and you find it difficult to attend to the main thrust of the argument for resentment at the word that has been thrown at you. I think it was something like that with these Jews. 'Free,' they might have been saying to themselves, 'free. Whatever is the man talking about?' Then with a superb disregard for the realities of life, as shown by the Roman soldiers in their very midst, they exclaimed, 'We are Abraham's descendants and have never been slaves of anyone. How can you say that we shall be set free?' Jesus' answer

119

was, 'I tell you the truth, everyone who sins is a slave to sin' (or as some manuscripts have it, 'everyone who sins is a slave'; Jn. 8:33–34).

And that is all too terribly true. Sin makes slaves of all of us. Take, for example, the person who has a temper (and which of us is guiltless?). He finds that his outbursts cause trouble and unhappiness to all sorts of people and more particularly to those he cares for most in life. So he repents. He decides that he will control himself and not say those harsh words. And if he is a strong person, perhaps he succeeds – for a time. But then one day along comes the provocation and before he knows what is happening he has burst out in those angry words and deeds which bring so much unhappiness to others and deep sorrow to him. Do you see what is happening? He is not free. As far as this thing is concerned he is a slave.

And in greater or less measure the same is true of every sin. Perhaps you can remember the first time you committed a particular sin. It was quite a struggle. You resisted the temptation, but in the end you lost. Next time there was not the same struggle. And later there was less still. In time you came to do the wrong thing almost easily and naturally. Do you see that the evil made a slave of you?

The trouble is that we are still in this situation. Sin is simply too strong for us. I know that from time to time we can chalk up a victory. Every one of us knows what it is to overcome a bad habit at some time or other. It is not easy, but it can be done. What cannot be done is to break all our bad habits, so that there is no evil at all that we do. And because we cannot do this it becomes clear what Jesus means. To sin is to become the slave of sin.

CHRIST THE REDEEMER

Now let us see what all this amounts to. God created man, created him to be his own. Man belongs to God. God set him in Eden to live in fellowship with him. But man sinned. Man became the slave of evil. He cannot break free. This is precisely the situation that the ancient world saw as calling for an act of redemption. We who belong to God have gotten into the power of a strong enemy from which we cannot break free. If I can say it reverently, God, if he wants us back, must pay the price.

And the great teaching of the New Testament is that God has paid the price. He has redeemed us. Christ has become our

Redeemer. Jesus told us himself that this was the reason for his coming to earth: 'For even the Son of Man did not come to be served, but to serve, and to give his life as a ransom for many' (Mk. 10:45). His word 'ransom' is the technical term used of the money paid to release a prisoner of war or a slave. To release the slaves of sin he paid the price. We were in captivity. We were in the strong grip of evil. We could not break free. But the price was paid and the result is that we go free. 'Sin shall not be your master' (Rom. 6:14).

Paul can use the redemption terminology in a slightly different way. 'Christ redeemed us from the curse of the law by becoming a curse for us,' he writes, 'for it is written: "Cursed is everyone who is hanged on a tree"' (Gal. 3:13). He is referring to the law which says of a man executed in this manner for a capital offence: 'anyone who is hung on a tree is under God's curse' (Dt. 21:23). Paul is saying that Christ's death on the cross meant that he bore the curse that would otherwise have rested on us. He suffered in our stead. He took what was coming to us. He bore the curse that sinners incurred and this is viewed as a paying of the price, an act of redemption.

The thought that Christ's death was a redemption, a setting of sinners free by payment of a price, is found elsewhere. Thus Paul writes to the Romans of 'the redemption that came by Christ Jesus' (Rom. 3:24) and in the next verse goes on to refer to his blood. In another place we read: 'In him we have redemption through his blood, the forgiveness of sins' (Eph. 1:7). The writer to the Hebrews speaks of Christ's work as 'eternal redemption' (Heb. 9:12), which brings out not only the element of cost, but also the permanent consequences of the payment of this price. In passing we might notice that, while this author does not often use the redemption terminology, the idea that Christ saves at cost runs through his epistle. He speaks of him in these terms: 'During the days of Jesus' life on earth, he offered up prayers and petitions with loud cries and tears to the one who could save him from death, and he was heard because of his reverent submission. Although he was a son, he learned obedience from what he suffered and, once made perfect, he became the source of eternal salvation...' (Heb. 5:7–9). This passage makes it clear that our redemption was not purchased cheaply, and the same is implied in other passages which speak of the sufferings Jesus endured (*e.g.* Heb. 2:10,18; 12:2–3; 13:12, *etc,*). The basic idea in redemption may be there even when the precise terminology is not used. It is certainly present in some passages where verbs like 'purchase' are used, as in Paul's speech at Miletus in which he exhorted the elders of the Ephesian church, 'Be shepherds of the church of God, which he bought with his own blood' (Acts 20:28).

There is a very important passage in which the writer to the Hebrews assures his readers that Christ 'has died as a ransom to set them free from the sins committed under the first covenant' (Heb. 9:15). The significant teaching here is that it was the cross of Christ that provided the way in which people who lived in the centuries before he came were redeemed from their sins. They had their sacrifices and the like, but these were not the means of putting away their sins: 'it is impossible for the blood of bulls and goats to take away sins' (Heb. 10:4). In the providence of God the one act of redemption provided the means of saving people in all ages. People do not have to live after Calvary in order to be saved. The death of Jesus is the sufficient ransom for all the redeemed, in whatever age they may live.

REDEMPTION AND THE FUTURE

Furthermore, if redemption reaches back into the past like this, it also reaches forward to the consummation of all things. Jesus spoke of the coming of the Son of man 'in a cloud with power and great glory' and went on to say, 'When these things begin to take place, stand up and lift up your heads, because your redemption is drawing near' (Lk. 21:27–28). There is a sense in which our redemption was perfectly and completely accomplished on the cross. The price was paid in full. Nothing more remains to be done. But here and now we see no more than the beginning of what redemption means. It is only when Christ comes again that we shall know it in all its fullness.

This is in mind also when Paul writes, 'we ourselves, who have the firstfruits of the Spirit, groan inwardly as we wait eagerly for our adoption as sons, the redemption of our bodies' (Rom. 8:23). The New Testament insists that bodily values will not be lost in the new state of things when our Saviour returns to set up his kingdom. The Christian idea of life in the world to come is not that of the immortality of the soul (an idea that was held by certain pagan Greeks), but that of the resurrection of the body. Paul makes it clear in 1 Corinthians 15 that bodies like ours cannot go straight into God's kingdom. Those who are alive when Christ comes will be changed before they can enter the final state. But that does not mean that the body is disposed of. What values it has will be retained in some way and in the passage of which we are thinking Paul connects this with redemption. Redemption means more than that our sins are put away. It is not a negative concept. It means that when Christ comes we shall take our changed bodies into the kingdom. Redemption looks forward to the life of the world to come and nothing appropriate to that life is beyond the scope of our redemption. Or to put the same thing in another way, redemption is so great and vast that its full potential cannot be realized here and now. For that we must await the coming kingdom.

There is something of the same thought when we read, 'do not grieve the Holy Spirit of God, with whom you were sealed for the day of redemption' (Eph. 4:30). There is no reference here to the body, but clearly the words are forward-looking. Christians have received the wonderful gift of the Holy Spirit. Indeed, the Spirit has 'sealed' them. In antiquity many people could not read. There was accordingly no point in writing one's name on one's property. To cope with this situation people used seals. A man would adopt a certain device as his own, say a stag or a triangle. He would have a seal made which enabled him to stamp his chosen symbol into soft material like clay or wax, material which retained the impress when it hardened. It then showed whose the object was on which the seal had been affixed. Paul is saying that the presence of the Holy Spirit is the 'seal', the mark that shows God's ownership. Those who have this seal belong to God. But there is also the thought here that this is not the final state of affairs. Believers have the Spirit now, but on the day of redemption, the day when Christ comes back at the end of the age, they will enter into all that their redemption means. The presence of the Spirit now is wonderful, but it is no more than a foretaste. There are greater things to come.

Another of the passages which look forward is of great interest, all the more in that it is not easy to see its full meaning in most English translations. It occurs in Hebrews 11 where the writer is summing up his discussion of faith with some generalized references to classes of people who had exercised faith. 'Women received back their dead,' he writes, 'raised to life again. Others were tortured and refused to be released, so that they might gain a better resurrection' (Heb. 11:35). The words translated 'refused to be released' mean more exactly 'not having accepted the redemption'. The point is that these people were not offered simple release, but release on conditions. Most commentators agree that the sort of thing the author has in mind is a situation that could arise in times of persecution.

Thus we read in 2 Maccabees of the deaths of seven brothers in a persecution initiated by Antiochus Epiphanes, each death taking place after the man had refused life on condition of apostasy. It is possible that the writer to the Hebrews had specially in mind the account of the death of the youngest of the brothers. After six of the young men had been executed for remaining steadfast in their allegiance to God, the persecuting king tried hard at least to secure the seventh. He promised him riches and high position if he would apostatize. Then he called on the young man's mother to help persuade him. She agreed, but when she spoke to her son she urged him to stand firm. She ended her appeal to him with these words: 'Do not fear this butcher, but prove worthy of your brothers. Accept death, so that in God's mercy I may get you back again with your brothers' (2 Macc. 7:29). This is surely refusing release at a price with a view to a better resurrection. In the end both son and mother were killed, both standing firm in their allegiance to God.

If the writer to the Hebrews had this kind of thing in mind it is clear that his use of the word 'redemption' is very apt. He was not referring to unconditional release, but release at a cost which a religious man could only regard as a very heavy price indeed. The use of the expression in this passage in Hebrews lends no support to the view of those who see redemption as meaning no more than 'deliverance'. In the New Testament redemption is deliverance on payment of a price and when men's salvation is concerned that price is the death of the Son of God.

NOT A TRUISM

There is an important passage in which Christians are exhorted in these terms: 'Since you call on a Father who judges each man's work impartially, live your lives as strangers here in reverent fear. For you know that it was not with perishable things such as silver or gold that you were redeemed from the empty way of life handed down to you from your forefathers, but with the precious blood of Christ, a lamb without blemish or defect' (1 Pet. 1:17–19).

The expression 'reverent fear' seems curious. Surely we might expect 'live your lives in *joy*, for you were redeemed....' But no. The writer urges his readers to reverent fear on account of the way they were redeemed.

I think he may be drawing attention the fact that redemption is something miraculous. It is a blessing that we could never have expected. Our sin had brought us into a hopeless position and we had no right to think that we could ever be delivered from it. We might be helped in our understanding of the passage if we go back to the thoughts of a godly man who lived on the other side of the cross. In Psalm 49 we have the meditation of a saintly man of old as he reflected on the limited power that wealth gives to wealthy men. He is thinking mostly of the impotence of even the rich in the face of death and he writes, 'No man can redeem the life of another or give to God a ransom for him – the ransom for a life is costly, no payment is ever enough' (Ps. 49:7–8). That is the position before Christ came. Of course, the Psalmist had in mind basically life here and now, but the principle is of wider application. If even the richest of us cannot ransom anyone from physical death, how much less from that death that is the wages of sin?

It seems that Peter has something like this in mind. 'Your sin', he seems to be saying, 'is a very serious matter. It set you in opposition to God and handed you over to eternal condemnation. From that situation there was no escape. You were hopelessly, irrevocably lost. There is no ransom from such a situation. And then, incredibly, unbelievably, a ransom was found. It meant a heavy price, the price of the death of the wonderful Son of God. But that price was paid and you have been redeemed. Never take your redemption for granted. Never count it a common, ordinary thing. It is the most incredible thing that has ever happened. But it did happen. Accept it, then, with gratitude and with awe. Live your life in reverent fear.'

And that is the attitude that we too should have. There is nothing automatic or axiomatic about redemption. Sinners have no reason for expecting that they can ever be delivered from their sin and its eternal consequences. That Christ died for them is so wonderful that it is always to be received with awe and wonder. We, too, should pass our time in reverent fear, for our redemption is not a matter of silver or gold or the like, but of 'the precious blood of Christ'.

CHRIST'S FREE PEOPLE

'It is for freedom that Christ has set us free,' wrote Paul. 'Stand firm, then, and do not let yourselves be burdened again by a yoke of slavery' (Gal. 5:1). His 'for freedom' is the formula of the documents of manumission at which we were looking earlier. The slave was purchased by the god, not to be a temple drudge but 'for freedom'. So the Christian is bought by Christ, not in order that he may enter some new form of slavery but in order that he may be free. Many of the manumission documents go on to affirm that the person set free shall never be made a slave again, and some of them attach heavy penalties to any attempt at enslaving the freed person. Freedom is precious and must not be lost. In the same way the believer is to live in freedom. He is not to 'be burdened again by a yoke of slavery'.

It is one of the curious things in life that Christians have all too often neglected this. Purchased at such great cost, they have promptly looked for some new servitude. Even in the early church it was not long before some people began to speak of Christianity as 'the new law' and to subject themselves to a legalism every bit as trying as that of which the New Testament writers complained in Judaism. And this has continued in the history of the church. Again and again it is not liberty in Christ which has characterized believers, but strict conformity to some new rule they have made or found. This may involve a rigorous asceticism or the firm conviction that the way forward is by observance of some sacramental discipline or the like. At the other extreme it may be by conformity to a new licence, so that all who prefer an ordered way are held to be false to true Christianity. Mankind has a fiendish ingenuity in discovering ways of bringing itself into bondage. Paul's words are far from being out of date.

The Christian way is never a way of rigid conformity to a system. This does not mean that rules are never helpful. Most Christians find it very helpful to have some rules, for example about the way they pray and read the Bible day by day and about regular attendance at worship. Many adopt a 'rule of life' which points them to useful paths of Christian service. I am not objecting to any of this. I am simply saying that believers can never take any such rule as sacrosanct. They cannot subject themselves to regulations as though they were of the essence of the Christian life. They are no more than subordinate helps. Believers are redeemed 'for freedom' and it is in freedom that they must live.

CHRIST'S SLAVES

This we must understand in connection with other sayings which paradoxically regard believers as slaves. Thus Paul writes, 'Do you not know that your body is a temple of the Holy Spirit, who is in you, whom you have received from God? You are not your own; you were bought at a price. Therefore honour God with your body' (1 Cor. 6:19–20). There is a sense in which the Christian is free. He owes no allegiance to a system, to any device of men. There is another sense in which he is not free. He has been bought by Christ and belongs to him. The very name 'Christian' is a reminder that he is 'Christ's one'. He is to live his life in conformity with his new status. Paul can point out that the person who is a slave when called by Christ need not worry unduly about his status, for he is the Lord's freedman, while the person who is free when called must always bear in mind that he is the Lord's slave (1 Cor. 7:22). In this context Paul can go on to say, 'You were bought at a price; do not become slaves of men' (verse 23).

Perhaps we should connect this with the fact that, before they were redeemed, believers were the slaves of sin (Jn. 8:34). They often try to disguise the fact with systems and rules of their own, but the basic thing about them is their bondage to sin. When Christ redeems, however, sin is no longer dominant. This may be spoken of in terms of freedom or described as slavery to Christ. Either way of putting it reminds us that sin has been defeated in the believer's life. He belongs to Christ. He is free.

The last book of the Bible contains the words of a 'new song' addressed to Christ: 'You are worthy to take the scroll and to open the seals, because you were slain, and with your blood you purchased men for God from every tribe and language and people and nation. You have made them to be a kingdom and priests to serve our God, and they will reign on the earth' (Rev. 5:9–10). This brings out the greatness of the price. He who is the object of the worship of heaven 'was slain' and with his blood he bought people for God. But in buying them he did not simply transfer them from one slavery to another. While in a sense they are his slaves, in another they are free. This is brought out with the affirmation that they are 'a kingdom' and 'priests' and that

127

'they will reign'. They have a royal state and are thus as far from being menials as can be conceived. They are priests and therefore have no need of priestly mediation. The death that bought them is all that is needed. And they will reign. They are not in bondage but on the contrary in a place of rule. The purchase that set them free from sin brought them into a glorious inheritance.

Redemption is a picturesque way of looking at what Christ did on the cross. Vividly it brought before first-century men some important aspects of the salvation Christ died to bring. Specifically it emphasizes three truths.

1. People are by nature slaves to sin

This means more than that they occasionally do evil things. In the state of the modern world it cannot be denied that there is a good deal of evil in the way people live. But it may be held, and it is held by some humanists and others, that this evil is not an insuperable object in the way of human progress. Man can do good. There is that deep down within him to which appeal may be made and when he responds he can rise above his lesser self and do deeds of altruism. In that lies the future of the human race, they say.

When Christians speak of redemption they are emphatically rejecting this whole position (though they do not, of course, deny that people sometimes act altruistically). They are saying that the evil that people do is simply the outworking of the evil that is part of their nature. Jesus put it this way: 'What comes out of a man is what makes him "unclean." For from within, out of men's hearts, come evil thoughts, sexual immorality, theft, murder, adultery, greed, malice, deceit, lewdness, envy, slander, arrogance and folly. All these evils come from inside and make a man "unclean"' (Mk. 7:20–23). The evil we do is not accidental and occasional. It arises out of what we are. And being what we are, we can never break free. Our victories are always comparatively small and incomplete; our defeats are always with us and their effects may be calamitous. Redemption reminds us to face the facts of life realistically.

2. Christ paid the price of freedom

We see, then, that breaking the hold of evil is not easy. But with people firmly under the control of evil we have the kind of situation that the ancient world saw as calling for redemption. It demanded a high price. Obviously the price is always proportionate to the redemption required. To ransom a lord would require a higher price than to ransom a common soldier. And when it is a question of the whole race of mankind, the price is very high indeed. But the price was paid. Christ's death was the price that made it possible for all mankind to be set free.

Sometimes in the history of the church the question has been asked, 'To whom was the price paid?' The early church Fathers tended to answer, 'To Satan.' Some of them worked out quite a theory of the way redemption works. They held that because of our sin we were all destined for hell. Sinners belong to Satan. In that situation God, in effect, offered to do a deal with Satan. He would give his Son in exchange for sinners. Satan realized that he would be making a fine profit on this transaction and was happy to accept the offer. The death of Jesus on the cross represented the handing of the Son over to Satan. But when Satan got Jesus down into hell he found (in the modern elegant idiom) that he had bitten off more than he could chew. On the third day Christ rose triumphant and Satan was left lamenting, having lost both the sinners he previously had and him whom he had accepted in exchange for them.

It did not take a profound intellect to work it out that God must have foreseen this. The theory means that he deceived Satan. But, bless you, that did not worry the Fathers. Indeed some of them gloried in it. It simply showed that God is wiser than Satan as well as stronger than he. Some of them worked out an illustration of the process along the lines of a fishing expedition. The flesh of Christ was the bait, the deity the fish-hook. Satan gulped down the bait and like any poor fish was caught on the hook of deity and destroyed.

Such theories do no more than amuse us these days. We cannot take them seriously when we are trying to work out what God has done for us in Christ. But they remind us that in the New Testament there is never any hint of a recipient of the ransom. In other words we must understand redemption as a useful metaphor which enables us to see some aspects of Christ's great saving work with clarity but which is not an exact description of the whole process of salvation. We must not press it beyond what the New Testament tells us about it. To look for a recipient of the ransom is illegitimate. We have no reason for pressing every detail. We must use the metaphor in the way the New Testament writers did or we fall into error.

This does not mean that we should water down the meaning of redemption. It is necessary for us to see the main thrust of the metaphor. This way of looking at the cross brings out the magnitude of the price paid for our salvation. It shows us that the death of Christ was meaningful. It was more than the martyrdom of a good man who was not strong enough to resist the machinations of evil people. Rather it was the outworking of the love of God. It was God's costly way of overcoming evil. Looked at in this way Christ's death was the effective payment that removed our bondage to evil.

3. The redeemed are free

Christians agree that evil is strong and that they cannot break free from it by themselves. But the wonderful thing about the Christian way is that it is the way of freedom. The evil that is part of human nature has been defeated in Christ. Believers live in freedom. Since the price has been paid the bondage is ended. They are no longer to live in slavery.

The Bible teaching on redemption then is a continuing call to Christians to live in all that freedom means. But freedom is demanding and too often we settle for some form of bondage. This may arise from excess of zeal as we give ourselves over to following some rigorous rule for living the Christian life. Or it may be the consequence of lack of zeal as we acquiesce in the power of evil and make no real attempt to do anything other than go along with it. Either way we are denying the fundamental freedom of the people of God. Neither is the way for those who have been redeemed at the cost of Christ's death. 'For freedom did Christ free us.'

For further study

1. What may we learn about redemption from the way the Greeks used the term?
2. How does the Old Testament usage of the word help us see the meaning of redemption?
3. In what ways does the Bible bring out the truth that people are naturally slaves to sin? (In a good concordance, look up words like 'redeem', 'redemption', 'slave', 'sin'.)

4. How does the 'redemption' picture help us to understand the meaning of the cross?
5. How can you preserve the freedom that Christ won for you?

6
Reconciliation

Paul tells us that God 'reconciled us to himself through Christ and gave us the ministry of reconciliation: that God was reconciling the world to himself in Christ, not counting men's sin against them. And he has committed to us the message of reconciliation. We are therefore Christ's ambassadors, as though God were making his appeal through us – we implore you on Christ's behalf: Be reconciled to God' (2 Cor. 5:18–20). The concept of reconciliation is taken by some scholars to be the best way of understanding the atonement. If this line is taken, it must be because reconciliation is seen as the thrust of many New Testament passages rather than from the specific use of the concept. The term 'reconciliation' is found in no more than a handful of passages, all of them in Paul, though certainly these few are important. But we should bear in mind that reconciliation is implied in places where it is not mentioned in set terms.

Reconciliation is a term we use quite commonly and in much the same way as people used it in Bible days. It means 'restore to friendship', 'make up after a quarrel'.

It is not a word to describe good relations in general. It means good relations which follow when an enmity has been overcome. Imagine that I were visiting you in your home and while I was there your friend Mr Brown dropped in. If your Mr Brown and I got along well you would not say to your other friends next day, 'Last night Mr Brown and Dr Morris were reconciled at my home.' 'Reconciled' would be quite the wrong word. This is the first time that your Mr Brown and I have met. It is impossible for us to be 'reconciled'. Of course, if this was not in fact our first meeting, if we had known one another in the past and had had a

132

thundering great row and if you were able to bring us to be of one mind, then reconciliation would be exactly the right word. That is the way we use the term. It means bringing people into a state of friendship after they have been at loggerheads. It means turning people from being enemies into being friends. It means replacing enmity with friendship. It means ending a quarrel.

If we use the word strictly, mindful of the 're-' with which it begins, it implies three states: first friendship, then a quarrel, then friendship again. We do not always insist that there be these three states before we use the term; if there are people who have quarrelled on sight and have subsequently been brought to agreement we use the term 'reconcile' quite happily. But in strictness 'reconciliation' means more than 'conciliation'.

Let us see how the Bible writers use this concept. We begin, as we did with redemption, right at the beginning of the Bible. When God created our first parents he created them to be in fellowship with himself. He put them in the Garden of Eden and the picture of bliss which results shows us how things ought to be. God and man were in complete harmony with nothing to spoil the picture. Nothing until sin came.

ENMITY

Fellowship is a wonderful thing. It is one of the enriching experiences of life and we are all indebted to it at some time or other. It enlarges our horizons and brings us well-being. But fellowship is a fragile thing. It must be looked after carefully or we lose it. For example, if you and I are getting along well and then for no apparent reason I call you a nasty name and punch you on the nose, it is difficult to see how a state of fellowship can continue. Of course, if that were to happen you would react like a good Christian (I certainly hope you would) and say to yourself: 'Poor fellow. He probably knows no better. I guess they are always doing that kind of thing where he comes from!' But your forgiving spirit would not mean that there was a state of friendship. It would mean only that from your side there was no obstacle. But for fellowship to exist there must be a right attitude on both sides. Without that we may have a kind of armed truce, a refraining from open conflict. But fellowship is more than that. It means warmth and goodwill on both sides. A one-sided kindliness is not fellowship.

But when fellowship does exist it can be ended. And there is no surer way of ending it than by one person thwarting the purposes of the other. Let us imagine that you are sitting in the park one day at peace with the world. A man and his little boy come strolling past. The little chap (let us say he is no more than two or three years old) sees a beautiful water-lily out there in the middle of the pond and he wants to go and get it. Dad says, 'No.' That does not suit the boy at all. He insists. So does Dad. The boy gets angry. He stamps on the ground. He screams and generally puts on quite a performance. A decided, though we trust temporary, coolness develops between father and son.

What we see, naked and unashamed, in the case of the small boy, we see in one form or another throughout life. We all like our equivalent of the pretty water-lily and are incensed when we are not allowed to have it. Whenever anyone stops us from doing something we want to do, or from getting something we want to have, we are always tempted to be angry. And if we have set our heart on that thing our anger can be terrible to behold.

In the illustration I used we should say that the father was quite right. He could not allow the little boy to jump into the lily-pond. The boy was wrong. It was necessary that his will be opposed because his desire was not a good one. But it is just as true that we destroy fellowship and develop anger if it is a good desire that is thwarted. Thus a social reformer may come across a situation in which rich or influential people are making money out of other people's misery, perhaps landlords refusing to do the right thing by their tenants and condemning them to live in hovels while they themselves flourish. The reformer sets himself to alter this state of affairs and immediately he meets strong opposition. He gets angry. We would not think him a better man but a worse one if he did not. Indeed we often do not call his emotion anger at all, but righteous indignation. There can be strong and praiseworthy opposition to evil.

OBSTRUCTING GOD'S PURPOSES

God's purposes are always righteous. God's purpose is that people have rich and full lives. But sinful man, because he is sinful man, sets himself against those purposes. The result is the dreadful thing the Bible speaks of as 'the wrath of God'. God is angry when his righteous purposes are obstructed. We should be clear that sin always obstructs those purposes of God in some way.

First, sin obstructs God's purposes in the sinner. Sin always makes us less as people. If I tell a lie I become a liar – and God does not mean me to become a liar. If I steal something I become a thief – and God has better purposes for me than to become a thief. And so through all the range of evil. Every sin pulls me down and makes me less of a person. This is true of what we see as great sins, like murder, and what we see as smaller sins, like cheating or gossiping. Sin makes us proud and self-centred. Whatever the sin it cuts us down; it prevents us from being the best that we can be. We must not think that God does not mind this. He does. The Bible makes it clear that God 'expresses his wrath every day' (Ps. 7:11). For God it is important that we be the best that we can be, and when we make ourselves into lesser people we arouse his wrath and destroy all hope of fellowship with him.

Secondly, we bring about the same consequence when we sin against others, for our sin is harming them in some way and affecting God's purposes for them. I think of a very lazy man I once knew. Where I come from there is a proverb, 'Laziness is no good unless it is properly carried out.' Don't believe it. I have seen a thoroughly lazy man only once and it is not an attractive sight. This man lived in a very isolated place. It was seven miles away from the railway line and another ten miles along the line to the nearest town. He was not on a road that led to any place, so that people did not drop in in passing. Callers were few. The man lived on a farm and was supposed to be a farmer, but when I shook hands with him the first time I called I was intrigued to find that his hand was softer than mine. I subsequently found out that, though he called himself a farmer, he did practically no work on his farm. He had discovered that there were government subsidies, allowances and handouts of various kinds. There were relief agencies whose object was to help people in need. He had found out that by diligent application and the proper methods of approaching the various authorities he could get by practically without doing any work. In a way it was a remarkable feat.

But what made all this matter so much was the fact that the man had taken to himself a wife and they had a large family. These children were growing up in that isolated place where they rarely saw any visitor. They were all too strongly influenced by the example of their father. He was the man they saw more than anybody. In fact they rarely saw any other man at all. It was natural for them to think from their earliest days that the way their father lived was the normal and right way to live. Cleverness for them meant working out ways of sponging on the government or on other people – anything but work. It is the one time that I have seen little children growing up without ideals and it is not a pretty sight.

Now I cannot think that the God and Father of our Lord Jesus Christ looks on such a man with equanimity. I know that God often overrules evil and brings good out of unpromising situations. I acknowledge that it is possible for children to react against the evil they see in their parents, so that from such a home as the one to which I refer there may emerge hard-working citizens with clear aims and strong characters. But when I make full allowance for all such possibilities I cannot believe that our God does not mind those little children having their outlook warped, their lives influenced for evil. The sin of the father all too often has its results in the lives of the children. And God is angry.

Much of our sin has its effects on other people. This is obvious in sins against the person, robbery, violence and the like. But whether we see it or not it is there. 'No man is an island.' It is impossible for us to live to ourselves in such a way that the evil we do harms no-one but ourselves. Our lives affect other people for good or for evil. When we affect them for evil we are obstructing God's purposes in them and arousing God's wrath against ourselves. We are making ourselves into the enemies of God.

ENEMIES OF GOD

James tells us that 'friendship of the world is enmity towards God' (Jas. 4:4; NIV translates 'hatred towards God', but the Greek word is *echthra* which means 'enmity', 'hostility'). From the standpoint of the saved Paul looks back and says, 'For if, when we were God's enemies, we were reconciled to him through the death of his Son, how much more, having been reconciled, shall we be saved through his life!' (Rom. 5:10). So he writes to the Colossians, 'Once you were alienated from God and were enemies in your minds because of your evil behaviour. But now he has reconciled you...' (Col. 1:21–22).

It is thus plain that the New Testament speaks of God and sinners as enemies. Now an enemy is not simply someone who falls a little short of being a good and faithful friend. He belongs in the opposite camp. He is opposed to what one is doing.

Sinners are putting their effort into the opposite direction to that of God. We should be clear on this. The sin we do inevitably arouses the hostility of God.

Sometimes people emphasize the fact that when the language of reconciliation is used the New Testament writers always speak of *man* as being reconciled, never God. They argue accordingly that we should not think of any attitude of God as needing to be modified. God is love and he is always ready for men to return to him. The hostility arises in our own minds and the moment we get rid of it all is well.

There is truth here, for God is love and he is always ready to receive repentant sinners. But there is also error, for it is the demand of God that causes the hostility. In this connection it is not always taken into account that man has no conscious hostility to God. Sinful man is always ready to let bygones be bygones. He is not greatly concerned by those small sins he perceives in himself and he cannot imagine why God should be. He is quite ready to let the past remain in the past and simply be friends with God in the present. There is nothing from his side that demands that there be enmity.

Now if here on earth among men we find a situation in which Jones says, 'Smith is my enemy' while Smith says, 'No, no. I am not hostile. I am quite ready to let the past rest so that we can be friends', it is not easy to see how it can be contended that all the hostility comes from Smith. It is Jones, not Smith, who speaks of enmity. Clearly it is he who sees an obstacle to friendly relations. It is his attitude, not primarily that of Smith, that must be dealt with if there is to be reconciliation.

There is an example of this use of our terminology in the Old Testament. On one occasion David was serving with Achish of Gath and this service in the Philistine army was questioned: 'how could this fellow reconcile himself to his lord?' they asked (1 Sa. 29:4, RSV). David consistently denies hostility to Saul and his actions back up his words. It was Saul's hostility that must be removed, though 'reconcile himself' is used of David.

It is something like this with God and man. If man is not greatly concerned about the problem then we cannot say, 'All the hostility is on the manward side. All that needs to be done is for man to change.' Clearly it is God's demand that we live holy lives that is the root cause of the problem. As long as he is angry with the selfishness, the disregard of the needs of others and the general attitude of lovelessness that the Bible calls sin, the attitude of God is going to be an important factor, indeed *the* important factor. We cannot get a glimmering of an understanding of what the New Testament understands by Christ's atoning work unless we see that God is hostile to every evil thing and every evil person. 'One died for all,' Paul writes, 'and therefore all died' (2 Cor. 5:14). But why should all die? The incidental reference to the death of sinners shows us something of God's hostility to evil as well as something of the way he procured forgiveness of sin. If men are to be forgiven, something must be done about this hostility. There can be no fellowship between God and man as long as God is persisting in a demand to which men are indifferent. That is simply to perpetuate the enmity.

Reconciliation takes note of the realities of the situation brought about by sin. When Article Two of the Anglican Thirty-Nine Articles says that Christ 'truly suffered, was crucified, dead and buried, to reconcile his Father to us...', it is certainly using language that goes beyond that of the New Testament. But it is not giving expression to teaching that is foreign to that of the New Testament. It is taking seriously what the New Testament writers tell us about the hostility of God to all that is evil.

HOW DOES RECONCILIATION TAKE PLACE?

Quarrels and enmities are unfortunately part and parcel of life here and now. We are all familiar with them. But it is also part and parcel of life here and now that quarrels are not necessarily permanent. It is quite possible to become friends again after there has been a quarrel. It is worth looking into the process.

Let us suppose that you have had a quarrel with a friend. In the heat of the moment strong words were spoken and the friendship you have so valued has been strained. Perhaps when you cool down you say to yourself: 'I was a fool to quarrel with him. He is a wonderful person and a valued friend.' Then you think, 'I'd love to be friends again. I'd like to have things as they used to be.' You decide that you will try to repair the damage. You will take the initiative. Then what do you do? You take steps to deal with the root cause of the quarrel. If it was a matter of harsh words spoken you go along to your friend and say, 'I am very sorry about what I said. I apologize sincerely. I withdraw that statement entirely.' As far as you can you remove the cause of the enmity. You take it out of the way. If any action is required you perform that action. If it was a matter of a letter that had to be written you write it. If it was a document to be signed you sign it. If it was money that had to be paid you pay it. You give thought to what the root cause of the trouble was and take it out of the way. It is only when the root cause is identified and dealt with that there can be a genuine reconciliation. Without that it is possible to have no more than an uneasy, patched-up truce. But not peace, not a reconciliation. In passing it is worth noticing that in many of the modern world's trouble-spots this seems to be overlooked. People concentrate on the symptoms and do not get to grips with the deep-seated causes of the trouble. This can never lead to long-lasting peace.

REMOVING SIN

We have seen that the root cause of the enmity between God and man was the sin of man. It is always sin that arouses the wrath of God and that is the barrier in the way of good relations between God and man. If there is to be a reconciliation then that barrier must be done away. God did not adopt half-measures in dealing with the problem. He sent his Son to live among men and show us how we ought to live. He sent him to die on a cross and so put away our sin. Why his death should take away sin this way of looking at the cross does not say. Each of the great picture-words makes its own contribution to the whole story. None is the whole story. What reconciliation is saying is that the root cause has been dealt with; it is not saying how. But the cross means that sin has been taken away. There is no longer any barrier to fellowship between man and man's Creator.

We should perhaps take notice of the fact that the Greek equivalent of 'reconciliation' can be used in a way slightly different from that in which we use the English term. With us it signifies that the quarrel is over and that full harmonious relations have been re-established. But Paul can write to the Romans, 'we also rejoice in God through our Lord Jesus Christ, through whom we have now received reconciliation' (Rom. 5:11). This implies that reconciliation had in some sense been accomplished by what Christ did on the cross and only then was it offered to those who received it. Reconciliation was wrought on the cross before there was anything but evil in the hearts of sinners. It is on the basis of a reconciliation that can be spoken of as already accomplished that an offer can be made to men, who then 'receive' the reconciliation. This means that there is more to the process than man's response (though that response is important, as we shall see a little later). When Paul speaks of reconciliation as something we have received he is clearly referring to more than a change of heart on the part of sinners. In the same context he has referred to Christ as dying for us 'While we were still sinners' (Rom. 5:8). This is true whatever our reaction. It is a statement about what God in Christ has done for the salvation of sinners, not about any human reaction.

Some scholars overlook this and argue that because God is love nothing is required for our salvation other than that we turn from our sin. Nothing is needed from God's side. He is there, simply waiting for us to come to him. Reconciliation is a term that refers to nothing more than a change of attitude on the part of sinful man. One writer equates reconciliation with 'the flooding of human hearts with the love of God, the disappearance of hostility, the joyful acceptance of forgiveness'. Another tells us that in Romans 3:23–26 'as always, it is taken for granted that, if man repents, the "wrath" of God dies'. Yet another explains reconciliation in this way: 'Reconciliation to God may be defined as a recognition of God's gracious relation to us through blessedness in our use of the world, our dealings with our fellow-men and our loyalty to His Kingdom.' Obviously there is some truth in all these statements. If anyone fills his heart with the love of God, accepts forgiveness joyfully and repents of his sin, if he recognizes God's gracious relation to men and makes the appropriate response, nobody is going to quibble about his being reconciled to God.

But it is quite another thing to hold that this is what the New Testament writers have in mind when they refer to reconciliation. All three of the statements quoted find no place for what Christ did. They leave everything to human activity: it is man repenting, man recognizing God's gracious relation and the like.

But to leave Christ out of Christianity is to start a new religion. That is certainly not what the New Testament preachers preached. For them Christ's death on the cross was the central thing. That death dealt effectively with sin so that it no longer features as an obstacle. It is what Christ has done, not what man does in changing his attitudes, that brings about reconciliation. On the view of the scholars we have just noticed, reconciliation is little more than the clearing up of a misunderstanding. People did not realize that God was not hostile to them. They made the discovery that his love is all that matters and so came to understand that all they had to do was to change their own attitude. Nothing more was needed. But Christ has a greater part in the Christian way than merely to point out to men that they have some wrong ideas about God. He is at the very centre of Christianity and his death on the cross is the heart of it all. As Paul put it, 'we preach Christ crucified' (1 Cor. 1:23). The habitual message of Christian preachers, the essence of the gospel, is Christ's death.

MAKING PEACE

Sometimes this is put in terms of making peace. There is a notable discussion of this in Ephesians 2. Here the writer is concerned with two different divisions, that between God and men and that between Jew and Gentile. He tells us that the Gentiles were 'separate from Christ, excluded from citizenship in Israel and foreigners to the covenants of the promise, without hope and without God in the world' (Eph. 2:12). But because of what Christ has done, and specifically because of his death, all that is changed. Now 'in Christ Jesus you who once were far away have been brought near through the blood of Christ' (verse 13).

Then comes the notable statement, 'For he himself is our peace' (verse 14). So closely is Christ identified with the peace-making process that he can be identified with peace. We have no peace apart from him. He is our peace.

Peace is an important concept in the Bible, where it has a somewhat different content from that which we give it in contemporary use. We are apt to miss this because the classical education that has shaped so much of our understanding in English has given us a concept different from that in the Bible. We have simply taken over the idea of peace from the ancient Greeks. With them (and consequently with us) it is basically a negative term. It means the absence of war or strife or turmoil. If we do not happen to have a conflict on our hands at any given moment, then we are at peace.

But the Bible understanding of peace is much fuller than that. The New Testament writers took their idea of peace from the Greek translation of the Old Testament. There the Greek word *eirēnē* was the regular translation of the Hebrew *shālôm* and it picked up something of the meaning of that Hebrew term. Now *shālôm* is not a negative term at all. It has a positive meaning. It

141

denotes not the absence of war or strife or anything, but the presence of something. It means the presence of God's rich and full blessing. We may see this in the way the word was used as the normal greeting, *shālôm lᵉkha*, 'Peace to you'. When one Hebrew was walking down the street and said to another Hebrew *shālôm lᵉkha*, 'Peace to you', he did not mean, 'I hope you don't get into a fight.' He meant, 'I trust that God's rich blessing will rest on you in all its fullness'; 'I wish you prosperity in the fullest sense.'

There is considerable agreement that the basic idea in *shālôm* is completeness, wholeness, soundness, well-being. It points to the well-rounded life, the life that lacks nothing good. Now and then *shālôm* is used in the Old Testament in much the same way as we use 'peace', for the Hebrews regarded war as an evil and one ingredient in the blessing for which they looked was the absence of war. The Hebrews were unusual in the ancient world in that their great men for the most part were not warriors. David is the exception, but apart from him the great people of the Hebrews were men of peace, like Abraham, Moses and the prophets. The Hebrews did not glorify war but looked for the blessing of peace. The absence of war is no more than one ingredient in a well-rounded peace. But peace is more than that one ingredient. It was that wonderful thing that we speak of as 'the peace of God that passes all understanding'. The absence of war was included, but so were other things like material prosperity. And spiritual prosperity was a necessary ingredient in the well-rounded peace which the Hebrews sought.

When we read that Christ is our peace we are being told that completeness, wholeness, soundness in our lives depend on him. What he has done provides for our deep needs. We were alienated from God, but he has brought us near. He 'has destroyed the barrier, the dividing wall of hostility' (Eph. 2:14). There has been a good deal of discussion about the meaning of this 'barrier' or 'wall' and a final resolution is not easy. But it is worth noticing that a symbol of the bitterness between Jew and Gentile was the wall in the temple at Jerusalem that separated the court of the Gentiles from the court of the women. The court of the Gentiles was as far as any Gentile could go into the temple, and in the wall separating this from the next court notices were set up to make this plain. The inscription reads:

No foreigner may enter within the balustrade and enclosure around the Sanctuary. Whoever is caught will render himself liable to the death penalty which will inevitably follow.[1]

It would be too much to say that Paul is writing about this wall. But the wall and its inscription allow us to see something of the depth of the division between Jew and Gentile and that is certainly before us in Ephesians 2.

There is a problem in following the thought because, as we have seen, the passage has in mind two divisions, that between Jew and Gentile of which the inscription just noted is so vivid a symbol, and that between God and man which is before us constantly in the New Testament. Both are done away in Christ. His death meant preaching 'peace to you who were far away and peace to those who were near' (Eph. 2:17). Christ's death enabled both Jews and Gentiles to draw near to God and as they did so they drew near to each other. Reconciliation with God means also reconciliation with man, as Jesus himself taught. 'If you are offering your gift at the altar', he said, 'and there remember that your brother has something against you, leave the gift there in front of the altar. First go and be reconciled to your brother; then come and offer your gift' (Mt. 5:23–24). It is impossible to enter into the reconciliation that Christ died to accomplish and at the same time to nourish grudges against other people. The two reconciliations are closely connected. So it is not surprising that it is difficult to untangle them in Ephesians 2.

That peace has a very different content in the Bible from that which we normally give the term is clear from some words towards the end of Romans. The writer assured his readers that 'The God of peace will soon crush Satan under your feet' (Rom. 16:20). God is characterized as 'the God of peace' by the very fact that he performs a warlike action! This is strange language to us, but the overthrow of Satan was a necessary ingredient in peace as the men of the New Testament understood it. So it is quite natural for one of them to speak in this way of God as the God of peace as he crushes the evil one. What could more vividly show what 'peace' means?

Peace means the defeat of evil. Peace means breaking down the barrier between man and God. Peace means the presence of

---

[1] Cited from Jack Finegan, *Light from the Ancient Past* (Princeton, 1946), p.246.

God's rich and abundant blessing. Peace means positiveness; it is not the absence of anything – the barrier that separated us from God or anything else. Peace is presence, the presence of God. Christ 'is our peace'.

MAN'S PART IN RECONCILIATION

So far we have been taken up with what God has done to bring about reconciliation. I have been emphasizing the truth that it is the action of God that is important in reconciliation, not that of man. I have rejected the idea of some scholars that it is really a work of man who simply turns from evil and finds himself in fellowship with God. That is not adequate for an account of New Testament teaching, and in particular it does not do justice to the New Testament insistence on the place of the cross. What Christ did is of central significance.

But this does not mean that man is passive in the whole process. Early in this study we noticed that for a state of fellowship to exist there must be good relations from both sides. There is no doubt about God's attitude. He is love and his attitude towards those he has created is always one of love. He sent his Son to die for sinners so that they might be reconciled to him. That is basic. But it is not the whole story. There is also the attitude of man to be considered and if he is set on his own selfish, sinful way reconciliation is not going to be consummated.

Let us go back to the illustration we were using of your quarrel with your friend. We saw that if you want to take the initiative in bringing about reconciliation you face up to the cause of the quarrel and as far as in you lies you take away the cause. Without that there can be no reconciliation. So you put your pride in your pocket and apologize or do whatever else it is that has to be done.

But suppose that, when you eat humble pie in this fashion, your friend will have none of it. Suppose he looks you in the eye and says, 'Look, I've met your sort before. After what you said and did the other day I don't care what you do. I'll never call you friend again.'

What can you do? You have apologized. You have removed the cause of the trouble as far as it is in your power to do so. You have shown clearly that you want to be friends and that from your side there is no barrier. You believe that you have demolished the obstacle that had been keeping you apart. But just as surely as it takes two to quarrel it takes two to make a reconciliation. If your friend will not have it there cannot be a reconciliation. The most you can say is that the way to reconciliation is open wide. There is no barrier. But there is no reconciliation either.

There is an equivalent in this matter of reconciliation with God. God was never in the wrong, but he took the initiative all the same to get the cause of the enmity out of the way. He has dealt with our sin and from that point of view it can be said that the reconciliation is complete.

But from another point of view the story is not ended. Paul can write movingly, 'God was reconciling the world to himself in Christ, not counting men's sins against them.' Then he continues, 'And he has committed to us the message of reconciliation. We are therefore Christ's ambassadors, as though God were making his appeal through us – we implore you on Christ's behalf: Be reconciled to God' (2 Cor. 5:19–20). Do you see? The whole thing has been accomplished by Christ. Nothing remains to be done. And yet there is something to be done. This reconciliation has no effect in the life of any individual sinner until he receives it, until he himself is reconciled to God. That Christ has accomplished the reconciliation means that the way is open wide. 'Whoever will, may come.' But come he must if he would be there. It is like the invitation in Revelation 22:17, 'Whoever is thirsty, let him come; and whoever wishes, let him take the free gift of the water of life.' The word translated 'wishes' means 'wills'; it is the expression of the will that is meant, not some moment of fleeting desire. The passage indicates that the water of life is freely available but also that it must be 'taken'. There is not the slightest reason why the sinner should not enter the fullness of the blessing of God. But until he does, he is outside it. Nothing happens for the person who waits passively. So with reconciliation. Paul 'implores' the Corinthians that they 'be reconciled'. Christ has made the way open for them. Let them enter.

People are not like inanimate things or even like dumb cattle. They are thinking, feeling entities. They are not arbitrarily drafted into salvation, though, of course, they are elected into it. There is mystery here, for the New Testament is clear that turning to Christ is never a purely human decision. The saved are those whom God has elected to salvation. Nothing should be said to obscure the importance of the divine initiative. Indeed from the point of view of election it may well be said that our whole salvation is of God.

145

But our whole salvation is the salvation of thinking, feeling people, people to whom God has given wills of their own. That we must be reconciled brings before us the thought that in the process of salvation those God-given wills must be used aright. When Christ has accomplished the reconciliation we can yet be called on to be reconciled to God.

Each of the ways of looking at salvation brings out something that the others do not. Each gives us particular insights into what Christ has done for us. Reconciliation brings out six thoughts in particular.

1. Sin is the barrier

It is not peculiar to reconciliation that sin is the problem in the relationship between God and man, but reconciliation must begin here. Had man not sinned there would have been no need and no place for reconciliation. But man sinned and men sin. The evil we share with the race and the evil we do ourselves both put up a barrier between us and God. Even among men sin alienates one from another. And sin always alienates us from God. This needs emphasis in a day like our own when people take sin so lightly. It does not worry us and for the life of us we cannot see why it should worry God. But the Bible is clear. Sin forms an impenetrable barrier, shutting off blessing. Sin keeps us away from God.

2. Sin must be dealt with

There is no ignoring reality. A barrier remains a barrier until it is taken away. At the heart of the idea of reconciliation there is the thought that getting people together means dealing effectively with whatever it was that was keeping them apart. This way of looking at the cross then reminds us that there can be no real fellowship between God and men unless and until the barrier of sin has been taken out of the way. It will not go away by wishing. We seem often to act on the assumption that, if we sit quietly and wait, any unpleasant thing will go away. It will not. It does not happen in the ordinary affairs of everyday life and it does not happen in the matter of the sin that separates us from God. Modern man finds this difficult to accept. It is not difficult for us to see that we must change our attitude and turn away from such things as selfishness. But that sin constitutes a very real barrier shutting us off from God, and that it must be effectively dealt with, is not at all obvious to us. But the New Testament keeps telling us that it was the death of Christ that effected reconciliation, that it was the cross that made peace between God and man (and for that matter, between Jew and Gentile).

3. There is a real hostility between God and sinners

We must not think that 'the wrath of God' is no more than a figure of speech which we may safely ignore. God hates every evil thing. But we are not comfortable with the New Testament teaching on the consequences of our sin. Partly at least this is because we have so well learnt that God is love. It is accepted today as axiomatic that God's attitude to us is one of love and that it always will be. I wish to affirm this in the strongest of terms. But it is love and not sentimentality that is in question. And what we do not always see is that love is capable of very strong action. Real love will always be resolutely opposed to evil in the beloved. Nearly a century ago E. H. Gifford wrote: 'Human love here offers a true analogy: the more a father loves his son, the more he hates *in him* the drunkard, the liar, or the traitor.'[2] We must never overlook the fact that real love has its stern side toward the beloved.

Nor should we overlook the fact that sin puts us completely in the wrong with God. When we sin we set ourselves in opposition to him and we invite his wrath against us. We make ourselves into God's enemies. We have seen that the New Testament does not hesitate to speak of sinners as enemies and that it uses terms like 'enmity' to describe the relationship of sinners to God. People today are inclined to accept sin as a normal and not particularly serious aspect of life, but we should not read such an attitude back into the New Testament. The first Christians saw sin as 'normal' in the sense that all people do sin. But they did not regard it as the normal thing in a world created by a good God. They saw it as the result of an invasion by an alien power. Sinful people are aligning themselves with that alien power. They are setting themselves in opposition to God.

This is serious, because of what it does to the sinners themselves. It removes them from the simplicity and the love for others for which they were meant. It makes them into people

[2] E. H. Gifford, *The Epistle of St. Paul to the Romans* (London, 1886), p.114.

concerned primarily with their own success (however they may understand success). It limits their horizons and makes them less as people. It leads them to produce a world like the one in which we live, where oppression and deception flourish, where the strong prosper at the expense of the weak, where the rich get richer at the expense of the poor, where millions lack necessary food even to the extent that they die of starvation while the nations (incredibly including the poor nations) spend astronomical amounts on armaments. The evil we do is our ruination. It cuts us off from the full and rich life that God would give us. Sin limits us, stops us being the best we could be, prevents us from enjoying life to the full.

And sin is serious because it alienates us from God. For some people this might be more intelligible if I were to say it alienates us from the ground of our being. We are not made to sin. We are made to live in harmony with one another and with God. When we turn to sin, as we do so freely, we alienate ourselves from all that we ought to be and from the God who made us and has given us so much richly to enjoy. There is a deep and very real hostility brought about by the sin of the race.

4. Reconciliation is God's work

There is never the slightest hint in the New Testament that reconciliation can be brought about by what we do. We created the barrier that separates us from God (and from one another), but we cannot break it down. There are theologians who stress the element of human responsibility in such a way as to indicate that man brought about the alienation from God and that man can and should end it. On this view God's attitude was always the same. He has always loved us and he is simply waiting for us to return to him. As soon as we do, reconciliation is effected.

But this is not what the New Testament is saying. The New Testament insists that something must be done about sin. It is not possible simply to ignore it, to count it as something that never happened. It did happen. Its results are with us. It has established a continuing enmity. For reconciliation to take place that enmity must be dealt with. And Paul emphasizes that this is what Christ did. Under this figure it is not said *how* the death of Christ put away sin, but it is said emphatically that it does. In redemption this is seen by way of paying the price, in justification by the bearing of penalty, and so on. There is no equivalent in reconciliation. But this way of looking at the atonement takes it that whatever had to be done was done. The important thing was the removal of the cause of the enmity and when Christ died on the cross he removed it.

This is something that he alone could do. Man is so immersed in sin that he does not even make the motion of wanting to leave it, let alone do away with it. And even if he wanted to it is so big a task that it is more than he can accomplish. It is beyond him. But it is not beyond Christ. It is the measure of his greatness that he was able to accomplish this great task and he did. 'He is our peace.'

5. *Reconciliation proceeds from the love of God*

As Paul understands it reconciliation is not simply a work of mighty power or something that we are to connect with the majesty or the holiness of God. It is a work that God accomplishes because he loves us. The love of God is the great fact that undergirds the whole New Testament. God is love and he always acts in love. It is perhaps significant that the first mention of reconciliation in the New Testament comes in a passage in which Paul is emphasizing the love of God and where he sees the cross as a demonstration of that love. Not simply the love of Christ, but the love of God. 'God demonstrates his own love for us in this: While we were still sinners, Christ died for us. Since we have now been justified by his blood, how much more shall we be saved from God's wrath through him! For if, when we were God's enemies, we were reconciled to him through the death of his Son...' (Rom. 5:8–10). The thought of the love of God seen in the cross leads immediately to the thought of justification by Christ's blood and reconciliation through the death of the Son. The love and the reconciliation go together. The reconciliation is the outworking of the love.

This must be insisted upon as it is easy to put too much emphasis on passages which speak of 'enemies' and of 'the wrath of God'. From the preceding discussion it will be obvious that I hold that such passages must be taken with full seriousness. But they must not be understood in such a way as to cast any doubt on the truth that the great, fundamental fact in this universe is the love of God. It is the love of God for us that leads him to be so hostile to our sin. If he loved us less he would not care about it. But he loves us with all the fervour of his holy nature and because

149

he loves us he provided the reconciliation. Love and reconciliation go together and the biblical concept of reconciliation cannot be understood without the love.

6. *The reconciliation must be received*

This way of looking at the atonement puts some emphasis on the necessity for the human response. That response is, of course, always implied. Without the response we are lost. But the imagery of redemption, for example, puts no great emphasis on it. There the stress is on the payment of the price and the liberation of the captive. Reconciliation, however, is meaningless without a change of attitude. Reconciliation is accomplished by Christ, indeed, but it must be received if it is to be effective. 'Be ye reconciled to God' is an integral part of the process. So the imagery of reconciliation always presents us with a challenge. It calls us away from our contentment with our sin. It reminds us that it takes two to make up after a quarrel. It emphasizes the greatness of what Christ has done to take away the cause of the enmity. It stresses the greatness of the love that impelled him to do this. In the light of that it is an imperative call to respond. 'We implore you on Christ's behalf: Be reconciled to God.'

For further study

1. How do people become enemies of God?
2. In what sense can we speak of God as being reconciled to man? Of man as being reconciled to God?
3. What part does the death of Christ play in the processes of reconciliation?
4. What does the Bible mean by making peace? With the help of a concordance, study as many references to peace as you can find in Scripture.
5. What will you say to someone who asks how people become reconciled to God?
6. What does reconciliation mean in your own life?

7
Propitiation

It is my pious hope that this chapter will not prove too heavy for the ordinary reader (and my private fear that this hope will be disappointed!). The trouble is that nobody seems to have been able to make propitiation simple. To most of us the term is just plain incomprehensible. Accordingly, it does not seem to matter much what it means and the result is a pronounced disinclination to make the effort needed to see whether anything much is at stake. But there is in fact quite a lot at stake; the concept is important for biblical religion. So, if we are serious about our Christianity, we must at least make the effort to attempt to understand it.

First, let us notice that neither the verb 'to propitiate' nor the noun 'propitiation' is of frequent occurrence in the New Testament. Indeed, if you are using a modern translation the chances are that you won't find them anywhere. Favourite replacements these days are the verb 'to expiate' and the noun 'expiation' (as in RSV, NEB, etc.). To most of us the change does not seem to matter much, as we don't understand 'expiation' very well either. We tend to inquire, 'What's the difference?' 'Does anyone know what either means anyway?' And, as neither is exactly of common occurrence in everyday speech, it is not difficult to come to the conclusion that no great issue is involved, so that it does not matter greatly which alternative we choose.

But this is superficial. The two concepts are really very different. Propitiation means the turning away of anger; expiation is rather the making amends for a wrong. Propitiation is a personal word; one propitiates a person. Expiation is an impersonal word; one expiates a sin or a crime.

151

When we are speaking about Christ's atoning work it makes a great deal of difference which meaning we understand. If we speak of expiation our meaning is that there is an impersonal process by which the effects of sin are nullified. We may be ready to think of the process as a remedy for defilement, a means of forgiveness, or a sacrifice that takes sin away, but we resolutely refuse to see any reference to the wrath of God. But if we speak of propitiation we are thinking of a personal process. We are saying that God is angry when people sin and that, if they are to be forgiven, something must be done about that anger. We are saying further that the death of Christ is the means of removing the divine wrath from sinners. The issue is far from being superficial.

We may perhaps feel that 'propitiation' is not a good word. It is a long word, a word which most of us rarely use, which many of us do not understand, and which some of those who do readily confuse with 'appeasement'. It is natural that translators often feel that it should be replaced by something more intelligible. I go along with this, with the sole proviso that the essential meaning of the term must be preserved. My quarrel with almost all modern translations is that they do not retain the essential meaning; specifically, they adopt some rendering that glosses over the wrath of God. But this is a very important concept (as I shall try to show), and it cannot be ignored in any satisfying understanding of the work of Christ.

THE USE OF HILASKOMAI

I'm afraid that we cannot study this subject seriously without a little linguistic work. We must examine the meaning of the Greek verb that has traditionally been translated 'to propitiate' or 'to make propitiation' (for example, in RV, ASV), and which is rendered in some other way in most recent translations. This verb, *hilaskomai*, is in common use in Greek in general and it means the turning away of anger. As far as the general run of Greek literature is concerned, there cannot be the slightest doubt that the meaning is 'to propitiate'.

A few scholars, it is true, raise an objection. They point out that in days well before the New Testament period it was often held that the gods became angry with their worshippers and that they had to be appeased by choice offerings. But more worthy ideas were making their appearance by New Testament times, they suggest, and the older, cruder ideas were fading away. They reason that we should go along with this trend and remove 'propitiation' from our New Testament.

Now it may well be that the trend of which these scholars write did in fact exist. I am not prepared to deny it. But the interesting thing is that the scholars who hold this view do not come up with any real evidence that *hilaskomai* and its related words were used to express it. Wherever these words occur they have the meaning of the turning away of wrath. As far as I know there are only two passages in the whole range of Greek literature that are suggested as possible exceptions and neither of these is convincing.[1] The *hilaskomai* words consistently mean propitiation. It is, of course, quite possible that the Bible writers evolved a new meaning for some well-known words and then used the words in their new meaning, without telling anyone what they were doing and without making their new meaning clear in the way they used the words. We must look at the evidence to see whether this in fact happened. Though it is worth pointing out that if they did this they concealed what they had done very effectively, because until our day no-one has suspected the new meaning. But the first point to notice is that there can be not the slightest doubt that the word-group means propitiation in Greek writings generally. This creates a presumption that it will be used in similar fashion in the New Testament.

THE WRATH OF GOD IN THE OLD TESTAMENT

Before we look at the passages where the propitiation words occur, it will be useful to notice the way the Bible speaks about the wrath of God. It is this wrath that is called into question when people deny that the Bible speaks of propitiation, so it is important to notice that the Bible makes it very clear that this wrath is a reality and that it says a great deal about it.

In the Old Testament more than twenty words are used of the wrath of God (in addition to a number of others which are used only of human anger). The total number of references to God's wrath exceeds 580, so that it cannot be said to be an occasional topic. There is a consistency about God's wrath in Scripture which we do not find in similar expressions used about the gods

[1] I have examined these passages in *The Apostolic Preaching of the Cross* (London, 1965), pp.145–147, and have, I think, shown that neither demands a meaning other than the usual 'propitiation'.

of the heathen. The heathen worshipped capricious gods. The worshippers could never guess what the gods would be up to next. They could never tell when their gods would be angry or what it was that annoyed them. The Hebrews were not in doubt. They knew that one thing and one thing alone aroused God's anger, and that was sin. They knew that God was always angry with sin – the reason there are so many references to the divine wrath is that they had so much experiential knowledge of the subject! God was angry with sin generally (Jb. 21:20), or with specific sins, including the shedding of blood (Ezk. 16:38), adultery (Ezk. 23:25), afflicting the widow or orphan (Ex. 22:22–24), violence (Ezk. 8:17–18), covetousness and falsehood (Je. 6:11–13). Most of all God's wrath is aroused by idolatry and this is frequently brought out (Ex. 32:8–10; Dt. 6:14–15, *etc.*).

The idea of the wrath of God is so widespread in the Old Testament and so strongly emphasized that one would have thought it would be taken as basic that God is angry when people sin. But no. C. H. Dodd, for example, notices that 'the wrath of God' is an expression frequently found in passages telling of disaster following sin. He develops the ingenious argument that the expression is a kind of shorthand. It is a quick way of describing an impersonal process in which sin is followed by disaster. Where we might think of an automatic process the ancients preferred to speak of 'the wrath of God'. Thus Dodd says that the work of the prophets is such that

> 'the Wrath of God' is taken out of the sphere of the purely mysterious, and brought into the sphere of cause and effect: sin is the cause, disaster the effect... in speaking of wrath and judgment the prophets and psalmists have their minds mainly on events, actual or expected, conceived as the inevitable results of sin; and when they speak of mercy they are thinking mainly of the personal relation between God and His people. Wrath is the effect of human sin: mercy is not the effect of human goodness, but is inherent in the character of God.[2]

This idea has been widely taken up. The wrath of God is not a highly popular concept and it appeals to us when an outstanding scholar suggests that we may do away with it. We like to feel that

[2] C. H. Dodd, *The Epistle of Paul to the Romans* (London, 1944), pp.22–23.

we have nothing to fear from God, whatever sins may trouble our consciences.

But the trouble is that, for all its attractiveness, Dodd's hypothesis will not fit the facts. In the Bible the wrath of God is intensely personal. The prophets did not think of an absentee God, benevolently allowing the universe to go on its way with all kinds of impersonal mechanisms in operation. They emphasized the sovereignty of God. They saw him as active in the affairs of men. Specifically they were sure that the punishment of sin was due to God himself. They could ask, 'When disaster comes to a city, has not the LORD caused it?' (Am. 3:6; *cf.* 'he flashes destruction on the stronghold', Am. 5:9). They spoke of a God who could say, 'I form the light and create darkness, I bring prosperity and create disaster; I, the LORD, do all these things' (Is. 45:7). Right through the Old Testament it is implicit, and quite often explicit, that God is supreme in the affairs of men. He is active in bringing his purposes to pass, whether they are purposes of blessing on his people or of judgment on the sins of men.

This is very clear in some of the 'wrath of God' passages. Take, for example, these words:

See, the Name of the LORD comes from afar,
  with burning anger and dense clouds of smoke;
his lips are full of wrath,
  and his tongue is a consuming fire.
His breath is like a rushing torrent,
  rising up to the neck.
He shakes the nations in the sieve of destruction;
  he places in the jaws of the peoples
  a bit that leads them astray....
The LORD will cause men to hear his majestic voice
  and will make them see his arm coming down
with raging anger and consuming fire... (Is. 30:27–30).

Or these from Ezekiel:

I am about to pour out my wrath on you and spend my anger against you; I will judge you according to your conduct and repay you for all your detestable practices. I will not look on you with pity or spare you; I will repay you in accordance with your conduct and the detestable practices among you. Then

155

you will know that it is I the LORD who strikes the blow
(Ezk. 7:8–9).

Or this cry from the Psalmist:

You have rejected us, O God, and burst forth upon us;
  you have been angry....
You have shaken the land and torn it open....
You have shown your people desperate times;
  you have given us wine that makes us stagger (Ps. 60:1–3).

It is not easy to see how words could more clearly express the
truth that the wrath of God is seen as personal. Such passages
telling of the wrath of God are vivid and frequent.

It is true that in the Old Testament disaster is seen as the
inevitable consequence of sin. But that is not because some
impersonal process is at work; it is because a moral God will not
allow man to sin with impunity. Because God is the moral God
he is, he is angry when people sin, people whom he created for a
higher destiny than that. Again and again it is emphasized that
God is personally at work in the execution of his anger, just as he
is in the showing of his mercy. Dodd distinguished between
wrath and mercy, regarding wrath as an impersonal process and
mercy as God's personal action, as we have seen. But the prophets
make no such distinction. Micah prays, 'You do not stay angry
for ever but delight to show mercy' (Mi. 7:18). Similarly the
Psalmist can speak of forgiveness and wrath in the same breath:
'You forgave the iniquity of your people and covered all their
sins. You set aside all your wrath and turned from your fierce
anger' (Ps. 85:2–3). I do not see how it can seriously be contended
that in such passages mercy is to be regarded as personal and
wrath as impersonal. The same kind of language is used of both.

I repeat, such passages are frequent. We should not think that
the 'wrath of God' passages represent a minor aberration, found
occasionally in obscure passages not known to most writers. The
idea that the wrath of God is exercised against sin runs through
and through the Old Testament. I have already pointed out that
more than twenty different words are used by the Old Testament
writers to convey the thought of the wrath of God, with a total of
more than 580 occurrences of the words. That is a large number.
If we cut them all out, our Old Testament is left with quite a few

holes. The statistics themselves show that the wrath of God is an important Old Testament concept. If we are to be true to the Old Testament we cannot lightly discard or overlook the teaching that God is personally angry in the face of all evil. It is one of the facts of life that God is always hostile to evil. Wrath may be his 'strange work' (Is. 28:21), with the implication that mercy is more congenial. But it is his work. We do ourselves a disservice if we shut our eyes to the fact.

The conclusion to which all this drives us is that in the Old Testament the wrath of God receives some emphasis. It is invariably aroused by human sin and, if people are to be forgiven, then the fact of that wrath must be taken into consideration. It does not fade away by being given some other name or regarded as an impersonal process. There are too many vividly personal passages for that. Perhaps we should notice that ten times God is said to be 'slow to anger' (Ex. 34:6, *etc.*). He is not an irascible deity, ready to become angry at the slightest provocation. But, slow though it is, his anger is real. His wrath is certain if we continue in sin.

We should finish this section by noticing that, as the Old Testament writers see it, God's wrath is not put away by some human activity. The gods of the heathen might be expected to respond to bribes from their worshippers. Not so the God of Israel. His anger against sin is a grim reality and, if it is to be removed, its removal is due to none less than God himself. In the wilderness 'Time after time he restrained his anger' (Ps. 78:38). We might translate as the American Standard Version, 'many a time turned he his anger away' (the verb is that used in the expression, 'A gentle answer turns away wrath', Pr. 15:1; again in 29:8). So also, 'For my own name's sake I delay my wrath' (Is. 48:9). Also relevant are a couple of passages we noted earlier, 'You do not stay angry for ever but delight to show mercy' (Mi. 7:18), and 'You set aside all your wrath and turned from your fierce anger' (Ps. 85:3). The Old Testament is clear about the extent and the seriousness of God's anger. But it is clear also that God will put that anger away. There is a paradox here which must be preserved if we are to understand biblical religion. God's attitude to evil is not passive. He is vigorously opposed to it. But he is also a merciful God and it is to him that we owe the forgiveness which means that we are no longer the objects of his wrath. Wrath and mercy both belong to God.

PROPITIATION IN THE SEPTUAGINT

Dodd has another string to his bow. He examines the use of our words in the Septuagint, the translation of the Hebrew Old Testament into Greek. It was this that was the Bible of the first Christians, so that it is to be expected that they used the words in the way the Septuagint did and with the meanings those words had in the Septuagint. Dodd's argument is that in the Septuagint the *hilaskomai* words do not mean 'propitiation' at all. The Septuagint translators, according to him, evolved a new meaning for the old word-group and the New Testament writers took it up.

It is not easy for anyone without a knowledge of Hebrew or Greek to follow the intricacies of Dodd's argument. But it is important to make the attempt because (a) a concept of prime importance for our understanding of the New Testament is at stake, and (b) many people hold that Dodd has settled the issue. Let me try, then, to set out the issues in such a way as to bring out Dodd's essential argument and my objections to it.

In the Septuagint *hilaskomai* and its related words are most often the translation of words from the Hebrew root *kpr*. But this is far from invariable and Dodd finds three groups of passages to consider:

1. Passages in which words from the Hebrew root *kpr* are translated by words other than those from the *hilaskomai* group.

2. Passages in which the *hilaskomai* words are the translation of other Hebrew words than *kpr*.

3. Passages in which *hilaskomai* and related words translate the Hebrew root *kpr*.

The third group is the largest group and it is clearly very important. In particular the verb from *kpr* occurs quite often and this is the word normally translated into English by 'to make atonement'. We have already looked at this in connection with the offering of sacrifice and there is no point in going over the ground again. We saw then that the meaning is generally something like 'to put away sin by the death of a spotless victim'. This does not necessarily mean 'to avert the wrath of God', but it is certainly consistent with it. It would be very dangerous to argue that it implies that there is no such thing as a personal wrath of God to be reckoned with. Dodd's case gets no support from this group.

The strength of his case is in the other two groups. Basically the argument is that you can tell the meaning of a word from the company it keeps – words that can be linked with *hilaskomai* in the translation process must be of similar meaning to *hilaskomai*. Dodd argues from passages in the first group that the words other than *hilaskomai* that translate *kpr* have nothing to do with anger. They have meanings like 'to sanctify' or 'to cancel (sins)'. He reasons that *hilaskomai* must have a similar meaning and that it likewise has nothing to do with anger.

He has the same kind of argument with the passages in group 2, the words other than *kpr* which *hilaskomai* translates. These have meanings like 'to cleanse from sin' or 'to have mercy'. They do not mean 'to remove anger'.

Both groups, Dodd says, class *hilaskomai* and its related words with words like 'grace' or 'forgiveness', not words like 'wrath' or 'anger'. He finds that *hilaskomai* keeps company with the grace and the mercy words, not with the anger words. Therefore it has a meaning like 'be gracious' or 'forgive', not 'avert anger'.

The argument sounds impressive and it is not surprising that many have been convinced. But it has some fundamental weaknesses. One is that it completely ignores the realities of translation. Any word has a range of meaning; its meaning is like the area in a circle rather than like a point. It is rarely the case that the circle of meaning of a word in one language exactly overlaps that of a word in another language. The translator will select one word for the overlapping area and other words for the areas where the two do not overlap. Dodd is arguing that where the areas do not overlap there still must be a similar meaning. But as soon as we examine the way translation is done we see that this is simply not the case. In many instances, perhaps in most, the meanings will not be similar.

Let us take an example from translation into English where the non-specialist can appreciate the point more easily. The Greek word *kosmos* means very nearly what the English word 'world' means and in the overwhelming number of cases we translate *kosmos* by 'world'. But there are some places where these two words do not overlap, where 'world' is not the meaning of *kosmos*. An example is 1 Peter 3:3, where *kosmos* is translated 'adornment' (we derive our word 'cosmetic' from this way of using *kosmos* and its cognates). Nobody doubts that 'adornment' is the correct understanding of *kosmos* in this particular passage any more than that 'world' is the normal English equivalent of the term. Dodd's method of argument would require us to maintain that in English 'world' and 'adornment' are of similar meaning; they can both be used as translations of the one Greek word. But of course they are not similar. The method is fallacious. While we can say that the English equivalent of *kosmos* is mostly 'world' (and that the Greek equivalent of *kpr* is mostly *hilaskomai*), we cannot say that other English words which translate *kosmos* are of similar meaning to 'world' (or that other Greek terms which translate *kpr* are of similar meaning to *hilaskomai*). They may be very dissimilar.

Even if we were to allow a limited validity to Dodd's method, certainly Dodd goes beyond any limits we can assign to it. We see this from the fact that he groups words with meanings as diverse as 'to sanctify' and 'to cancel'. I do not understand why he does not draw attention to the fact that these words are not of similar meaning at all. If *hilaskomai* has a meaning like 'to sanctify', it cannot have a meaning like 'to cancel' (and so the other way round). The range of meaning is too wide to prove anything. And even then Dodd has not shown how wide the range of words involved in the translation of *hilaskomai* really is. Dr Roger Nicole maintains that Dodd has not taken into account quite a large number of Greek words used to translate members of the *kpr* group and that in fact he notices no more than thirty-six per cent of the evidence. If all the evidence is included Nicole holds that we should re-write Dodd's conclusion in these words:

> Where the LXX translators do not render *kipper* and its cognates by words of the *hilaskesthai* class, they render it by words which give the meaning 'to sanctify', 'to forgive', 'to remove', 'to cover with pitch', 'to ransom', 'to contribute', 'to give', 'to veil', 'to anoint', 'the village', 'the myrrh', or they have failed to render it altogether. We should therefore expect to find that they regard the *hilaskesthai* class as conveying similar ideas.[3]

This, of course, makes the statement meaningless, which is Nicole's point. He holds that the argument is so inherently defective that it proves nothing. Dodd is ignoring one of the basic truths about translation.

[3] *Westminster Theological Journal*, xvii, 1955, p.129.

PUTTING AWAY WRATH

If we are to discover the meaning which the Septuagint translators saw in *hilaskomai*, the way to do it is to look carefully at the meaning required in the contexts in which the word is found, not to drag in the meanings of words used when *hilaskomai* is held to be inappropriate. The interesting fact which emerges from the examination is that quite often in the contexts in which *hilaskomai* is used there is a reference to the divine anger. Take, for example, its use in Lamentations 3:42. There our verb translates the Hebrew *slh* and is rightly rendered 'you have not forgiven'. But the passage reads, 'We have sinned and rebelled and you have not forgiven. You have covered yourself with anger and pursued us....' The word may indeed be translated 'forgive', but the people to whom it is applied are the objects of the divine wrath. The kind of forgiveness the word denotes here is a forgiveness which includes the averting of the wrath of God. Propitiation is not out of mind.

Exodus 32:14 is another place where the Septuagint translators used *hilaskomai*. The NIV translates the original Hebrew as 'relented', and I am not going to quarrel with that translation. But notice that what happened was in response to a prayer of Moses in which he said, 'O LORD, why should your anger burn against your people...?...Turn from your fierce anger; relent and do not bring disaster on your people' (verses 11–12). There is wrath in the situation. The relenting in question means that that wrath will not be given full reign. Similarly the Psalmist says of God, 'Yet he was merciful; he atoned for their iniquities and did not destroy them. Time after time he restrained his anger and did not stir up his full wrath' (Ps. 78:38). And so we could go on. Again and again we find that, however the word is translated, there is the thought of the divine wrath in the context. Let me quote my summing up after an examination of every occurrence of the verb *hilaskomai* in the Septuagint:

> six times there is explicit mention of wrath in the immediate context, once the people are under sentence of death, twice the psalmist is greatly afflicted, and on the other occasion the action is that one above all others which the Old Testament regards as provoking God's wrath [*i.e.* idolatry]. We cannot say that the concept of the wrath of God is certainly absent

161

from any of these passages, and in every one the rendering 'propitiate' is quite appropriate. In the face of all this it is manifestly impossible to maintain that the verb has been emptied of its force.[4]

I do not see how an examination of the way any of the words from this word-group is used can get rid of the thought of the divine wrath. Translate how you will, the words are used of situations where God's wrath against sin is being manifested, but as a result of the action this word-group denotes that wrath no longer operates. Do we have a better word than 'propitiation' for this?

I am not arguing for the crude, heathen view of propitiation as a process of celestial bribery. There is an example of that when the Moabites were in great trouble. The king of Moab took 700 swordsmen to break through the Israelites, but they could not do it. 'Then he took his firstborn son, who was to succeed him as king, and offered him as a sacrifice on the city wall. The fury against Israel was great; they withdrew and returned to their own land' (2 Ki. 3:26–27). Plainly the king of Moab believed that his god was angry with him and that the greatest sacrifice he could offer was his son. He offered him and felt that his god responded in the subsequent withdrawal of Israel. This kind of thing is absent from the religion of Israel. There is no crude propitiation of an angry deity in Old Testament religion.

But there is a recognition that the wrath of God is real. Nothing in the Old Testament allows us to hold that God is indifferent to the evil we do. He demands uprightness: '"These are the things you are to do: Speak the truth to each other, and render true and sound judgment in your courts; do not plot evil against your neighbour, and do not love to swear falsely. I hate all this," declares the LORD' (Zc. 8:16–17). His opposition to the wicked is of the strongest: 'the wicked and those who love violence his soul hates' (Ps. 11:5). We do not do justice to the Old Testament unless we see that God is an incurably loving God and a God implacably opposed to evil. And that implacable opposition is what is in mind when the Old Testament writers speak of his anger, an anger that is inseparably bound up with his love. It is because he loves us that he is so opposed to the evil in us, that evil that makes us so much less than we ought to be and cuts us

---

[4] L. Morris, *The Apostolic Preaching of the Cross* (London, [3]1965), p.158.

off from so much blessing. The wrath of God is not a reaction born of pique at being slighted. It is God's strong opposition to that which cuts us off from the best that we can be. God's love is not a mindless sentimentality. It is a purifying fire, a force in the strongest opposition to everything that mars those whom God loves.

If we think of wrath as uncontrollable passion, then of course there is no way of applying this concept to the God of Israel. But when we see that there is a wrath that goes with a holy love it is a different matter. The old Prayer Book version of Psalm 36:4 says of the wicked man, 'neither doth he abhor any thing that is evil.' That is a dreadful condemnation. And perhaps we see what the Hebrews meant by God's wrath when we reflect that they did not ascribe that kind of moral indifferentism to God. God loves the right and therefore he is in vigorous opposition to every evil. But because God loves he provides the way whereby his beloved are delivered from the wrath that would otherwise engulf them.

THE WRATH OF GOD IN THE NEW TESTAMENT

We have noticed that there are some writers who think that the concept of the wrath of God should be removed from the Old Testament, so it does not surprise us that even more is this the case with the New. C. H. Dodd held that in the teaching of Jesus 'anger as an attitude of God to men disappears, and His love and mercy become all-embracing'. He thinks that Paul agrees with this in substance and that he uses the concept of God's wrath 'not to describe the attitude of God to man, but to describe an inevitable process of cause and effect in a moral universe'.[5] With charming dogmatism he says of Romans 3:25, 'the meaning conveyed... is that of expiation, not that of propitiation. Most translators and commentators are wrong.'[6] Many have followed Dodd and the concept of the wrath of God is widely questioned in the Christian scene.

Let us begin by noticing that Greek has two words which are used of anger, *orgē* and *thymos*. These are often used in much the same way and indeed in New Testament times it would be very difficult to find a consistent difference between them. There is a distinction in the New Testament, however, at least as regards

[5] C. H. Dodd, *Romans*, p.23.
[6] C. H. Dodd, *The Bible and the Greeks* (London, 1954), p.94.

God, for outside Revelation with its vivid imagery, the word *thymos* is applied to God once only; *orgē* was evidently seen as much more suitable for the divine anger.

This word *orgē* is connected with *orgaō*, which has a meaning like 'to be growing ripe for something'. It is used, for example, of the swelling of buds when the sap rises and of the swelling of fruit as it gets ripe. It points to that which proceeds from the inner nature of a thing and it accords with this that lexicons tend to give 'natural impulse' or the like as the first meaning of *orgē*. It is the anger that arises from what a man is; it proceeds from his settled disposition. When it is applied to God it means that his wrath is due to his settled opposition to every evil thing. By contrast, *thymos* is connected with *thyō*, 'to seethe'. The imagery lends itself to the idea of an anger which is like a boiling over, a sudden loss of control, a passionate outburst. As I said earlier, the two words cannot be consistently distinguished, but there is certainly a different feel about them. G. Stählin has an interesting comment on the different usages of Revelation and of Paul: 'one might very well say that *thymos*, to which there clings the concept of passionate outburst, was well adapted for describing the visions of the seer, but not for delineating Paul's concept of the wrath of God.'[7] I am not arguing that there is a difference between the two words on every occurrence. I do not think there is. But a consideration of the way the New Testament writers use the two words leads to an important consideration with regard to the wrath of God. What is meant is not an outburst of passion, but the settled opposition to evil that arises from the fact that God is who and what he is.

The word 'wrath' does not occur often in the Gospels. But it is there and the idea of the divine anger may be present when the word is not. John the Baptist warned his hearers of 'the coming wrath' (Mt. 3:7) and Jesus spoke of 'wrath against this people' (Lk. 21:23). In the Fourth Gospel we find that 'God's wrath remains on' him who 'rejects the Son' (Jn. 3:36). Jesus himself is said to have been angry on one occasion (Mk. 3:5). More important, however, are passages which do not use the term 'wrath' but which clearly have this in mind. Thus Jesus spoke of hell quite a number of times and this implies the outworking of the wrath of God. He referred to 'the fire of hell' (Mt. 5:22, *etc.*), to

[7] G. Friedrich (ed.), *Theological Dictionary of the New Testament*, v (Grand Rapids, 1967), p.422.

'eternal fire' (Mt. 18:8), and to that dreadful place 'where "their worm does not die, and the fire is not quenched"' (Mk. 9:48). He spoke of 'him who, after the killing of the body, has power to throw you into hell' (Lk. 12:5). There is much more about such themes as judgment, the outer darkness, the 'weeping and gnashing of teeth' and the like. It is impossible to take the Gospels seriously and yet maintain that Jesus did not teach the reality of the wrath of God.

It is the same with the rest of the New Testament. There are passages in which God's wrath is explicitly referred to and there are places where the term 'wrath' is not used but the idea is present. Sometimes it is urged by way of objection that the expression 'the wrath' occurs quite often with no explicit connection with God. Few would go so far as to say that this means that wrath is personified, regarded as an independent entity separate from God. But some would certainly affirm that this shows that not all of the New Testament writers were happy to associate 'the wrath' closely with God. For some of them, it is said, there was a sense in which 'the wrath' operated more or less independently.

But the conclusion being drawn from this usage is not necessarily the right one. It overlooks the fact that 'the wrath of God' is certainly a New Testament expression (Jn. 3:36; Rom. 1:18; Eph. 5:6, *etc.*). Other expressions are also relevant, such as 'his wrath' (Rev. 14:10; 16:19) and 'your wrath' (Rev. 11:18) with reference to God. 'The wrath of the Lamb' (Rev. 6:16) also links wrath with a divine person. The anger denoted by *thymos* is linked with God on a number of occasions in Revelation (see Rev. 14:10, 19; 15:1, 7, *etc.*). All in all it is pretty plain that the New Testament writers did not hesitate to speak of 'the wrath of God' when it suited them. The places where the expression 'the wrath' is used without special mention of God do not necessarily point to hesitation about divine wrath. They may mean that the men of the Old Testament had written of God's wrath so effectively that it was sufficient in New Testament times to say 'the wrath'. Nobody doubted whose wrath that was.

But it is not only a question of passages which specifically use the term 'wrath'. There are others which clearly make use of the concept, even though the word does not occur. Thus Paul writes to the Thessalonians about the day 'when the Lord Jesus is revealed from heaven in blazing fire with his powerful angels.

165

He will punish those who do not know God and do not obey the gospel of our Lord Jesus. They will be punished with everlasting destruction and shut out from the presence of the Lord and from the majesty of his power' (2 Thes. 1:7–9). This is certainly the same stern reality as is elsewhere called 'the wrath of God' and it must be reckoned with, even though Paul does not choose to use the word 'wrath' to express it.

In view of Dodd's idea that 'the wrath of God' is used of an impersonal process of cause and effect, it is worth drawing attention to Romans 1. There Paul is speaking of the degradation of the sinner as the result of his sin. It would be the easiest possible thing for him to leave this as a natural process, to say something like 'the punishment of sin lies in being a sinner'. But he does not. Three times he says 'God gave them over' to the result of their sin (Rom. 1:24, 26, 28). In this passage Paul goes out of his way to emphasize the divine activity. He could so easily have expressed himself without this.

The wrath of God then is a topic not to be neglected in a study of New Testament teaching. It is found sometimes in express words and sometimes in the general thrust of passages. It is found in the teaching of Jesus and in that of his followers. The New Testament leaves us in no doubt but that God is vigorously hostile to sin and that he will punish the unrepentant sinner.

It is important to see that 'the wrath of God' is a significant category in the New Testament. The process of salvation must accordingly take into account this aspect of the human predicament as well as other aspects. Concepts we have looked at so far, such as the new covenant, redemption or even reconciliation, do not adequately cover the overcoming of wrath. The propitiation words do not occur very often, but in view of the widespread occurrence of 'the wrath' and the like they must be given serious consideration as we reflect on what Christ's death has done for us. We turn accordingly to passages which speak specifically of propitiation.

CHRIST SET FORTH AS PROPITIATION

The first such passage is that in which Paul tells us that God has set forth Christ as 'a propitiation [*hilastērion*] through faith in his blood' (Rom. 3:25, AV). The word *hilastērion* clearly belongs to the propitiation word-group, but its interpretation in this passage has been a subject of dispute. NIV translates 'a sacrifice of atonement' (with a marginal alternative, 'the one who would turn aside his wrath'), RSV 'an expiation', NEB 'the means of expiating sin by his sacrificial death' (which apparently includes the reference to the blood), and GNB 'the means by which people's sins are forgiven'. We are not short of suggestions and the variety of translations shows that the meaning of the passage is not obvious. At the same time one suspects that part of the problem arises from modern objections to using 'propitiation'. These days we do not like the idea of the wrath of God, and still less do we care for propitiation with its suggestion of appeasement. The variety in the translations amounts to a number of different ways of finding a substitute for propitiation.

But whether we like it or not, it is propitiation to which the linguistics point. The word is a member of the word-group we have been examining in the Old Testament and which we have seen to denote the turning away of wrath. There is no reason, either in the Greek Old Testament or in non-biblical Greek, for seeing it as meaning anything other than 'propitiation'. The form of Paul's word in this passage could give the meaning 'means of turning away wrath' or 'place of turning away wrath'. Some hold that it is the latter meaning that we should see in Romans 3 and they point to the use of the word in the Septuagint for the cover of the ark, the 'mercy-seat'. They think that this is the way we should translate it in the present passage. But there are substantial reasons for rejecting this. In the Septuagint *hilastērion* is used for other things than the mercy-seat, such as the ledge on Ezekiel's altar (Ezk. 43:14, 17, 20, *etc.*) and a rather obscure reference in Amos 9:1. In Symmachus's translation it is used of Noah's ark. We need more than the simple use of the word to convey the idea of 'mercy-seat'. The Septuagint always has something in the context to give us the clue when this is meant, but there is nothing corresponding to this in Romans 3. The word means 'propitiating thing' or the like. There is nothing in the context in Romans 3 to show that the 'propitiating thing' in question is the mercy-seat. 'Means of turning away wrath' is better.

RSV's 'expiation' seems to be due to nothing more profound than the rejection of the biblical idea of propitiation. We have seen this idea in the writings of C. H. Dodd and it has been widely accepted in some circles. But the linguistics are against it. The word *hilastērion* is one which refers to the act of persons. It signifies the means of turning away someone's anger. It is not the impersonal expiation of a sin. NIV and GNB are better, but neither reckons with the fact that the word had a recognized meaning and this meaning was linked with the turning away of wrath. None of these translations fits the essential meaning of the word or the way it is used in the Old Testament.

It is sometimes said that we should understand our passage as a reference to the Day of Atonement ceremonies. I am a little more respectful of this, but I find it not demonstrated. Basically it rests on the view that *hilastērion* means 'mercy-seat'. From this starting-point it goes on to the reminder that this article of tabernacle furniture was used only on the Day of Atonement. On no other day could the high priest go into the Holy of Holies where the mercy-seat was (and of course no-one else could go into it at any time). The conclusion is that Paul was using the solemn fast day and its ceremonies to illustrate what Christ did for us.

But I have already noted that there is not sufficient evidence that the word means 'mercy-seat'. Granted that the mercy-seat could be regarded as 'a propitiating thing', there is nothing to show that Paul had in mind this particular 'propitiating thing'. We should also bear in mind that this apostle does not make use of Levitical practices in the way that the writer to the Hebrews does. It would be out of character for Paul to throw in just one reference to a priestly practice without explanation and without anything to follow it up. It is not that Paul would not suddenly make use of one concept which he uses nowhere else. He does this, for example, with the Rock in 1 Corinthians 10:4. But there he can be readily understood. Here he could not be so easily understood, if the reference is to an article of temple furniture which in any case was not in existence in his day. It is last mentioned in 2 Chronicles 35:3 and it is not known what happened to it after that. But it was not in the the temple in New Testament times; it had long since vanished. The sprinkling of the blood was carried out on the Day of Atonement, but it was not the mercy-seat that was sprinkled. It was a stone on the traditional site of the ark, a stone three finger-breadths high called Shetiyah. The difficulties in the way of interpreting Paul as referring to the Day of Atonement are simply too great.

A cogent argument in favour of 'propitiation' (in addition to the normal meaning of the word) is the context. In the opening section of Romans Paul has argued powerfully that the wrath of God 'is being revealed from heaven against all the godlessness and wickedness of men' (Rom. 1:18). He proceeds to document this with respect both to the Gentiles and to the Jews and he backs up his argument with an appeal to a list of scriptural passages (Rom. 3:10–18). It is not too much to say that, after his salutation and introductory remarks, the whole of the early part of Romans is a massive indictment of all mankind with a view to showing that all people are sinners (Rom. 3:23) and accordingly that they are under the judgment of God and are the objects of his wrath.

In Romans 3:21 Paul begins a most important section in which he shows how the death of Christ deals with the problem of sin. Part of the process is his dealing with the wrath. That the wrath is important for Paul is shown by the way he has ordered his argument to show that all are the objects of the wrath (Rom. 1:18; 2:5, 8; 3:5; *cf.* 4:15). But unless *hilastērion* means 'propitiation', Paul has put men under the wrath of God and left them there. He uses other terms like redemption and justification, but these have nothing to do with wrath. These two refer respectively to the paying of a price to set people free and to the paying of a penalty. Nothing deals with salvation from the divine wrath other than *hilastērion*, which means 'the averting of wrath'.

If we reduce *hilastērion* here to the sub-personal 'expiation', as do some modern translations and commentators, then what has become of God's wrath? Paul has undoubtedly put emphasis on it in the earlier stages of his massive argument. This understanding of the term leaves the wrath unaccounted for. Are we to understand that, though we are in some sense saved, God's wrath is still in force? Or that in the last resort God's wrath can simply be ignored? How can we fit such ideas into Paul's argument? To do justice to what the apostle is saying we must include in our understanding of this passage the idea that part of the meaning of salvation is that God's *wrath* is averted.

I am not concerned to contend for the word 'propitiation'. I do not find it an elegant word, nor one which is easily understood by most people today. By all means let us abandon it if we can find a better way of expressing what it stands for. But if I am not greatly concerned about the word, I am greatly concerned about the idea that it conveys. The plain fact is that *hilastērion* signifies 'the means of averting wrath' and the new translations miss this.

And in missing it they pass over a very important biblical concept. The other words they use do not bring out the truth that in one aspect Christ's atoning work dealt with the wrath of God against sinners. This is too important a biblical theme for us simply to ignore it. So far, the alternative translations suggested do just that.

THE VERB 'TO PROPITIATE'

The corresponding verb 'to propitiate' is not common in the New Testament. In connection with the atonement it is used but once, namely in Hebrews 2:17, where the writer speaks of Christ as becoming 'a merciful and faithful high priest in service to God, and that he might make atonement for the sins of the people'. Here NIV has our verb as 'make atonement for' (with a marginal alternative, 'that he might turn aside God's wrath'), while RSV renders it 'to make expiation for', and NEB is similar, 'to expiate'. GNB paraphrases with 'so that the people's sins would be forgiven'. Again we see behind all these translations an unwillingness to recognize that the word-group has to do with the putting away of wrath.

There is one point in favour of translations such as 'to expiate' in this passage, namely that the verb has 'the sins' as its direct object. This is a very unusual construction. In all of Greek literature outside the Bible it is cited once only and in the Greek Old Testament once more. There are half a dozen examples in the apocryphal book Sirach and these are sometimes claimed confidently as part of the background of the New Testament writers and as supporting the meaning 'expiate'. The basic idea in the whole argument is that 'propitiate' has a person as its object, while 'expiate' has a sin. Since the object here is 'the sins', the reasoning runs, the meaning is 'expiate'.

But it is not easy to make the argument stand up. The passages in Sirach, for example, do not prove the point and these are important, for this is apparently the only book which has more than one example of 'sin' as the direct object of our verb. Let us look at a typical passage: 'Do not say, "His mercy is great, he will forgive [really 'be propitiated for'] the multitude of my sins," for both mercy and wrath are with him, and his anger rests on sinners' (Sirach 5:6). The fact that 'sin' is the direct object of our verb does not signify that the meaning 'expiate' is in order and that the idea of wrath has been abandoned. The verse quite plainly means that if anyone goes on calmly in his sin, relying on the compassion of God to see him through, he will be in deep trouble. There are explicit references to 'wrath' and 'anger'. The evil-doer will find that God's anger is a reality resting on sinners. The passage makes no sense without the concept of the divine wrath. That wrath against a man's 'multitude' of sins cannot be held to be averted simply because God is compassionate. The passage lends no support to the view that the verb has lost its meaning of the turning away of anger. On the contrary, it requires just this meaning.

There is no point in going through the entire list. It is enough to say that in most of the other cases the context makes it clear that the verb has to do with the removal of wrath. If a passage speaks of the wrath of God as at work and then uses our verb with respect to the bringing in of a happier state of affairs, then, translate it how you will, the meaning is that wrath is averted from the sinner.

Since the meaning 'expiate' cannot be demonstrated anywhere we should understand the verb in Hebrews 2 as elsewhere in the sense 'to make propitiation', 'to turn away anger'. The passage will mean, 'to make propitiation with respect to the sins of the people.' This understanding of the word agrees with the meaning of the verb elsewhere and with the teaching of Hebrews as a whole. It should further be noted that the immediate context favours it, for Christ is spoken of as 'a merciful and faithful high priest in service to God'. If mercy is specifically required and if Christ is acting 'in the service of God' who is totally opposed to sin, then sinners are in trouble. The turning away of wrath is very much in place in a situation which can be described in these terms.

THE PROPITIATION FOR OUR SINS

The noun 'propitiation', *hilasmos*, is found twice in the New Testament, both in 1 John. The first passage assures the reader that 'we have one who speaks to the Father in our defence – Jesus Christ, the Righteous One. He is the atoning sacrifice for our sins' (1 Jn. 2:1–2). Here NIV translates *hilasmos* with 'atoning sacrifice', but has a marginal alternative, 'He is the one who turns aside God's wrath'. The other passage says, 'This is love: not that we loved God, but that he loved us and sent his Son as an atoning sacrifice for our sins' (1 Jn. 4:10). Again there is a marginal reading, 'as the one who would turn aside his wrath'. In both passages (as elsewhere) this version's margin recognizes the true meaning of the term.

Scholars like Dodd and the translators of the RSV (who have 'expiation' in both places) reject the idea of the wrath of God here as elsewhere. But as far as I know there is nothing to be added to the case they have made in the earlier passages. If we feel that it has not been made out for those passages, it has not been made out here. And there are some additional objections. The first is context. In the case of 1 John 2:2 even Dodd admits that 'in the immediate context it might seem possible that the sense of "propitiation" is in place'.[8] It seems not only possible but demanded. Christ is described as 'an advocate with the Father' (AV, RSV; NIV has 'one who speaks to the Father in our defence'). If we need this kind of help, then clearly we sinners are in trouble. We are facing the opposition of God against us for the evil we have done, or, as Scripture would put it, the wrath of God. Notice further that Christ is called 'the Righteous One' and that there is a reference to his blood a few verses earlier (in 1:7). We recall that in Romans 3:25, where another 'propitiation' word occurs, there are several references to the righteousness of God in the context and the propitiation is in Christ's blood. Such resemblances strengthen the conviction that this passage too refers to propitiation.

In the case of 1 John 4:10 there is no compelling reason in the context why 'propitiation' should be chosen as the translation, though at least we can say that 'propitiation' is quite suitable. If we accept it we have another of the vivid paradoxes which lead us into a deeper understanding of Christ's atoning work. If we reduce it to 'expiation' the passage is less colourful.

CONCLUSION

From all this it seems clear that the words traditionally understood as 'propitiation' should not be watered down to 'expiation' or the like. They are fully personal words: they have to do with the way a person acts. They tell us of the wrath of a great Person, whereas 'expiation' operates on a sub-personal level. It means no more than the wiping out of a crime or a sin or whatever. It does not take into account the fact that persons are involved.

Suggestions other than 'propitiation' thus give an inferior

[8] C. H. Dodd, *The Johannine Epistles* (London, 1961), p.26.

sense. They overlook the personal factor which is so important with 'propitiation'. In addition they fail to square with the linguistic facts. We have seen that in both the Old Testament and the New there is good reason for understanding the relevant Hebrew and Greek words to mean the putting away of the divine wrath. The Bible is insistent that the wrath of God is the grim reality which the sinner must ultimately face. God is not neutral in the face of evil, but is strongly and personally active in opposition to it.

Probably a good part of the modern objection to the use of the term 'propitiation' arises from the widespread feeling that 'wrath' is not a good word to use about God. He is above our petty angers and what he feels must be so different from human anger that we easily come to think that we should abandon the concept when we talk about God. I for one feel the strong attraction of such a view. Nobody wants to attribute to God the weakness we know so well from human anger.

But such an approach is not fully convincing. What it amounts to is no more than the reminder that we cannot attribute to God an anger like our own. With us anger always involves elements of passion and lack of self-control. We speak of losing our temper and the like. No-one wants to attribute to God the worst elements in human anger.

But whenever we say anything about God there must always be the implied qualification, 'of course, without the defects that we see in people even at their best.' This applies not only to wrath but to everything we say about God. We do not hesitate to speak of the love of God. But can anyone say that that puny thing human love is at best is really what we mean when we speak of God? And is it not the same with goodness, mercy, and indeed every quality which we ascribe to God? The use of a term in human life may well be a guide to the quality in God of which we wish to speak, but in no case can it be said that God exercises the quality with all our human weaknesses.

It is the same with wrath. We know among men a quality which we speak of as 'righteous indignation' and this gives us a glimpse of what a pure and selfless anger might be. It is something like this that is in mind when we speak of 'the wrath of God'. We mean 'wrath without the imperfections that characterize human wrath at its best'. We use the term, not because it is a perfect word, but as Augustine said long ago, 'lest we remain silent'. It is not ideal but it is the best we can do. It expresses the strong and personal opposition to evil that God shows and the alternatives so far suggested do not. We have no better word for the divine repulsion against every evil thing.

This does not mean that we should accept crude ideas about 'anger' and 'propitiation'. It is abundantly clear in the Bible that God cannot be propitiated in the way the pagans held that their deities could be. The God of the Bible is not capricious or arbitrary. He does not impose punishments without reason on bewildered worshippers who must then bribe him back into a good mood with their costly offerings. To argue that we must take propitiation seriously is not to resurrect unacceptable, sub-Christian ideas. It is simply to accept the idea that runs through the Bible, New Testament as well as Old, that God is vigorously opposed to every form of evil. It is to face the implication of that fact, namely that forgiveness of sin must take into account that divine opposition. Why should we think that we can ignore it?

Some find a difficulty in that they see wrath as incompatible with the fact that 'God is love'. They are so sure of the love of God that they say that there can be no such thing as the wrath of God. But this is faulty reasoning. The opposite of love is not wrath. It is hate. We can say that, if God is a God of love, he will not hate those that he has made, but we cannot say that he will never be angry with them. Indeed, the opposite may well be the case. The more he loves the more he will be angry with everything that mars the perfection of the beloved, that is with every sin. God's wrath is identical with God's love. God's wrath is God's love blazing out in fiery indignation against every evil in the beloved.

I am arguing that if there is divine hostility to evil, then this must be taken into account in the process whereby forgiveness is brought about. This does not mean that we must bribe God to be kind. But it does mean that the way in which God brings about our salvation will necessarily take account of God's strong opposition to evil. He will not forgive with an airy wave of the hand. His wrath will be reckoned with.

This is all the more important in that those who reduce our term to no more than 'expiation' rarely face the questions that result. If there is no 'wrath of God', if 'wrath' is the wrong term and there is nothing corresponding to this teaching of Scripture, then the question arises, 'Why should sin be expiated?' And another question, 'What would happen if sin were not expiated?'

And another, 'Would there be any unpleasant consequences?' If there are to be such consequences, yet another question must be faced, 'Would God be active in those consequences?' Unless we are prepared to say that there are no significant consequences of sin, that evil people will always get away with their wrongdoing, that in the end wickedness will triumph, it seems that we are shut up to the view that in the end God will take action to deal with sin and with sinners. Call it what you will, the wrath of God must be included in any serious consideration of the ultimate destiny of the human race.

The impersonal expiation view is up against another difficulty. By taking the personal out of the process of forgiveness it raises the question, 'What is the meaning of an impersonal process in a genuinely theistic universe?' If God made this universe and if he ordered it to run as it does, with sin being punished in one way or another, then God cannot be absolved of responsibility when this happens. If there is a process of putting away sin (expiation), then God must be in that too. We cannot bow God out of his creation. It seems impossible to get rid of the idea that salvation comes about because of God's personal activity. And that means propitiation rather than expiation. It means salvation on personal terms, not the end-product of an impersonal process.

We should also bear in mind that the idea of the wrath of God is a genuinely Christian idea. Some of those who criticize it seem to suggest that it was an idea imported into Christianity from its pagan environment. But this is not the way of it at all. Greek philosophy had long since abandoned the idea that deity could experience anger. Deity, it was held, is passionless, quite without disturbing emotions of any sort. The Christians held on to the idea of the wrath of God in spite of the criticisms that came from their environment. It was not an idea that penetrated their system from that environment and which they were unable to resist.

We should also notice that early Christian writers like 1 Clement and Hermas undoubtedly had the idea of propitiation. They use the verb with the accusative of the Deity and in the sense 'propitiate'. With this construction there is no possible doubt. I have been arguing that there is continuity of meaning, that there is the wrath of God and a forgiveness that takes account of it in both the Old Testament and the New and this, of course, goes on into the early church. But if those who hold that the Septuagint translators and the New Testament writers worked out a new meaning for the word-group are correct, then nobody understood them until our own day. Their new understanding perished with them. We do not find it in the literature of the early church or anywhere else until our own day. It is a big claim that every Christian generation but our own has failed to understand this not unimportant piece of biblical teaching.

It is difficult to resist the impression that the claim arises basically from the outlook of our generation. We do not like the concept of the wrath of God and we are happy to accept an argument that enables us to get rid of it. But the wrath of God is real and the writers of the New Testament books no less than the Old make this clear. We must reckon with that wrath. Unpalatable though it may be, *our* sins, *my* sins, are the object of that wrath. If we are taking our Bible seriously we must realize that every sin is displeasing to God and that unless something is done about the evil we have committed we face ultimately nothing less than the divine anger. God has given us every opportunity, but we have sinned. His wrath is the consequence.

But, of course, the important teaching at which we have been looking in this chapter is that the divine wrath is not the last word. Part of what Christ did on the cross was propitiation, the taking of such action that that wrath no longer works against us. He has made the offering that turns away wrath and as we put our trust in him we need fear it no more. This means a wonderful assurance of peace for the Christian. In the end we have nothing to fear, for 'he is the propitiation for our sins'.

For further study

1. Make a summary of Old Testament passages you know which refer to the divine anger. (Use a concordance if necessary.) Notice what it is that causes this anger.
2. What do you see as the meaning of 'the wrath of God'?
3. Where can you find the idea of God's wrath in the New Testament? In the concordance, look up 'wrath', 'anger', 'punish', *etc.*) What conclusions do you draw from this?
4. How does the concept of propitiation help us to see the meaning of the cross?
5. Carefully trace Paul's argument in Romans 1–3. Notice how it requires us to see that there is a divine wrath against sin with which Christ deals in his atoning work.

8
Justification

Justification has been the subject of a good deal of attention from Christian thinkers, especially from the Reformation period onwards. But these days it is more common to have people get excited about the place of justification than to give careful attention to its meaning. For some it is the be-all and the end-all of Christian salvation. Understand justification and you understand everything that matters. For others it is an irritating piece of legalism. It takes attention away from the personal categories that mean so much in the New Testament and reduces us to a discussion of hair-splitting legal quibbles. We would be better without it. There are, of course, all sorts of gradations in between. But, like it or not, it is an important biblical topic, especially in the Pauline writings.

The position is complicated by the fact that, where in English we have two word-groups to express the concepts of 'justice' and 'righteousness' (which seem to us quite different ideas), in Hebrew and in Greek and for that matter in a number of other languages the one word does duty for both concepts. This means that if we are to study justification we must include some notice of the righteousness words as well. This entails a lot of work, for the New Testament has ninety-two examples of the noun *dikaiosynē* ('justice' or 'righteousness'), thirty-nine of the verb *dikaioō* ('justify' or 'reckon as righteous'), ten of the noun *dikaiōma* (concrete expression of the root idea – 'ordinance' or 'sentence of justification'), eighty-one of the adjective *dikaios* ('just' or 'righteous'), and five of the adverb *dikaiōs* ('justly' or 'righteously'). A good deal of this will in the end be found to have little bearing on our understanding of the atonement, but the number

177

of passages to be looked at is impressive. There cannot be any doubt but that this category is deserving of the most serious study.

THE ATTITUDE TO LAW

Nor can we confine ourselves to the vocabulary of justification. I have pointed out that justification is a legal term and this means that we must take notice of the way people viewed law in Bible times, for this is the context in which justification is set. In those days and in those places people did not look at law in quite the same way as we do. With us 'legalism' is a dirty word. We do not like what we see as excessive concentration on legal niceties of no great significance. We firmly believe that experts in legal matters can find all sorts of loopholes in the law to benefit themselves, but also all sorts of restrictions which the law provides to bind other people. We do not like it and we tend to become suspicious of any emphasis on law. If in a discussion we can fasten the label 'legalist' on our opponent we are home and dry. No-one these days is going to take notice of a legalist.

But we should not read this attitude back into the thinking of people in antiquity. For the men of the Bible law held a special place. They kept using legal terms in ways that we find strange. This probably arises from the fact that they were so used to oppression and tyranny. Everyone knew that there was one law for the rich and another for the poor. Indeed, this was sometimes written into the statutes. There is a well-known law code of Babylon called 'The Code of Hammurabi' (*c.* 1792-1750 BC) which provides for punishment for a variety of offences. Take as an example these three sections dealing with an identical offence, the differences being in the offender and his victim:

> If a citizen has struck the cheek of his superior, he shall receive in the council sixty strokes with a thong.
> If one of citizen status has struck the cheek of his equal, he shall pay one mina of silver.
> If a vassal has struck the cheek of a fellow vassal, he shall pay ten shekels of silver.[1]

The immediately preceding regulations provide that, if a citizen

[1] Cited from D. Winton Thomas (ed.), *Documents from Old Testament Times* (London, 1958), p.34.

knocked out the tooth of a fellow citizen, his own tooth be knocked out. But if it was only a vassal's tooth it is sufficient for him to pay a third of a mina of silver. W. J. Martin thinks it likely that the provisions of this code were not carried out in practice, but that they remained as the ideal.[2] If this was the ideal, then in practice there must have been a very great deal of injustice indeed.

Over against this kind of practice the observance of strict justice was a consummation devoutly to be wished. A firm administration of even-handed justice looked to people in that situation very much like mercy does to us. We tend to be critical of a regulation like 'life for life, eye for eye, tooth for tooth, hand for hand, foot for foot' (Dt. 19:21). But to the people of the day this must have seemed a wonderful advance. It meant that the wealthy and the powerful could not get away with crimes against the lowly. They must be punished with strict justice in exact proportion to the crimes they had committed, no matter against whom. And for poor and friendless sinners it meant that punishment should not be excessive. No more than an eye was to be exacted for an eye, or a tooth for a tooth. Strict justice was important. Especially was justice looked for in kings. It is worthy of notice, for example, that David practised justice and judgment (2 Sa. 8:15).

It is not surprising that people who thought like this did not hesitate to use legal terms when writing about their God. Abraham's question is recorded, 'Will not the Judge of all the earth do right [or 'do justice']?' (Gn. 18:25). Here God is addressed with the legal title 'Judge', and in that capacity he is relied upon to act rightly (or with justice). A similar way of thinking underlies many statements about God in the Old Testament.

GOD WORKS BY LAW

It fits this way of looking at life that God is seen to work by the method of law. 'Even the stork in the sky knows her appointed seasons, and the dove, the swift and the thrush observe the time of their migration. But my people do not know the requirements of the LORD' (Je. 8:7). The word translated 'requirements' is the plural of *mishpāt*, the normal Hebrew term for 'judgment'. It is a legal term. If we translate it as 'requirements' we should under-

---

[2] *Ibid.*, p.28.

stand this in the sense 'legal requirements'. God works by the way of law. Just as he has put into the birds a 'law' that covers their migrations, so he has provided laws for his people. In both he is concerned for law.

The Old Testament writers often prefer legal to any other imagery when they are referring to what God does. His delivering of Israel from Egypt might easily have been described as a defeat of Pharaoh or as a work of power, and it sometimes is. But it is also an act of justice. God says, 'I will lay my hand on Egypt and with mighty acts of judgment I will bring out my divisions, my people the Israelites' (Ex. 7:4; so also 6:6). What God did was certainly a series of powerful acts, too powerful for the mighty Egyptians to counter or ward off. But the sacred writer sees them as 'judgments'. It was 'just' that God should smite the Egyptians and deliver the oppressed Israelites. When God struck down the first-born he was bringing 'judgment' (Ex. 12:12; Nu. 33:4).

Another well-known example of this way of thinking occurs in the Song of Deborah, when that redoubtable woman called the mighty deliverance of God 'the righteous acts of the LORD' (Jdg. 5:11). God's deliverance of his people was not arbitrary. It was right that he should overthrow the oppressor. But the same attitude meant that Israel had no immunity. The punishment of this nation was also a matter of executing judgment (Ezk. 5:8,10; 'punishment' in NIV in both verses is the translation of *sh^ephātîm*, 'judgments').

This love for legal imagery comes out again and again when the Israelites spoke of the acts of God. There is a tremendous judgment-scene in Micah where God is depicted as the counsel for the prosecution (or perhaps as the initiator of a civil action): 'Stand up, plead your case before the mountains; let the hills hear what you have to say. Hear, O mountains, the LORD's accusation; listen, you everlasting foundations of the earth. For the LORD has a case against his people; he is lodging a charge against Israel' (Mi. 6:1–2). Legal terms abound. The mountains are pictured as assessors or as a jury before whom the case will be heard. God sets forth his complaint in the accepted legal fashion.

There is a similar invitation to the nations generally: 'Let them come forward and speak; let us meet together at the place of judgment' (Is. 41:1). Or again, '"Present your case," says the LORD. "Set forth your arguments," says Jacob's King' (Is. 41:21). Or the prophet may wish to affirm his confidence and he may do this in legal language: 'He who vindicates me is near. Who then will bring charges against me? Let us face each other! Who is my accuser?' (Is. 50:8). The LORD's complaint against 'the nations' and against 'all mankind' is put in legal terms (Je. 25:31) and there are many passages like, 'The LORD takes his place in court; he rises to judge the people. The LORD enters into judgment against the elders and leaders of his people' (Is. 3:13).

This list is quite long enough, but the material is by no means exhausted. We should not think that the use of legal categories with respect to God is no more than occasional and that it is more or less accidental. It is frequent, so frequent indeed that it is plain that it corresponds to something deep-seated in Hebrew thinking. Law and the LORD went together. Law is congenial to God and it must be to his people.

THE LAWS OF GOD

It should not surprise us, then, that the actual laws given in the Old Testament are often associated with God. The great word for 'law' in the Old Testament is *tôrah*. Modern scholars usually see the fundamental idea conveyed by the word as 'instruction'. They may well be right, all the more so as the term is used of the instruction the priests give. Thus Malachi lays it down that 'the lips of a priest ought to preserve knowledge, and from his mouth men should seek instruction' (Mal. 2:7). Again we read, 'the teaching of the law by the priest will not be lost, nor will counsel from the wise, nor the word from the prophets' (Je. 18:18). But *tôrah* is frequently used of 'law' in our sense of the term, as when we read, 'The same law applies to the native-born and to the alien living among you' (Ex. 12:49).

The interesting thing for our present inquiry is that either way *tôrah* is constantly associated with the LORD. It is said to be 'the law of Yahweh' or 'his law' or, if God is speaking, 'my law'. In prayer one may say 'thy law'. Sixteen times we read of 'the law of Moses' which amounts to much the same thing. No-one held that Moses originated the law; he simply passed on what God said to him (*e.g.* Ex. 20:1–17). As for the priestly *tôrah*, this too came from God, as we see from some words in Hosea, 'Because you have rejected knowledge, I also reject you as my priests; because you have ignored the *tôrah* of your God...' (Ho. 4:6). Constantly *tôrah* is associated with God. The word occurs 220 times in the Old Testament and there seem to be no more than seventeen occasions when it is clear that it is not God's *tôrah* that is in mind.

This phenomenon is repeated with other law words. There are a couple of words for 'statute'; *hōq*, which is linked with the LORD in eighty-seven of its 127 occurrences, and *huqqah* which is so linked in no less than ninety-six cases out of one hundred and four. The term *mishpāt* is the usual term for 'judgment', but it may also be used in the sense 'law'; it is usually in the plural when used in this sense. The word is linked with Yahweh about 180 times and it agrees with this that the participle of the corresponding verb is used to refer to God as 'Judge'. In this or in some other way the verb is used of God over sixty times.

The list could be continued with other law terms, but there is scarcely the need. Enough has been cited to show that the Old Testament writers did not regard law as a burdensome requirement, devised by human ingenuity to make life difficult. Rather it was the wise provision of a loving God to ensure that his people had the guidance they needed to enable them to live well-adjusted lives, lives pleasing to God and which fulfilled the best purposes for men.

In an earlier chapter we saw that covenant was a dominant concept among the Hebrews. It should not be overlooked that covenant is another legal term. A covenant was a legal document. The centrality of the covenant puts law in an important place. Qualities like goodwill (even love) and loyalty were looked for in those who made covenants, but this should not blind us to the fact that a covenant was not an informal expression of goodwill. A covenant was essentially a legal arrangement. This is illustrated by what Joshua did when he brought the people into Canaan: 'Joshua made a covenant for the people, and there at Shechem he drew up for them decrees and laws' (Jos. 24:25). Or again, of the covenant God made with Abraham we read, 'He confirmed it to Jacob as a decree, to Israel as an everlasting covenant' (Ps. 105:10). The parallelism makes 'decree' (or 'law', *hōq*) very close in meaning to covenant.

All this shows plainly that the Old Testament writers delighted to apply legal categories to the working of God. We cannot say that this is confined to a few writers or a small section of the Old Testament. It is widespread, indeed practically universal. This has important consequences for our understanding of Hebrew religion. Israel's neighbours appear to have had no such conception. Their gods were capricious beings who might act in bewildering ways. They were completely unpredictable. But the linking of law with God delivered the Israelites from such moral and religious chaos. It was not that they thought of law as hanging over God in some way, as something to which he must submit. Such an idea is nonsense. God is superior to everyone and everything. Rather law was seen to be, so to speak, part of God. It was the way he worked. God is essentially righteous. He is just. He may be relied upon. He will always act in accordance with justice.

It is important to bear all this in mind as we approach the subject of justification. Justification is not to be viewed as an isolated topic which is to be studied as a self-contained concept. It belongs to a whole way of viewing God and the acts of God. If a God like the God depicted in the Old Testament is to save men, then he will do so in a way that is right, a way which takes due notice of the place of law and justice. We cannot dismiss the New Testament references to justification as so much superficial legalism which may be discarded without loss. The use of legal categories in the Old Testament as a means of setting forth religious truth, followed up as it is in the New Testament with its references to justification, means that we must take with full seriousness the legal way of setting forth what God has done to bring salvation to his people.

THE MEANING OF JUSTIFICATION

In the light of our examination so far it should not surprise us that righteousness, as the Old Testament writers understand it, is closely connected with justice. Indeed the one word does duty for the two conceptions. Traditional education in the modern English-speaking world perhaps makes it more difficult for us to grasp this. Much of our understanding is derived from the classics, and in the classical Greek writers righteousness is an ethical virtue. Something like this may, of course, on occasion appear among the Hebrews. The man who had right standing with God will always have a deep concern for ethical uprightness and the Hebrews might express this with the righteousness terminology. But it still remains that for them the basic meaning of these words is legal rather than ethical. Long ago J. Skinner wrote, 'the forensic element preponderates' in the Old Testament idea of righteousness and he went on to explain:

what is meant is that questions of right and wrong were habitually regarded from a legal point of view as matters to be settled by a judge, and that this point of view is emphasized in the words derived from *tsdq*. This, indeed, is characteristic of the Heb. conception of righteousness in all its developments: whether it be a moral quality or a religious status, it is apt to be looked on as in itself controvertible and incomplete until it has been confirmed by what is equivalent to a judicial sentence.[3]

It is conformity to the law of God that is in mind, not conformity to an ethical norm. It is a religious, not an ethical term.

The legal basis is plain in such a passage as Isaiah 5:22–23, though our translations do not always reflect this. NIV has it that the prophet says: 'Woe to those who are heroes at drinking wine and champions at mixing drinks, who acquit the guilty for a bribe, but deny justice to the innocent.' The words rendered 'deny justice to the innocent' more literally mean 'take away the righteousness of the righteous from him' (as AV). Now it is not possible to take away righteousness in the ethical sense. If a man is ethically righteous he is ethically righteous, no matter what corrupt judges do. What Isaiah is saying is that certain judges who are mighty drinkers refuse to give the verdict according to justice. They take away the 'right-standing' from the man who has justice on his side; they rob him of the acquittal to which he is entitled.

Similarly to justify the wicked and to condemn the just are both abominable to the LORD (Pr. 17:15); the one is the wrong conferring of a status, the other the wrong removal of a status. The procedure that ought in justice to be followed is given: 'When men have a dispute, they are to take it to the court and the judges will decide the case, acquitting the innocent and condemning the guilty' (Dt. 25:1). The verb translated 'acquitting' could be rendered 'they will justify'. In this verse justification and condemnation are set over against one another as contrasting legal terms. Justification means much what we mean by 'acquittal' (which is the basis of the translation in NIV). We see the legal basis again when we read in Isaiah, 'Let them bring in their witnesses to prove they were right ['that they may be justified',

[3] In James Hastings (ed.), *A Dictionary of the Bible*, vol.iv (Edinburgh, 1904), p.273.

RV]' (Is. 43:9). The ground of the justification is the bringing forward of witnesses to establish the legal proof.

Many passages could be cited. The legal basis of justification is clear. This is not to minimize the importance of passages in which the word-group is used in a non-legal way. There are many such. The situation is not unlike the way we use the English word 'judge'. Both the noun and the verb are used for a wide variety of non-legal activities. But that does not alter the fact that 'judge' is a legal term, nor that it is the legal use that gives us the clue to all the other uses. What I am saying is that, while 'justify', 'justification' and the like may well be used in a variety of ways, including the ethical, the basic meaning is legal and it is the legal that gives us the clue to all the other uses.

Take, for example, the prayer of the Psalmist: 'Do not bring your servant into judgment, for no-one living is righteous [=will be justified] before you' (Ps. 143:2). The writer is facing the important question: 'How can sinful man be accepted by a just God?' The Psalmist recognizes his limitations, his sheer inability to reach the standard God requires of him. He looks for mercy (verse 1), he relies on God's 'unfailing love' (verse 8). And in the verse in which we are primarily interested he puts his plea in legal terms. He asks that he be not involved in a lawsuit with God, for he knows that he has no way of getting the verdict in such a lawsuit. Clearly he is not thinking of a literal lawsuit, but he uses the legal metaphor as a way of bringing out his deep conviction of his unworthiness. And this, he says, applies not only to him. No-one on earth will ever be accepted before God on the ground of his merits. We are all sinners and our sins prevent us from ever being justified in God's sight.

THE JUSTIFICATION OF GOD

Now and then there is a striking use of the terminology when it is God who is said to be justified. There is the well-known prayer in which the Psalmist addresses his Maker in these terms: 'you are proved right when you speak and justified when you judge' (Ps. 51:4). There is no question of anyone putting God on trial. But the Psalmist can use the imagery of the lawcourt to make his point. When anyone is acquitted in a court of law he is shown to have right on his side. So whenever God engages in judgment one result is that he is invariably shown to be in the right. He is 'proved right'; he is 'justified'. There is no question here of the verb having a meaning like 'make righteous', as some suggest. It cannot have such a meaning in this passage. The process of judgment shows that God is just, or perhaps is a vivid declaration that he is just.

The same essential meaning of 'justify' is seen elsewhere, as when Elihu accused Job of 'justifying himself rather than God' (Jb. 32:2). His complaint was not that Job had in some way 'made' himself righteous instead of making God righteous. Rather he is complaining that, whereas Job should have been concerned to declare that God is righteous, to show that God is just, he had instead been preoccupied with showing that he himself was just. Whether Job or God is the object of the verb the context makes it clear that it is a declaratory process that is in mind.

God's activity as judge and his character as just are often before us. 'The heavens proclaim his righteousness, for God himself is judge' (Ps. 50:6); the LORD 'comes, he comes to judge the earth. He will judge the world in righteousness and the peoples in his truth' (Ps. 96:13). In an interesting linking of legal terms 'the LORD Almighty will be exalted by his justice (*mishpāt*), and the holy God will show himself holy by his righteousness (*ts^edāqah*)' (Is. 5:16). The two legal terms are joined with holiness in an impressive statement about the character of God. For our present purpose the significant thing is that, even when speaking about the divine holiness, it was quite natural for the prophet to express his meaning in legal terms.

RIGHTEOUSNESS AND SALVATION

A further feature of this terminology is the way it is linked with salvation. It is a just, a righteous thing with God that he bring salvation. The Psalmist can sing, 'The LORD has made his salvation known and revealed his righteousness to the nations' (Ps. 98:2), where the parallelism makes 'salvation' and 'righteousness' very close in meaning. The Psalmist is speaking about essentially the same thing in both parts of the verse, but he brings it out in two different ways. God's righteousness may well be exercised (and recognized) in his delivering of his people. So is it when the LORD says, 'my salvation will last for ever, my righteousness will never fail' (Is. 51:6). Or when the Psalmist prays, 'My mouth will tell of your righteousness, of your salvation all day long' (Ps. 71:15).

We may fairly infer from such passages (and there are many of them) that righteousness and salvation go together. Where there is true righteousness, salvation follows. It would not be going too far to say that in one aspect God's righteousness brings salvation. We may also infer that salvation, as the Bible writers understand it, is right and just. They do not see God as delivering his people quite apart from moral considerations. The gods of the heathen might be thought of by their worshippers as mighty deliverers who would rescue their devotees quite irrespective of their moral worth. But for Israel God is just. When he delivers the people it is because it is just and right that he should do so. If they continue in sin they can look for no deliverance, only punishment. But when they are fulfilling their role as the people of God they can confidently look to God to save them.

This is not the way the terminology is used in the New Testament. There we have the thought that God saves sinners. In the Old Testament the righteousness terminology is not used to bring out this thought. The two do not contradict one another. It is a question of terminology. And the fact is that in the Old Testament the righteousness terminology is used of the way God delivers his people, not of the salvation of sinners. That is expressed rather by terms like 'mercy'.

An important idea in the New Testament is that righteousness may be imputed. There are grounds for imputation in an Old Testament passage, that in which we read, 'Abram believed the LORD, and he credited it to him as righteousness' (Gn. 15:6). This presents a problem to some modern people, because we so firmly believe that righteousness is an ethical quality. It is 'being good'. In that sense it is nonsense to talk about righteousness being imputed. Everyone who aspires to this kind of righteousness must merit it for himself, by right living. It cannot be 'credited' or 'reckoned' or 'imputed' to him other than in some fictitious and fanciful sense. But when we see righteousness as basically legal, as 'right-standing', it is another matter. A standing or status can be conferred. The narrative says that God conferred this status on Abraham because of his faith. Paul uses this as his classic example of justification by faith. Abraham received his 'right-standing' not on account of any meritorious action but simply because he trusted God.

Phinehas was another to whom righteousness was imputed: 'Phinehas stood up and intervened, and the plague was checked. This was credited to him as righteousness for endless generations to come' (Ps. 106:30–31). There is this difference from Abraham,

187

nehas performed a rather vigorous action, namely the
f the two chief sinners at Baal-Peor (Nu. 25:6–8). He can
be cited as a convincing example of righteousness on the
grounds of faith alone. But his attitude was not unimportant and
he was commended on the grounds of his zeal for the LORD's
honour (Nu. 25:11).

MERCY AND TRUST

Those who read the New Testament can scarcely refer to justification without adding 'by faith'. This has become one of the
great doctrines which Christians discuss endlessly. As far as the
terminology goes it is a New Testament doctrine. We never find
it explicitly set forth in the Old Testament. But that does not
mean that in those days God saved people by a different method.
The way of expressing it is different, but the basic thought is the
same. It is just as clear in the Old Testament as it is in the New
that people are accepted by God because of his forgiving grace
and mercy. They are exhorted to godly living, but it is God's
mercy that is decisive. A great passage in Isaiah makes it clear
that God's good gift is not earned by human merit: 'Come, all
you who are thirsty, come to the waters; and you who have no
money, come, buy and eat! Come, buy wine and milk without
money and without cost' (Is. 55:1). The prophet goes on to an
exhortation, 'Seek the LORD while he may be found; call on him
while he is near. Let the wicked forsake his way and the evil man
his thoughts. Let him turn to the LORD, and he will have mercy
on him, and to our God, for he will freely pardon' (Is. 55:6–7).
Such a passage makes it very plain that the sinner may look to
God for mercy and salvation. Salvation comes by God's grace.
This conviction is widespread.

Thus Micah exults in God's forgiveness: 'Who is a God like
you, who pardons sin and forgives the transgression of the
remnant of his inheritance? You do not stay angry for ever but
delight to show mercy. You will again have compassion on us;
you will tread our sins underfoot and hurl all our iniquities into
the depths of the sea' (Mi. 7:18–19). There is no room for human
merit in such a view of forgiveness. And when Micah goes on to
say, 'You will be true to Jacob, and show mercy to Abraham, as
you pledged on oath to our fathers in days long ago' (verse 20), he
is taking us back to the days of the patriarchs as one who would
say, 'God has always dealt with men in mercy. We may rely on

188

him who showed mercy to Jacob and to Abraham.' A very moving expression of trust comes from the aftermath of the destruction of Jerusalem: 'Because of the LORD's great love we are not consumed, for his compassions never fail. They are new every morning; great is your faithfulness' (La. 3:22–23). The pious man of the Old Testament could rely on God's compassion even in the ruins of his beloved city.

The Old Testament says little in set terms about faith. There is the well-known passage in Habakkuk, 'the righteous will live by his faith' (Hab. 2:4). Most recent scholars emphasize that the Hebrew here means faithfulness rather than faith. They see it as indicating the man who can be relied on rather than the one who relies. Let us grant the point. But it still remains that for the prophet (and indeed for the Old Testament saints generally) faithfulness in trying circumstances arises from a trustful reliance on God. The two concepts are not really far apart. Habakkuk is certainly not envisaging a self-made man, proud in his self-reliance. He is speaking of one who walks humbly with God.

This thought is explicit in the frequent references to trust. If 'faith' is not a common Old Testament word, 'trust' is and the two are not so very different in meaning. 'I trust in your unfailing love; my heart rejoices in your salvation' (Ps. 13:5). So again, 'Surely God is my salvation; I will trust and not be afraid. The LORD, the LORD, is my strength and my song; he has become my salvation' (Is. 12:2). Or consider these words of comfort: 'You will keep in perfect peace him whose mind is steadfast, because he trusts in you. Trust in the LORD for ever, for the LORD, the LORD, is the Rock eternal' (Is. 26:3–4). It would not be difficult to compile a lengthy list of such passages, for trust in God is one of the leading Old Testament ideas.

Sometimes the trust words are linked with the righteousness words. Thus the Psalmist exhorts his readers: 'Commit your way to the LORD; trust in him and he will do this: He will make your righteousness shine like the dawn...' (Ps. 37:5–6). We have just noticed the 'trust' saying in Isaiah 26:3–4; it is worth adding that these words are introduced with 'Open the gates that the righteous nation may enter, the nation that keeps faith' (verse 2). Again, 'Those who trust in the LORD' appear to be identical with 'the righteous' to whom the land is allotted (Ps. 125:1, 3). Negatively, the man who 'trusts in his righteousness' will be in great trouble (Ezk. 33:13).

From all this it is clear that in the Old Testament period it was made quite plain that people must trust in God. The way of acceptance depends on his saving activity and the attitude for which he looks is one of trustful dependence. While the actual expression 'justification by faith' does not occur in the Old Testament, the essential doctrine is there. God saves people. They do not save themselves. And the attitude they should bring is faith (or trust). They did not know the terminology of the New Testament, but they did know that trustful reliance on God is the essence of the matter.

JUSTIFICATION IN JUDAISM

In the rabbinic writings it is everywhere assumed that men are accepted before God on the grounds of their merit. The legal language we have seen in the Old Testament is often used to express this conviction. It is God's judgment that determines whether a man is righteous or not, but there are various ways in which this judgment is manifested. A number of times it is said that God judges the world four times a year: at Passover there is judgment in respect of produce, at Pentecost of fruit, at Tabernacles of rain, while at New Year God weighs men's merits and assigns rewards and punishments. They then have until the Day of Atonement (a period of ten days) to repent of their sins; if they have not done so by then, God's decree becomes unalterable.

God appears to be bound by these decrees and there are some extraordinary provisions to meet cases where he would prefer not to be. Thus if the nation was adjudged wicked at New Year's Day and allotted scanty rain as a result, but repented after the Day of Atonement, there was a problem. God's decree could not be altered. But could God withhold blessing from his penitent people? The Rabbis did not see this as a possibility. They taught that in this case God so arranged things that the scanty rain fell at the best time and on the places that needed it, so that it did maximum good. On the other hand if the people were adjudged righteous on New Year's Day and had good rain allotted to them, but subsequently backslid, then God saw to it that the abundant rain fell at the wrong time and on barren land (Rosh Hashanah, 17b).

But it is final judgment at the end of the world that is most significant. There are many references to this judgment and it is clear that among the Rabbis it was accepted without question that men will be judged on the basis of their deeds: if a man has done good he will enter Paradise, but if his deeds were evil Gehenna awaits him. We might cite some words from R. Eliezer:

> When R. Eliezer fell ill, his disciples went in to visit him. They said to him: Master, teach us the paths of life so that we may through them win the life of the future world. He said to them: Be solicitous for the honour of your colleagues, and keep your children from meditation, and set them between the knees of scholars, and when you pray know before whom you are standing and in this way you will win the future world.
>
> (Berakoth 28b)

This Rabbi is dated around the end of the first century and the beginning of the second, so he is not far from the New Testament period. The attitude of the man and of his students shows plainly that it was not doubted that the way of acceptance with God was the way of human merit. There might be dispute about the way merit was accumulated, but that this was what was required was not in doubt.

Every deed meant a certain quota of merit or demerit. Judgment day saw a weighing of the merits and demerits and often the imagery of the balances is employed. When the good deeds outweighed the bad the man was righteous and when the bad were too heavy the man was wicked and went to Gehenna. What happened when the scales were evenly balanced? The learned were not agreed. R. Eliezer (or perhaps R. Eleazar) maintained that God then pressed down the merit side of the scales in accordance with Micah 7:19, 'he will press down our iniquities' (this is not the way our translations run, but it is a possible understanding of the Hebrew). But R. Jose b. Hanina taught that God raised the demerit side of the scales, for which he quoted as scriptural support Micah 7:18, 'raising iniquity' (Rosh Hashanah 17a). It is easy to get lost in the wonders of this learned debate and overlook the fact that is significant for our inquiry, namely that both sides accepted without question that to be righteous meant to get the verdict on judgment day, just as to be wicked meant to miss it. Clearly for such scholars 'righteous' is a legal term and the obtaining of the verdict on the day of judgment was all-important.

One consequence of this whole system was the impossibility of assurance. Nobody knows how much weight is attached to any good deed or bad deed and thus nobody can know whether his celestial account is in credit or in debit. The great Hillel said, 'trust not in thyself until the day of thy death' (Aboth 2:5). One may be in good standing at this moment, but who can tell what sin one will subsequently commit and what weight of demerit it will carry? When R. Johanan b. Zakkai was on his deathbed his disciples came to visit him and they were distressed because he began to weep. They asked why this was and he replied, 'when there are two ways before me, one leading to Paradise and the other to Gehinnom, and I do not know by which I shall be taken, shall I not weep?' (Berakoth 28b). He was simply taking seriously the creed by which he had lived. To be righteous was not to have attained certain known ethical standards but to get the verdict before God. And R. Johanan had no idea whether he had lived well enough to get the verdict or not.

The Rabbis built their teaching on the Old Testament. We may fairly comment that at many points they misinterpreted it and in particular that they did so at this point of overestimating the saving power of human effort. But for our present purpose the important thing is their terminology. They certainly carried on and developed the Old Testament legal use of terms like 'righteousness' and 'justification'. They helped establish the way these words were used by the New Testament writers.

JUSTIFICATION IN THE NEW TESTAMENT

Some have gone astray in their understanding of the New Testament teaching on justification because they have ignored the Old Testament and rabbinic background. Assuming that 'righteous', 'righteousness' and the like have the meanings we commonly give them, they have not uncommonly gone on to see justification as a process whereby men are rescued from their sin by being 'made righteous'. It is, of course, true that all Christians understand salvation in part as making people righteous. But it does not follow that the justification terminology is used to express this aspect of Christ's saving work.

What I am contending is that righteousness, justification and the associated words are to be understood from the way they are employed in the Old Testament and developed in the usage of the Rabbis. G. Schrenk emphasizes the difference from the Greek approach, 'There is a deep gulf between the NT *dikaios* and the Greek ideal of virtue, which isolates man in independent achievement'; 'In content, *dikaios* in the NT is very largely determined by the OT.'[4] The first Christians were Jews and took a good deal of their terminology from accepted Jewish usage. Immersed in the teaching of the Old Testament from their earliest years as they were, and accustomed to the way the Rabbis used concepts like righteousness, we should expect nothing else. Specifically they started from the Old Testament with its legal understanding of righteousness, a usage accepted without question among their contemporaries. They rejected the particular way in which the Rabbis saw people as justified, the way of human merit, but they retained a good deal of the terminology. They were familiar with the concept of judgment day, a day when all people will be tried before God with the result that some will be adjudged righteous (*i.e.* be justified) and others condemned.

I am not arguing that every occurrence of the 'righteousness' terminology in the New Testament is of this kind. There are passages in which the words are used in much the normal Greek way. For example, both Pilate's wife and the centurion at the cross refer to Jesus as 'righteous' (Mt. 27:19, where NIV translates 'innocent', and Lk. 23:47). Pilate himself calls Jesus 'righteous', according to many manuscripts (Mt. 27:24). But these are all Romans and we should not expect them to use the words in the typical Hebrew way. The early Christians were another matter, and they preferred to follow the Old Testament and Jesus himself.

We see the way Jesus used the terminology when he spoke about what will happen on judgment day. 'I tell you that men will have to give account on the day of judgment for every careless word they have spoken. For by your words you will be acquitted, and by your words you will be condemned' (Mt. 12:36–37). Justification (= acquittal) and condemnation are seen to reflect the judicial process. It is a question of getting the verdict when tried before God.

Another good example is in the passage in which Jesus refers to the judgment that will take place when he comes 'in his glory, and all the angels with him'. Then 'he will sit on his throne in heavenly glory' and judge the nations, putting some people on his right (for acceptance) and some on his left (for condemnation) (Mt. 25:31–33). Those who thus get the verdict are called 'righteous' and the culmination is expressed in these terms:

[4] G. Kitel (ed.), *Theological Dictionary of the New Testament*, vol. ii (Grand Rapids, 1964), pp.187, 188.

'Then they [*i.e.* the wicked] will go away to eternal punishment,
but the righteous to eternal life' (Mt. 25:46). Quite clearly the
'righteous' in this passage are those who get the verdict, those
who have 'right-standing' when tried before God.

The same kind of usage is found in the Pauline writings. Thus
the apostle writes, 'through the obedience of the one man the
many will be made righteous' (Rom. 5:19). The many 'righteous'
are obviously the multitude of the saved, those accepted by God.
And the ground of their acceptance is the work of Christ.

The legal thrust of this language is seen from a somewhat
different angle in passages in which the adjective 'righteous' is
applied to God. Thus Paul looks for the crown (the crown, moreover, 'of righteousness') which 'the Lord, the righteous Judge'
will award him on judgment day (2 Tim. 4:8). There are also the
words of the angel, 'You are just in these judgments' (Rev. 16:5).
In both cases it is the activity of judging in which God is seen as
'righteous' or 'just'. One of the very important passages in the
New Testament includes the term, namely when Paul says that
God brought about salvation in Christ 'to demonstrate his justice
[other translations have 'righteousness'] at the present time, so
as to be just and the one who justifies the man who has faith in
Jesus' (Rom. 3:26). The passage has the thoughts of redemption
and of propitiation, but at this point there is strong emphasis on
justification. No explanation is adequate which does not see God
as shown to be just or righteous, legally in the right, in the way in
which he provides salvation for sinners.

This passage uses the noun 'justice' (or 'righteousness') and
the verb 'to justify' as well as the adjective. Paul is emphasizing
the topic of justification, and he is saying that the way God saves
sinful man accords with what is right. God is just, not only in
saving, but in the way he saves. Some commentators have missed
this point. Thus C. Ryder Smith writes, 'To put Paul's meaning
in modern terms, he is saying: "God pleased to make man so that
it was possible for him to sin; He also made man so that every sin
should spread its evil infection through the mass of mankind; we
have just seen the hideous result (Romans i.18–iii.18); God, who
must have foreseen this, would not even be righteous if He did
not find a way to save men from this; He has found such a way by
sending His Son."'[5]

[5] C. Ryder Smith, *The Bible Doctrine of Salvation* (London, 1946), p.218.

Do you see? The question that is worrying Ryder Smith is, 'How could God be righteous if he did not forgive?' But the question that worried Paul was just the opposite, 'How could God be righteous if he *did* forgive?' He has just said that God 'presented him [Christ] as a sacrifice of atonement [the expression means 'propitiation'], through faith in his blood'. He goes on: 'He did this to demonstrate his justice, because in his forbearance he had left the sins committed beforehand unpunished' (Rom. 3:25). Often and often people had sinned. You would expect that a just God would punish them. That is what justice means. Paul is arguing that sinners deserve to be punished for their sins; but in the past God has not invariably punished sin. Sinners have gone on living, just as they were. Now you can argue that this shows God to be merciful, or compassionate, or kind, or forbearing, or loving. But you cannot argue that it shows him to be *just*. Whatever else the absence of punishment of sins shows, it does not show us justice. Because God had not invariably punished sinners, people might be tempted to think that he is not a just God.

Not any more, Paul is saying. The cross demonstrates the righteousness, the justice of God. In the very act by which sin is put away decisively, the death of Christ on the cross, God is seen to be just. It is not the fact that God forgives that shows him to be righteous, but the fact that he forgives in a certain way, the way of the cross. It is the cross that shows God to be righteous in the very act of forgiveness.

Traditionally this has been taken to mean that the cross represents the paying of the penalty of sin. The law has no more claim on those whom Christ saves. Paul does not say this in set terms, but it does seem to be the meaning of his words. After what Christ has done the law has no more claim on those whose trust is in him. What is beyond all doubt is that Paul is saying that God forgives in a way which accords with right. God does not set aside the moral law when he forgives. It can never be said that he forgives simply because he is too strong for the devil. That would mean that in the end with God might is right. The language of justification is a perpetual protest against any such view. It provides an emphasis on the truth that our God is just, is righteous, that he has regard to moral considerations even when he saves people who do not deserve salvation. God saves in a way which is not only powerful but which is right.

On a number of occasions Paul speaks of 'the righteousness of God' and this has caused a good deal of discussion. Some hold that the expression points to a quality in God himself, while others suggest that it means rather 'a righteousness from God' (a meaning which the Greek construction might well have). It seems that in some contexts the former meaning is needed, for example, when Paul asks, 'But if our unrighteousness brings out God's righteousness more clearly, what shall we say?' (Rom. 3:5). Here there can scarcely be doubt that 'righteousness' is a quality of uprightness in God.

But on other occasions the expression signifies the righteousness or 'right-standing' that God gives. Thus Paul writes, 'But now a righteousness from God, apart from law, has been made known, to which the Law and the Prophets testify. This righteousness from God comes through faith in Jesus Christ to all who believe' (Rom. 3:21–22). Once again we see that Paul delights to express the Christian salvation in terms of justice. We see this again when he refers to 'the gift of righteousness' (Rom. 5:17), for in the sense of an ethical virtue righteousness cannot be a gift. Ethical virtues must be earned by moral achievement in daily life. Paul is clearly referring to a legal status, a standing before God. A status can be given and the apostle says that this status *is* given.

Justification then means the according of the status of being in the right. Sin has put us in the wrong with God and justification is the process whereby we are reckoned as right. In one way or another all religions must face the ultimate question: 'How can man, who is a sinner, ever be right with a God who is just?' Most religions answer, in some form, 'By human effort.' Man committed the sin, so man must do what is required to put things right and undo the effects of his sin. It is the great teaching of the New Testament that we are justified, not by what *we* do, but by what Christ has done. Paul puts it simply when he says that we are 'justified by his blood' (Rom. 5:9). He links our justification directly with the death of Jesus.

FAITH

But if Paul can argue strongly that sinners do not obtain right standing before God by their own efforts, he can argue just as strongly that it is necessary that they exercise faith. Thus he contrasts the way the Gentiles entered salvation with the Jews' struggle, a struggle which left them lost, and stresses the place of faith as he does so: 'What then shall we say? That the Gentiles, who did not pursue righteousness, have obtained it, a right-eousness that is by faith; but Israel, who pursued a law of righteousness, has not attained it. Why not? Because they pursued it not by faith but as if it were by works' (Rom. 9:30–32). Faith is the one way into this God-given righteousness. Indeed, in the culmination of what most students hold to be the statement of the thesis of the epistle to the Romans Paul cites the prophet Habakkuk: 'The righteous will live by faith' or perhaps better, 'He that is righteous by faith will live' (Rom. 1:17).

In view of Paul's emphasis on the inability of works of any sort to bring about salvation, it is perhaps unnecessary to labour the point that faith is not being depicted as a different kind of work. Paul is not saying, 'To be saved by works is too hard. So God allows you to produce something easier – faith.' He does not see faith as a merit at all. Rather it is the abandonment of all reliance on merit. Faith is the recognition that there is nothing in the sinner that can avail to bring him salvation. Faith is the casting of oneself wholly on God. Faith is the hand that reaches out to God for salvation. Faith is no more than the means through which salvation is received.

Let me try to illustrate this. In my youth there were Sunday Schools in most churches and each Sunday School normally had an annual picnic. In its way it was the highlight of the year. On one occasion at one such picnic it fell to my lot at the time of the midday meal to move around among the children with a four-gallon can of a cool drink and ladle out portions to the thirsty. I came to a small boy who had evidently had a busy morning. He was red in the face, sweating profusely, obviously quite hot. I would think at that moment he probably had Australia's no.1 thirst. And there I was with four gallons of the reviving liquid and the single desire to get rid of it speedily. Nothing would have given me greater pleasure than to give my young friend all he could drink. But he had no mug. He had no way of receiving what I was offering freely. Fortunately someone was able to come up with the necessary utensil and the lad did not die of thirst in the midst of plenty. But the mug he eventually held out in no way merited the gift. True, it was indispensable. Without it he could not receive the cooling drink. But the mug was no more than the means by which he received it.

Faith is something like that. It is not a merit. It is the means by which we receive the gift. It is the abandonment of all reliance on self, all attempts to achieve salvation by our own endeavours. Faith is the hand stretched out to receive God's good gift, stretched out in the assurance that God will not fail to keep his promises.

JUSTIFICATION AND THE LOVE OF GOD

Some object to the whole concept of justification on the grounds that it does not fit in with the basic idea of the love of God. A God who loves people, it is argued, will not go through all the non-sense of complying with some law before he forgives. It is further argued that the whole idea of justification is unsatisfactory. It rests salvation ultimately in legal categories and yet it involves something like a transfer of penalty, which is legally impossible. So, the argument runs, it is better to abandon the whole concept and concentrate on the fact that God loves us and saves us as the outworking of his love. He has no need of penalty or satisfaction. He simply loves and forgives.

To this a number of things could be said. One is that those who follow the teaching of the New Testament in this matter have often harmed their cause by the way they have argued it. They have stressed the analogy with the kind of law they know and have even used police court analogies. I have heard now and then the illustration of a judge who finds before him a former classmate who has become guilty of a serious crime. Because he is just the judge imposes the full fine demanded by the law. But because he is still a friend he pays the fine himself.

There is this in the illustration that it shows that even on our level it is sometimes possible to combine a sense of justice with the love of friendship. But it overlooks some important truths. One is that our legal systems differentiate between the kind of crime for which a fine is the suitable penalty and those for which imprisonment, in some jurisdictions the death penalty, is laid down. With a fine it does not matter much who pays the money. I have known cases in which a man very much wanted to go to prison so that he could be a martyr for his cause, but who could not because some enemy paid the fine. The requirement of the law is satisfied no matter who pays the fine. When once it is paid there is no more penalty.

But with imprisonment or the death penalty it is another

matter. There no substitution is allowed. It is not only a matter of the penalty being paid; it is important that the right person, the guilty person, pays it. In this matter of sin the penalty is death (Rom. 6:23). This is the kind of penalty which in our legal systems is not transferable. The offender must bear it himself. Our police court analogies break down.

But our salvation is not a matter of conforming to the legal system of some modern country. The law in question is the law of God. Our systems may find no place for the exercise of love and compassion, but God's certainly does. In fact with God love is the very basic thing (1 Jn. 4:8, 16). But God's love does not mean that God's law is set aside. The two work together. And in this matter of justification we must bear in mind that the Saviour is one with the Judge and one also with the condemned. God wills that the penalty be borne, but he wills also to bear it himself. And the sinner is forgiven, but not any old sinner; it is the one who is 'in Christ'. The situation is complex. What the New Testament writers are saying when they use the justification terminology is that our salvation has a legal aspect as well as other aspects. From this point of view it is the payment of penalty, the assurance that the law has no more claim on those whose trust is in Christ.

That justification and love go together is seen in the fact that it is Paul who uses the two concepts most frequently. He is far and away the most frequent user of the term justification. Indeed, there are some who think that justification is a purely Pauline concept. But Paul also puts great emphasis on love. It is not always realized that Paul has more to say about love than has any other New Testament writer. He uses the noun *agapē* seventy-five times, the verb *agapaō* thirty-four times and the adjective *agapētos* twenty-seven times. This makes a total of 136 uses of the three words out of 320 in the New Testament. John is usually thought of as 'the apostle of love', but the three words occur a total of 112 times in the five Johannine writings.

It is the writer who emphasizes the importance of justification who makes most use of the words for love. Why should we think the two are in opposition? Love is surely the mainspring of justification. It is because God loves as he does that he provides the means whereby sinners may be justified.

We should also bear in mind that love does not in fact necessarily make forgiveness easy. Even among us love can complicate the process of forgiveness. Let us suppose that some passing tramp breaks into your home and steals something you value highly. In due course he is arrested. He denies that he robbed you, but his guilt is clear. He is caught with the goods, let us say. There is no doubt whatever.

You say to yourself, 'Perhaps this poor fellow has never had much of a chance in life. I am a Christian. I have been forgiven much and I ought to forgive.' So you forgive him. It is as easy as that.

But suppose that the person who robbed you and lied to you was not a passing tramp, whom you have never seen before and will never see again, but your best friend. Now the way of forgiveness is harder. And the thing that makes it harder, the thing that complicates the situation is just the fact of your love. Your whole being cries out for the restoration of the earlier state of fellowship. With all your heart you want to forgive. But precisely because you love your friend so much the way to the forgiveness you are so ready to offer is not easy. And if instead of your friend the one who robbed you and lied to you was your son, one to whom you owe the duty of showing the best way in life as well as one whom you love with all your heart, then the way of forgiveness may well be very complicated indeed. Love will make forgiveness certain, but it will not make it easy.

So when people suggest that this talk about justification is a needless beclouding of the issue, we can only retort that they have not thought the problem through. When we have the authority of the Bible for the statement that from one point of view the salvation Christ brought about is a process of justification, it is better for us to try to understand what this means than to persuade ourselves that we know a better way. There is no better way than the way God has provided, the way of the cross. In deep humility let us accept what God has done.

Justification is a way of looking at the cross which says chiefly three things to us.

1. Guilt

The first is that before God we are guilty people. Each of the ways of looking at the cross we have seen starts from the premise that people are sinners. Without sin there would be no problem. But there are different ways of looking at sin. Redemption sees it as an enslaving force from which we need to be liberated. Reconciliation makes it the cause of a quarrel. Justification sees it from a legal point of view. Sinners are people who have broken the law of God, and the verdict on them must be 'Guilty'.

2. Penalty

The Bible has a good deal to say about law, the law of God and the like. It sees the sinner as under the divine condemnation. But because of the cross believers have nothing to fear. The requirements of the law have been met. From this point of view the cross represents Christ's receiving of that penalty of sin that was our due. The result is that those who come to Christ receive the gift of 'right-standing' or 'righteousness' before God.

2. Faith

And the third thing is that this justification is not something given indiscriminately to all. It is 'those who are in Christ Jesus' for whom 'there is now no condemnation' (Rom. 8:1). Faith is not simply a desirable adjunct to the Christian way. It is fundamental to that way. It is the indispensable means of receiving God's gift of justification.

Justification reminds us that there is a legal aspect to our salvation. In the last resort the law of God is not swept aside as though it did not matter. It mattered so much that Jesus died to bring salvation in a way that is right (Rom. 3:26). This needs emphasis in a day like ours when many people have lost touch with the moral values we see in the Bible and deny that there are moral absolutes. If all morality is relative, then righteousness has little to do with salvation, and sinners are not really blameworthy. 'To understand all is to forgive all' is the kind of maxim that appeals to our generation.

But it does not square with the New Testament. To understand and to make due allowance is important, but it does not make right what is wrong. The Bible is clear that some things are right and some things are wrong. Those who do not reach God's standards are sinners and deserving of punishment. The Christian way does not become meaningful to us until we see this and recognize ourselves for what we are – sinners who have not attained God's standards, sinners who are 'without hope and without God in the world' (Eph. 2:12). We are in trouble because God really means us to live up to the highest and best we know, not simply to find good excuses for not making it.

But when all the evidence goes to provide a verdict of 'Guilty' on Judgment Day, God intervened. This way of looking at salvation makes the cross indispensable, for it was there that the claims of God's law were fully discharged. God's salvation accords with right. God is just in the means whereby salvation is accomplished.

But the New Testament writers are clear that this salvation does not come to all indiscriminately. Sinners refuse God's good gift, shut themselves up to disobedience, and remain in the group of those on whom the verdict at the end of the day must be 'Guilty'. To be justified we must come in faith, believing, trusting. As we put our trust in Christ and only as we put our trust in him we are justified, for 'a man is justified by faith apart from observing the law' (Rom. 3:28). Justification touches our lives by bringing home to us two great truths. One is that we are saved in a way that is right, for the new and living way does not sit loose to moral realities. The other is that Christ's justifying work is a challenge to us to believe. 'It is with your heart that you believe and are justified.'

For further study

1. Using a concordance, make a list of ways in which the Old Testament writers bring out the 'rightness' or justice of God's actions.
2. What do you see as the basic meaning of justification? Write out your own definition.
3. What can you find out about the way of salvation from the book of Micah?
4. What influence does the Old Testament background have on the meaning of the justification terminology in the New Testament?
5. How does the cross bring about justification?
6. How do you relate faith to justification?

Epilogue

This study has brought before us some of the richness of New Testament teaching about the cross of Christ. We have seen it as the making of a new covenant: it completely superseded the old way and opened up an entirely new way which brings people to God. It means the appearing of a new people of God, an idea which comes out under some of the other figures also. We have seen that Christ's death is a sacrifice, fulfilling what all the old sacrifices hinted at but could not do, and this whether we think of sacrifice in general or of particular sacrifices like the Passover or the Day of Atonement. With the expression 'the Lamb of God' there seems to be a novel way of referring to sacrifice, a way which brings out from an angle peculiar to the Christians the fact that Christ has fulfilled all that sacrifice means. Then there are expressions which point to cleansing from sin, to access to God, to the freedom that the people of God enjoy. Sometimes the thought is that the sin of man had aroused the wrath of God or estranged man from God and there are thoughts of averting the wrath and of bringing about reconciliation. The concept of the law of God is not lacking and we are reminded that Christ saves us in a manner that is right.

There are many facets to the atonement. It may be viewed from any one of a number of angles, each of which brings to us an individual insight into the way of salvation. Some of them emphasize that Christ took our place. We are the sinners. We deserve the punishment. But we do not undergo it. Christ stood in our place and we are free. The New Testament witnesses to a multi-faceted salvation, one which may be regarded in many ways and which is infinitely satisfying. In whatever way our need be viewed, Christ has met it fully.

The great thing about the cross is that God saves us by his grace. We do not merit our salvation, but receive it as a free gift. But every one of the categories at which we looked reminds us that this has implications for the way we Christians are to live. The cross is the making of a new covenant, but this means that we are to live as the people of God. It is the perfect sacrifice, but we are to present our bodies as living sacrifices. If Christ died for us, we are to live for him. He has carried our sins away, as the Day of Atonement reminds us, and won for us access into the presence of God. And this means that we have a great privilege. We must neither neglect it nor use it carelessly. Christ our Passover has been offered for us so that we, the church, constitute the people of God, and so that we should cleanse out every evil thing. Passover warns us against complacency. The Lamb of God brings us back to the thought of the perfect sacrifice with all that that means.

When the New Testament writers use the language of redemption they are bringing before us the important point that a great price has been paid to set us free from evil. We are to live in freedom, a more demanding programme than many of us care to think. Or we can look at the problem of sin from the point of view of the enmity between God and man that it arouses. Reconciliation is a process in which we are not to be passive, even though we do nothing to bring it about. We receive it as a free gift, but this way of looking at the cross reminds us that it must be received. And when Paul thinks of the making of peace between God and man he thinks of the consequent necessity that there be peace between man and man, specifically between Jew and Gentile. There is a divine wrath against every evil thing and when that has been put away by what Christ did we must have a due horror of arousing it again. And in our final study we saw that Christ has won our salvation in a way which is right, a way which takes due account of the law of God. And if we are saved in a way which takes due account of the divine law, it is imperative that we live in a way which takes account of that law.

Each of the ways of looking at the cross then underlines the fact that the way of salvation is not a way of human merit. All is of grace, for all is of God. But also each of the ways of looking at it brings home to us the truth that the new and living way Christ has won for us makes demands on the believer. Christ has given all, including his very life, to open up the new and living way. It is demanded accordingly that we give all for him, so that we enter by that new and living way.

It is important to be clear that an understanding of what the cross means has effects on the way we live. It is easy to get the impression that studies of the atonement belong to some ethereal, far-off world of the academic theologian, interesting as intellectual exercises no doubt, but having nothing to do with the business of living here and now. That is not the way of it at all. I have tried to show in this book that the cross is relevant, that it speaks to our need and challenges us to new adventures of faith. We must not miss the truth the Bible writers are conveying to their readers because they use old-world imagery to convey it. It is easy to stay with the imagery and to dismiss what the writers are saying as old hat, interesting probably in an earlier day, but of no practical use to us in our very different circumstances. When we take the trouble to find out what these ancient writings mean we find that the cross speaks to twentieth-century people just as loudly and just as clearly and just as challengingly as it did to any previous generation.

It is a true instinct that has led Christians to see the cross as at the heart of their faith. It is at the heart of their faith for two reasons. The first is that it is by way of the cross and no other way that Christ brought about their salvation. That alone is enough to make a study of the cross a significant undertaking.

And Jesus said that if anyone, anyone at all, wanted to follow him, he must take up his cross daily (Lk. 9:23). The Christian way is the way of the cross. It means something markedly different from and something vastly better than the heartless self-centredness and the callous indifference and the violence and the lust and the oppression that are so much part of the modern scene. The cross is a denial that self-assertiveness can ever be a satisfying way. It is an affirmation that one must lose the life to gain it. The cross is many-sided, and one thing this book has done has been to show that, look at it which way you will, it challenges us still. Each of the great picture-words that we have examined tells us something important about the meaning of the cross for Christ and for our understanding of the way he has secured our salvation. It shows that the content of the Christian salvation is rich and satisfying. Whatever our need, Christ met it. But each of these words tells us, too, something about the meaning of the Christian life. The way of the cross is a way that reaches into every corner of the way we live. Those who have come to understand it know that Christ's new and living way puts meaning into every facet of life.

'We have confidence to enter... by a new and living way... let us draw near to God with a sincere heart in full assurance of faith... and let us consider how we may spur one another on towards love and good deeds....'

Index of biblical references

General index